christian family guide to

Parenting a Toddler

Series Editor: James S. Bell Jr.

by Sybil A. Clark, M.A., C. Psych., L.L.B, L.M.H.C.

ALPHA

A member of Penguin Group (USA) Inc.

International Standard Book Number: 1-59257-049-6
Library of Congress Catalog Card Number: 2003112961

05   04   03   8   7   6   5   4   3   2   1

Interpretation of the printing code: The rightmost number of the first series of numbers is the year of the book's printing; the rightmost number of the second series of numbers is the number of the book's printing. For example, a printing code of 03-1 shows that the first printing occurred in 2003.

Printed in the United States of America

Contents

Appendixes

Introduction

Toddlers! What a joy! These next years in the life of your family will be exciting, playful, challenging, exhausting, and rewarding.

These are the years that will form your child's personality, character, and moral thinking. You will help your child learn how to speak your language, how to have a conversation, how to resolve conflict with siblings and friends, and how to share. You will guide your child as he or she develops emotional intelligence and a healthy sense of both body and sexuality.

You will discover that play is one of the primary ways that your toddler will learn, grow, and develop brain power.

In this book, you will find valuable tips, guidance, and advice on everything from feeding to bathing, to teeth brushing, to potty training, to going to bed, to shopping in the mall, to training your toddler not to whine or indulge in other annoying behavior, to riding in the car, to introducing your toddler to your new baby, to hiring a "safe" babysitter.

This book also attempts to provide adequate answers for appropriate disciplinary measures related to various forms of unacceptable behavior.

You will be able to teach your toddler about God's living presence within and help develop his or her conscience. You will learn how to pray for your little one according to his or her needs. You will learn how to guide your tot through inner healing if he or she is ever traumatized by abuse or abduction. You will learn how to pray for your little ones to protect them from nightmares and things that go bump in the night.

And finally, in this book, you will learn the value of nurturing your marriage and yourself during these years, as well as how to identify when a professional consultation might be helpful for yourself, your marriage, or your children.

May the Lord richly bless you, guide you, and give you all that you need to raise your children to love him, find fellowship in him, and serve him.

Sybil A. Clark

What's in This Book

In **Part 1, "The Job and Joy of Parenting Little Ones,"** we look at the critical issues involved in raising a toddler, and provide valuable guidelines for understanding your child's personality.

Part 2, **"Development and Growth,"** covers such issues as communication, sexuality, play, and introducing your newborn baby to your potentially jealous toddler.

In Part 3, **"Everyday Routines with Your Child,"** we discuss the everyday fundamentals of childraising, such as healthy eating, potty training, and the importance of creating a bedtime routine for your child.

In Part 4, **"Spiritual Development of Your Child,"** you'll find guidance for helping you train your child to discern the Holy Spirit, helping them to develop their conscience, and dealing with nightmares and other nighttime disturbances.

Part 5, **"Protection for Your Child,"** focuses on such important topics as hiring a babysitter and protecting your child emotionally. We also provide valuable information about how children are targeted by sex offenders—information that will better enable you to protect your child.

In Part 6, **"Temper and Tantrums: Dealing Humanely with Our Humanity,"** you'll learn how to deal with temper tantrums and fighting kids—and also learn how to keep your cool when you get angry.

Bonus Bits of Information

You'll also find these sidebars:

Safety and Sanity Tips

These boxes contain warnings to help you keep your toddler safe.

Dr. Mom Speaks

These boxes contain tips from a professional perspective.

Toddler Tales

Here you'll find interesting and amusing stories that highlight different aspects of raising a toddler.

Word from the Wise

These boxes contain scripture, inspirational quotes, and devotional thoughts.

Part I

The Job and Joy of Parenting Little Ones

God the Father has charged us with the awesome responsibility of guiding and nurturing the children he gives us. This means caring for them physically, emotionally, and spiritually.

Parenting toddlers is a joy and a job. These years, while being among the toughest in the life cycle of your family, will also be filled with some of the most endearing, fun, tender, and joy-filled moments.

There are two primary goals for you and your spouse during these years: First, make sure that you are nurturing your marriage, that you are taking care of each other, and that you are getting as much rest as is reasonably possible. Second, get to know your toddler for the unique and wonderful person he or she is. When you understand your toddler, you will come to know how to be the most effective parent.

Chapter 1

Parenting Preschoolers: Your Job Description

What is the goal of Christian parenting? To raise our children to become emotionally competent, socially responsible, spiritually mature servants of the Most High God!

Moving our children toward this goal starts while our children are being formed in their mother's womb. While your son and daughter are yet preschoolers, the time is ripe for you to set the foundation upon which they will continue to build throughout their lives. As parents, you want to give them the firmest foundation you can.

To do this, you have to consider the following:

- Your child's God-given traits and unique personality
- Your child's emotional needs
- Your child's spiritual needs
- Your child's physical needs
- Your child's need for protection and care
- Your child's needs for play and social interaction
- Your child's need for healthy sexual development
- Your child's need for correction and discipline

As parents, you also need to consider your own needs:

- Your need to maintain and nurture your marriage
- Your need to parent cooperatively
- Your need to rejuvenate yourselves and maintain your sanity
- Your need to be self-aware
- Your need to keep close to God

The Lord has entrusted you with a big job. Raising his little ones, and bringing glory and honor to him while doing so, is no small task. But he will give you all you need and more. He is trusting you to do as good a job as Mary and Joseph did as they raised the Lord himself. Your job is no less and no more than theirs. Ponder this thought: If the son of the Most High God was a toddler in your home, how would you parent him? Your child is not divine and will not turn out perfect as the Lord Jesus did, but he or she is entitled to the same care and nurturing as the Lord himself.

Growing Healthy Adults Starts at Birth

Healthy adults are created and developed. God creates them; we develop them.

What greater accomplishment is there than for parents to raise their child to be a well-functioning, capable, competent, spiritually astute adult? Our children are the by-product of everything we say and do, every response we make, every expectation we have, every crisis we handle, and every prayer we pray.

As Christian parents, we are not just trying to raise responsible, healthy adults. We are trying to raise our children so that they can come to know God the Father, the Lord Jesus Christ, and the Holy Spirit. But more than that, we want our children to know God intimately, to hear his voice, to desire to do his will, and to serve him with their whole mind, body, soul, and spirit. We want our children's lives to bring glory and honor to our heavenly Father and his son, Jesus Christ.

We have an awesome and rewarding task!

We have years to accomplish this task. Sometimes it seems like those years will never end; sometimes it seems they are slipping away too quickly. As you face exhaustion and fatigue to a significant degree, and as you come to see that this is a round-the-clock job that never seems to end, remember, live in the moment, be flexible, laugh at yourself, keep your wits about you, and enjoy your munchkin. Soon enough you'll wish you had more time with your little one than you did.

> ### Word from the Wise
>
> "May the Lord richly bless both you and your children. May you be blessed by the Lord, who made heaven and earth. The heavens belong to the LORD, but he has given the earth to all humanity." (Psalm 115: 14–16)
>
> David's prayer is a prayer for the family. It is for you and your children. As you pursue the raising of your children to God's glory and honor, may you and your household be truly blessed.

Even though we have years to do our job, there is no time to waste. We can't wait until our kids are teens to think we'll get them in shape to be competent adults. No, we start right now. To toddlers, every day seems like their whole life. Every day we have an opportunity to move them one step closer to becoming the adult children we admire. Let's get started!

The Critical Developmental Issues of the Preschooler

Your preschoolers need to work through a few basic developmental tasks. They need your help. They can't do it alone. You need to establish in your son or daughter a sense of trust, a sense of autonomy, a sense of initiative, and a sense of God.

Failure to help children through these tasks can leave them distrustful not just of people, but of life. Children who aren't able to trust their parents grow up unable to trust God, too. Children who don't develop an autonomous view of themselves remain dependent. They find it difficult to leave their mom or dad. Going to school becomes a problem (so does getting married!). They won't feel secure in who they are and who God created them to be. They will struggle to please others instead of being satisfied that they accomplished what they were able to accomplish. They will have no joy in what they are able to do.

How do parents teach trust to their children? By responding to their children's needs in a timely fashion without causing them much frustration. Your children should be able to have a sense of security in their environment—in these years, that means their parents. Within the environment in which they live, your care should be predictable and consistent. They should know that when they are hurt, when they are hungry, and when they are sad, you will respond to them in a warm and appropriate fashion. When you do this, you teach your children that they can trust their environment and that they can have optimism for the future. When your children learn that they can trust you, they are simultaneously learning that they can trust God. Although the critical time for developing trust is during the first and second years of life, parents need to maintain a predictable environment for their children throughout the preschool years and beyond.

How do parents teach their children to be autonomous? By balancing how they control their children and how they encourage them to control themselves. Children become autonomous when they learn that they are a separate entity from their moms and dads but are still dependent on them. Children become autonomous by learning how to self-regulate, to reward themselves internally and correct themselves internally. As toddlers begin to assert themselves, your responses to them can encourage them to become independent and self-confident. Toddlers need to learn to cooperate and compete at the same time. They need to learn how to interact with the outside world. They need to start learning how to look after themselves (getting dressed, brushing teeth, and so on). When children learn to walk to the beat of their own drum instead of to the beat of someone else's, they also learn to trust the sense that God can give them about what he wants them to do. The critical time for developing autonomy is between the ages of one and three. Of course, we continue to reinforce our children's autonomy throughout their lives.

How do parents teach their children initiative? By guiding them to try new things and meet new challenges, to help them strive toward their potential. Moms and dads show that they believe in their children and what they can do. They set expectations for their children that they can achieve. They encourage a lively imagination and creativity, encouraging children's play when they imitate adults and the roles they have in life. You need to explain to your children the rationale behind certain decisions and problem-solving strategies, and challenge them to think on their own. At this time, you also can teach preschoolers the balance between their own interests and the interests of others. That is, you teach assertive behavior and point out the limits when they need to stop short of intruding on another person. You can encourage your children's spontaneity at times by implementing one of their ideas or suggestions. The critical time for developing initiative in children is between ages three and five, but parents encourage and reward initiative throughout their children's lives.

How do parents teach their children to have a sense for God? By giving them opportunities to be in the Lord's presence. You can teach your children about God's love for them and your love for God. You can create an excitement for learning about the miracles of God and the works of Jesus. You can make God a part of your everyday life and a part of their normal experience.

Virtually every interaction with your sons and daughters throughout the day involves one or all of these four developmental issues. It is important to handle them well so that your children can become everything the Lord wants them to be.

These few precious years set the stage for your children's entire lives. The deposits you make now are not only deposits for your children, yourselves, and your families, but they are deposits in the kingdom of God.

The great harvest is coming, and we must keep in mind that the Lord needs workers for the harvest. The most usable servants of the Lord are well-raised Christian children.

Dr. Mom Speaks

As you gaze on the face of your newborn baby, you have joy and sadness at the same time because you realize that your job as a parent is to love your child so that you can then let him or her go. Your goal is to love your child, give to your child, sacrifice for your child, and do all the right things so that one day you can release that child into the world to stand on his or her own two feet. When this happens, you will experience the satisfaction of a job well done.

The "Good Enough" Parents

What are "good enough" parents?

Back in 1965, Dr. Donald W. Winnicott wrote about the concept of the "good enough mother." He was attempting to articulate what is needed in the early pre-school years for a child to develop in a healthy way. He wrote back in the days when fathers weren't as involved with their preschool children as they are today. In essence, he concluded that "good enough" care-giving by parents occurred when the child had a need and the parent responded to meet the need in a timely fashion. As the child moves from being an infant to being a toddler, the care-giver needs to move from meeting every need immediately to allowing a slightly delayed response so that the child has the opportunity to use his or her own mind to figure out the solution. But the good enough parent never waits so long that the child becomes frustrated and gives up. The good enough parent finds the balance. When this happens, the child moves from utter dependency toward finding his or her own "self" as separate from the parent's. Children raised in this way learn how to comfort themselves, entertain themselves, solve problems, and form relationships. It is this ability to balance responses to preschoolers that ultimately readies them to leave for school and to leave home.

The Parental Team and Working Together

Moms and dads do the best for their children when they work together. It gives your children a great deal of inner stability when they see you working together and being at peace with each other. A tight marital bond brings children peace in their little souls.

You and your spouse were likely raised in different ways. When you become parents, the way you know is what you learned, for better or worse. If you didn't think your parents did a great job, you can be thankful that lots of good advice on child rearing is available these days.

It's a good idea for the two of you to talk about child-rearing practices and ideals and decide together how you will handle various situations. If you are at odds with each other and get into a power battle over how your children will be parented, seek a family therapist or talk to your Christian small group or pastor. Investing a few bucks now will save all of you a lot of grief later.

Just because Mom (or, increasingly, Dad) is at home with the kids doesn't mean that she makes every decision about how the kids should be handled, nor does it mean that Dad's way is always wrong. Mom doesn't always know what's best for Jr., even if she thinks she does.

Moms and dads should recognize that there are gender differences in parenting. Mothers usually connect with their children by providing emotional comfort and verbal interaction with their kids. Dads connect with their children by roughhousing and doing things outdoors. This doesn't mean moms don't play and dads don't talk.

I'm referring here to preferences. Moms tend to be more protective. Dads tend to be more risk taking. Moms are quick to console. Dads are quick to challenge. Your kids need both of you just the way you are!

Moms and dads have different roles and functions in the family just like they have different roles and functions as parents. Together you provide a balance for your child. It's not important that you do the same things with your child, only that you are working together and not opposing each other. You both bring something special into your toddler's life—you bring yourselves.

Toddler Tales

The young mom walked into the living room and saw her husband tossing their toddler into the air and catching him. The tot was getting quite close to the ceiling. Both the dad and the tot were laughing their heads off. The mom's instant reaction was to tell them to stop because it was too dangerous. But she knew that dads and their kids interact differently than moms and their kids. Even though her anxiety was high, she knew she needed to step out of the room, leave them alone, and let them have their fun.

The Necessity of Nurturing Your Marriage

Marital satisfaction ebbs and flows over the lifetime of the family. It is at an all-time high when two people first get married. If they never have children, couples report that their level of marital satisfaction remains high throughout the course of their lives together.

For couples who have children, soon after the birth of the first baby, their level of marital satisfaction takes a drastic drop. It drops further with each additional child born. When the youngest child starts school, the level of marital satisfaction begins to increase. When the children begin to leave home, marital satisfaction continues to rise. When all of the children have left home, marital satisfaction approaches the level it was when first married *if* the marriage has been maintained and nurtured.

What does this say for parents with preschoolers? It is well recognized that married years with preschoolers are the most trying, exhausting, and stressful years for your marriage. Many marriages fall apart during these years. How do you prevent this? By recognizing the needs your marriage has.

Try to see "the marriage" as an entity unto itself. There is you, your spouse, and your marriage. You must take care of yourself during these years, your spouse must take care of him- or herself during these years, and you both must work together to take care of your marriage.

 Word from the Wise

"Love wisdom like a sister; make insight a beloved member of your family." (Proverbs 7:4)

The odds of marital collapse during the years with preschoolers are greater than during other periods of marriage. So be wise and invest in your marriage during this period. Don't take it or your spouse for granted. Take care of each other.

Taking care of the marriage means taking care of each other and nurturing your relationship together. An exhausted mother doesn't make a good mate or lover. An exhausted father won't fare much better.

Try to avoid making any major changes in your family for a few years. These years are taxing enough, and your family may not have the energy for more change. Ask yourself these questions:

- Do we need to move to another house at this time?
- Do we need to move to another state or country at this time?
- Do we need to change jobs at this time?
- Do we need to take a promotion at this time?
- Do we need to start a new business at this time?
- Do we need to change churches at this time?
- Do we need to take as many trips at this time?
- Do we need to obligate ourselves to every family function at this time?

Young couples with small children are stretched every which way. Don't let other people stretch you until your marriage pops! Don't let *yourselves* stretch you too far, either.

How can you nurture your marriage?

- Have a good list of babysitters on hand at all times.
- Meet for lunch regularly (even if it's once a month).
- Go for short walks together (even if it's just around the block).
- Husbands, take over with child care Saturday mornings so your wife can sleep in. If you want to get lucky Saturday night, your chances will greatly increase if you give your wife a chance to get some rest.
- Book a "couple's night out" every couple of weeks and stay out for two to four hours. Pick a night, put it on the calendar, and keep the date.
- When the kids are napping, cuddle and have a quick catnap yourselves.
- A regular appointment with a marriage counselor is a good preventive measure to make sure you always have a place to deal with your grief and keep it away from the kids. This is a time when your marriage can grow and deepen, but a concerted effort has to be made.

The most important stuff going on in your house during the preschool years is …

- Faith development.
- Nurturing your relationship with your kids.
- Nurturing your relationship with your spouse.
- Nurturing your child's relationships with siblings and friends.
- Getting enough sleep.
- Working and developing a career.

The least important stuff going on in your home during the preschool years is …

- Housework (except laundry and dishes!).
- Meeting demands and expectations of friends, relatives, and others.
- Attending extended-family functions.
- Taking trips.

Maintaining your marriage relationship is important throughout your lifetime. Taking care of it during the preschool years may actually ensure that you do have a lifelong marriage!

Toddler Tales

As the young mom watched her five-year-old daughter and three-year-old son, faces beaming, pushing their newborn sister down the corridor in the hospital to her room, she thought: "Look, there are the three precious souls that the Lord has entrusted to me to raise up in such a way as to bring glory and honor to him and his son, Jesus Christ. Yes, Lord, may I be a worthy servant! May I be as worthy as Mary when you chose her to raise your son."

Single Parenthood and Its Challenges

Single moms or dads have their hands full with one preschooler, let alone two or more. Preschoolers are a concern all the time, except when they are asleep.

Single parents need to do everything possible to conserve their energy and get whatever rest they can whenever they can. They also need to make concerted efforts to ensure that they get help when they need it.

If your child's other parent has visitation rights, try to use your time alone to regroup and re-energize, not expend more energy.

If the other parent is not involved, or if his or her involvement is unpredictable and rare, find other people who can take your kids off your hands now and then. Single-parent co-ops, other parents of preschoolers, friends, family, and babysitters aren't a luxury; they are a necessity. If married couples need help from others to keep sane during these years, so much more is this need for the single parent!

Safety and Sanity Tips

Said a working single mother of four children when asked how she did it: "Babysitters." A whole book, not a list, of babysitters. She had all her babysitters categorized according to their availability and made sure she was never stranded. She never took any of her children shopping. That was one time she could be alone and have no demands on her.

The Big Yellow Bus

When the first child goes off to school, there is a certain amount of fear and trepidation for Mom and Dad. You are turning your child over into the vast unknown: a big building, a teacher, a ton of other kids.

You may be asking yourself: Are they ready? Are we ready? Did we do a good enough job to prepare them for school? This anxiety is normal. Every mom and dad feels this. The kids look so small to be getting on that big yellow bus!

Parental anxiety can be high on two planes: First, you are scared for your child and his or her ability to cope in this new environment without you. Second, you are stressed about not having anyone home with you anymore—you've lost your job! The latter will be postponed if there are more preschoolers at home. But when the last one leaves, the stress of being alone and unemployed may hit hard. Sometimes moms have more babies to avoid being alone at home!

When your last child leaves for school, there isn't the same anxiety as the first. There is often a sense of relief and accomplishment. You've gotten through *that* stage of development. You can finally sleep! No more diapers, no more strollers, no more preschool, and no more teaching how to brush teeth, comb hair, or tie shoes. It's time to move on to some really fun and active years—the industrious years.

If you are the mom or dad of an only child, your anxiety may be greater when the big yellow bus picks up your child. You don't have a little brother or sister still at home to tend to. You may feel a bigger loss than other parents. You may feel more anxiety. You may feel lonely! Only children don't have brothers and sisters to attach to; they have only you. Their anxiety may be greater than that of other kids because they are more accustomed to being around adults than other children for play and interaction. Making sure you help your child connect to the teacher will ease that anxiety. Your only child will feel like a fish out of water if he or she doesn't feel connected to the only adult in the classroom.

The Rewards of Parenthood— Now and Later

There are both human and spiritual rewards of good parenting. There are rewards both now and in the future.

Word from the Wise

"Teach your children to choose the right path, and when they are older, they will remain upon it." (Proverbs 22:6)

The greatest joy of Christian parents is seeing their child choose to accept the faith and learn to walk closely with the Lord.

While your children are in the preschool years, there is such delight in watching your sons and daughters grow and develop, laugh and learn. Such fun can be had! From wrestling around in the autumn leaves to seeing the look of surprise, joy, and delight on a child's face, preschoolers are precious and priceless. These are moments you can enjoy right now, as they happen.

It's during the tough times, the power struggles, the whining and crying, that you have to remind yourself how important it is to do the right thing right now. How you respond to your children at their worst moments—and yours—will shape them more than the fun and happy times because in these moments you are shaping their character, teaching them right from wrong, letting them know that they can trust you, and showing them how to handle their negative emotions without hurting themselves or others. It's in the tough times that the right decisions will produce young adults you are proud of.

The reward for your future spans many more years than your rewards while parenting them as little tikes. The reward of good parenting is an adult child who loves the Lord, is emotionally healthy, has learned how to be a good husband or wife, has learned how to be a good mom or dad, works hard and provides for his family, and can look to his parents with a smile and say "thank you."

Well-raised children know they got where they are because of the investment their parents chose to make in helping them become who they are.

Chapter 2

Understanding Your Child's Personality and Temperament

What a wonderful gift the Lord has given you—your son, your daughter! Now that your child has progressed from being an infant to being a toddler and is moving through the preschool years, he or she is starting to show personality. Just as you have a distinct personality, so does your little one. Your job, as parents, is to discover your child's personality traits and learn to work with them effectively.

When you understand how a child's personality works, you will be able to determine, among other things …

- What are disciplinary issues and what aren't
- How your child needs to be comforted
- How you can gain your child's cooperation
- How to maximize your little one's potential

Nature vs. Nurture: Traits and Types

You don't create your child's personality; you help your child develop it. Children are born with a personality type or temperament.

How do you discover your son or daughter's uniqueness? Observation. Pay attention and observe your child. Pay attention and observe yourself! Learn to work with your child.

Does your child move from activity to activity? Does your child find contentment being alone? Does your child show feelings to everyone? Does your child try to hide feelings? Does your child adjust quickly to new people? Does your child cower in new situations? Work to identify your child's temperament traits.

Discovering Your Child's Uniqueness

One personality component that appears to be hereditary is the introversion-extroversion trait. Your child will lean toward being more introverted or more extroverted by nature. Is Mom more extroverted? Is Dad more introverted? If you have learned to deal with your own introversion or extroversion (or your spouse's introversion or extroversion), it will give you clues to how to respond to your child when you discover whether he or she is an introvert or extrovert.

Identifying whether your child is an introvert or extrovert will tell you how he or she gets energy. Extroverts are energized by interacting with people. Introverts are energized by solitude and internal dialogue. Your child will seek either vast amounts of stimulation or quiet, subdued stimulation. The introvert can do extroverted things now and then, but these moments must be followed by quietness to rejuvenate.

It's important to get to know the personality of your child because you will need to adjust your parenting to fit that child. If you have a child who thrives on stimulation, that child may do much better shopping at the mall, for example, than an introverted child for whom the mall is an overwhelming experience.

Identify Your Child's Source of Energy

Use the following chart to identify your child's source of energy.

Extroversion (75% of Kids)	Introversion (25% of Kids)
Loves lots of stimulation	Loves quiet and solitude
Likes to be around lots of people	Prefers to be around small number of people or alone
Attends to others in social situations	Not attentive to others in social situations
Has more friends, enters groups	Has fewer friends, is slow to warm up to groups
Thrill-seeker	Peace-seeker
More prone to conduct disorders	More prone to depression
Wiggles, squirms, taps, twitches, or talks to self if understimulated	Mentally shuts down when overstimulated
Prefers contact sports/play	Prefers noncontact sports/play
More irritable	More complacent
Steps forward in new situations	Holds back in new situations
Outgoing, verbally quick, socially forward	Shy, quiet, nonintrusive
Responds immediately	Slow to respond, ponders, muses before responding, appears stubborn but is just processing information differently

Observe and pay attention to your child. From the information in this chart you should be able to identify your son or daughter as an introvert or extrovert.

Children start with a genetic personality disposition. Depending on how their parents respond to them, their personality will develop for the better or for the worse. We need to learn how to respond to the different personality types of our children so that we can learn how to take them from where they are and help them to become all that God wants them to be. When you get in sync with your child's personality type, you can learn how to help your child along the path of development more smoothly.

For example, your extroverted child will be much happier at a preschool with other children, whereas your introverted child may do better in a home-based child-care situation with a few other introverts. Your extroverted child will like action figures, but your introverted child would rather look at books or draw. Your extroverted child may prefer the amusement park, while your introverted child may prefer the zoo.

The extroverted daughter whose parents are extroverted will feel like she "fits in." The extroverted daughter growing up in a family of introverts may feel like there is something "wrong" with her if her introverted family doesn't figure out how to work with her temperament instead of trying to encourage introverted tendencies. In any event, the extroverted daughter will turn out differently depending on the family that raises her because she will learn different things about the world. The extroverted family may not be able to help her learn to enjoy time alone, quietness, and solitude, while she will inevitably gain the value of this if raised in an introverted family.

Likewise, the introverted son, if raised by a family of introverts, may feel like he "belongs" with the family but not with the outside world (where the other 75 percent, the extroverts, live). The extroverted family can make the introverted son feel like an "ugly duckling" because he is so different from them. While they will teach him something about "the excitement of life" and help him develop his verbal skills, they won't help him learn how to recharge himself and can run the risk of trying to make him become something he never can become—"just like them!"

Parenting the extrovert requires us to be aware of the extrovert's tendency to cross the line with physical behavior. Extroverts are more prone to act out against other children when frustrated. We need to watch this and provide guidance and instruction for interactions with others. We have to spend more time teaching our extroverts about sharing and not dominating others, about talking to resolve problems with other kids rather than intimidating them. Our extroverts need us to help them learn to reel themselves in now and then.

Parenting the introvert requires us to be more aware of introverts' tendency to withdraw from people and be alone in their emotional pain and turmoil. We have to watch for when they pull away, and we have to guide them in learning to talk about what is wrong and what has happened that bothered them. Our introverts need our help pulling them out of their shell to deal with the world so that they don't slip into depression.

Even though the traits of introversion and extroversion will be our children's primary disposition over their lifetime, our goal as parents of preschoolers is to help them balance their disposition and avoid the extremes in order to become healthy adults. Our little tikes shouldn't be made to feel that they are bad or that something is wrong with them because they are the way they are.

Identify How Your Child Gathers Information

Study the following table for clues that will help you discover how your child gathers information.

Sensory (75% of Kids)	Intuitive (25% of Kids)
Likes stories of adventure and action, with lots of detail, read over and over	Likes stories of fantasy and metaphor read over and over
Prefers active play	Prefers story time
Goes with the flow; canceling events is taken in stride	Anticipates future events; canceling promises or plans is devastating
Focuses on here and now, and is aware of everything going on nearby	Focuses on the future and the possible; uninvolved and inattentive to the present
A truck is a truck	A truck may be a space ship, a deep water craft, or an airplane
Concrete thinker	Imaginative thinker
Warms up to new people quickly, engages them, makes eye contact, verbally interacts	Cowers around new people, may look down, avoids eye contact, stands back, won't talk until comfortable
If vengeful, will act out in any way, often unplanned and unrestrained; leaves no doubt that he or she is the culprit	If vengeful, will find the jugular of the other and go for it; will be careful and sly so as to go almost undetected, so is hard to accuse of being the culprit
Is whatever anybody wants him or her to be; will rise to others' expectations	Is his or her own person; won't cooperate until ready; can't be pushed (to push the intuitive child is devastating)
What you see is what you get: cooperation is cooperation, and uncooperative is uncooperative	Can mistakenly appear to be uncooperative when does not understand
Extroverted sensor walks naturally and concretely in nearly any environment, eager to experience new things and people	Introverted intuitive can feel like ugly duckling if not handled well; has very vulnerable self-concept; can be devastated by those who don't understand him or her

Is your preschooler showing a more intuitive mind or a more sensory mind? The sensing child may speak right up. The intuitive child needs time to think before speaking. There is a delay in the response. This delay is not resistance. The intuitive child is busy in his or her own little mind trying to process information and then trying to find the right words to use to respond to you. These children are our sweet little daydreamers. When we learn to understand them, work with them, and affirm the way they process the world, they will be our visionaries of tomorrow. They will come up with great ideas that the sensory people will figure out how to make work!

Our sensory children will become the teachers, the doctors, the construction workers. They love being concrete in everything. Their temperament is relatively easy to deal with: What you see is what you get.

Word from the Wise

This was the report to Moses on the part of those called to evaluate the Promised Land: "We arrived in the land you sent us to see, and it is indeed a magnificent country—a land flowing with milk and honey. Here is some of its fruit as proof. But the people living there are powerful, and their cities and towns are fortified and very large. ... But the other men who had explored the land with him answered, 'We can't go up against them! They are stronger than we are! ... The land we explored will swallow up any who go to live there. All the people we saw were huge. We even saw giants there ... We felt like grasshoppers next to them, and that's what we looked like to them!' (Numbers 13: 27-33)

The men Moses sent out were all tribal leaders. The first group who responded to Moses were the intuitives. They spoke to Moses in an imaginative way without detail. They described the land as flowing with milk and honey. They spoke about their discoveries in a sort of romantic fashion. The second group, the sensors, spoke up with all the details. They didn't notice how beautiful the country was; they noticed only how huge the enemy was—they were giants, and it made them feel like grasshoppers. To them, the land was something that would swallow them up! It's a good thing Moses sent all of them. Between the two kinds of information gatherers, the intuitives and the sensors, he had a good idea of what the land looked like and what the people looked like.

Identify How Your Child Makes Decisions

Your child has to make decisions, lots of decisions, just like you. Often we see only the result of the decision and not how people came to the decision. The decision may be the same for both the thinker and the feeler, but how they arrived at the decision involves either objective fact finding or consideration of the child or others who will be affected by the decision.

Use this table to discover whether your child is a thinker or a feeler.

Thinkers (⅔ Boys, ⅓ Girls)	Feelers (⅔ Girls, ⅓ Boys)
Ask for and need objective explanation of why things need to be done before they cooperate	Cooperate to try to please others and gain their affections, to keep them happy
Detaches self from others' emotional pain and an emotionally painful environment	Pick up on other people's feelings and take on responsibility of "fixing" others who are feeling bad or mad or anxious
Unaware of others' distress	Aware when others are socially or physically uncomfortable
Don't like to be touched and have difficulty receiving parental affection	Openly need and receive parental affection
More likely to get constipated when emotionally distressed	Get physically sick when feeling conflicted and anxious
Block off facial expressions in a crisis	Let all their emotions be seen in a crisis
	High need for parents to show appreciation and recognition for the things they do for parents and others
Resistant to showing emotion when scolded, even though they hurt inside just as badly as the feeling child	Cry easily; show all emotions readily

A "feeling" mom or dad with a "thinking" toddler, or a "thinking" parent with a "feeling" toddler must adjust to the little one's disposition. Thinking parents have to make physical and emotional efforts towards their feeling child. Feeling parents have to resist just wanting to cuddle their thinking child and need to be prepared to be more verbal and explain more things.

Dr. Mom Speaks

What was Jesus' temperament? Was he an extrovert or an introvert? Was he intuitive or sensing? Was he a thinker or a feeler? Was he judging or perceiving? In Christ we find the perfect balance of all personality strengths.

As parents, we help our children to find the balance that Christ had in him. We guide our children away from the extremes and, over the years, help them develop the complementary side of their temperament.

The feeling child will lap up your praise, but your thinking child will become suspicious of why you are fawning over him or her and wonder what your motive is. It's not that the thinking child doesn't need praise; it's just that once is enough. Feeling children can hear over and over how much you love them or how great a job they did.

To gain the cooperation of a thinking child, you often must explain why the child needs to do what you're asking. The child wants to hear the logic of it. When his son asks why they are going to visit grandma, Dad says to his little thinker:

> We're going to Grandma's house because Grandma wants to make us lunch. She hasn't seen us for a long time, and visiting her is important to our family.

To the feeler, Dad says:

> We're going to Grandma's house because Grandma loves to cook for her grandkids. She hasn't seen us for a long time, and she really misses us.

Depending on his or her type, your child will talk with you in different ways. You can identify your child's type depending on how he or she tells you things:

Says the thinker to Mom:

> I want to go play with Amy because she likes dolls.

Says the feeler to Mom:

> I want to go play with Amy because she's a nice girl.

Knowing whether your child processes information in a thinking way or a feeling way will help you know how to explain things best. Feeling parents need to adjust their language so that their thinking toddler or preschooler will not have to keep asking "Why?" (It works the other way, too—feeling children will cooperate with you more quickly if you learn to speak their language and explain things in a way that makes sense to them.)

Identify Your Child's Orientation to Life

Is your child a judger or a perceiver?

Judger	Perceiver
Ready quickly; time-oriented	Late; delayed in getting ready; has poor concept of time
Neat and tidy	Messy
Anxious when things aren't ordered	Peaceful when things are not ordered
Less flexible	More flexible
Learns easily to do things on own initiative	Has to be reminded to do everything
If extroverted, is an obvious leader who likes to organize others	If introverted, is an idealist who enjoys a good mental challenge
Decisive	Tentative
More worried	More carefree
Clothes have to coordinate	Clothes don't have to coordinate
May be more concerned about hygiene and hair brushing	May be less concerned about hygiene and hair brushing

Understand right now that if you have a perceiving child, dealing with a messy room will be a life-long issue. You'll be dealing with it as long as the child lives at home, and when that child gets married, it'll be an issue for the couple! You cannot change someone from being a perceiving person to a judger. God made people the way he made them. We have to learn how to work with them and teach them how to deal with their natural inclinations. You will always have to help them get organized and work on one part of their bedroom at a time. You will have to provide ongoing and steady guidance on a regular basis for them to have a livable room (livable for *you*, that is—a perceiving child will be very comfortable in the mess).

A perceiving child will need you to remind him or her often of routine things. It's not that these children are dumb—they can have above average or superior intelligence—it's about how their brain works. Details are not important to them. They don't even see the details!

Toddler Tales

Plan for the slow poke! My daughter was a fast thinker, talker, and mover. My son thought slowly, talked after a pause, and couldn't move quickly. I could not expect my son to be ready to leave immediately if I said "Come on, let's go." If I knew we needed to leave at 10:00, I had to start telling him at 9:30 to find his mitts, get his hat, bring his shoes to the door, put his shoes on, and put his coat on. Each direction had to be given one at a time. Later tests showed that both children had the same intelligence level, but my son was learning-disabled. I needed to account for that. I needed to exercise much more patience with him because he could do only what he could do. His brain just didn't work like his sister's. Then I had a third child just like my son. "Lord, give me patience!" As parents, we need to discover our children and love them for who they are.

God made perceivers to show us all of the possibilities in life, to show us all the options, and to keep us from getting stuck.

You might think that your judging child is better behaved because these children tidy their room with little suggestion from parents. They like to brush their hair and teeth. However, the judgers can be seen as opinionated and controlling. They want things "their way" and see their way as better. They can be very particular, which can cause them great stress if something goes wrong or something happens that they don't anticipate. They aren't "better"—they are just who they are. If you are a judging parent, the two of you will get along on this dimension. If you are a perceiving parent, you will frustrate your child and your child will frustrate you, unless you find a way to work *with* him or her.

The goal for perceivers is to help them become "reasonably organized." The goal for judgers is to teach them how to relax!

Identify How Your Child Needs to Be Comforted

Do you have a cuddler or a noncuddler? Depending on your daughter or son's disposition, you need to respond accordingly. Here are tips for moms and dads:

Noncuddlers	Cuddlers
Soothed by sounds (parents' voice, peaceful music)	Soothed by physical contact
Soothed by visual stimulation (looking at new things)	Soothed by holding
Soothed by being walked	Soothed by restraint
More restless	Less restless
More physically active	Less physically active
More advanced in motor development	Slower in motor development

One of your preschoolers may be a noncuddler and one may be a cuddler. You need to respond to each differently. When your noncuddler is distressed, you can hold your child and walk, but you can't sit down with him or her in a chair—your child will scream louder and squirm harder. Your cuddler will just want to be held and, sometimes, restrained. What do I mean by "restrained"? Sometimes your cuddler feels that his or her little world is falling apart and needs to be held in such a way that he or she can't move. Cuddle these children tight, in love, and tell them softly that you love them.

Word from the Wise

"How precious are your thoughts about me, O God! They are innumerable! I can't even count them; they outnumber the grains of sand! And when I wake up in the morning, you are still with me!" (Psalm 139:17–18)

Just as we like to know that our heavenly Father thinks precious thoughts about us, we also want to know that our parents are thinking precious thoughts about us. Affirm your children for the unique people God created them to be. When a child knows his parent thinks well of him, it makes that child feel good about who he or she is.

Many books out now detail temperament in parent-child relationships. To learn more, refer to Appendix E.

The Temperamentally Difficult Child

Temperamentally difficult children's personalities are shaped through social interactions in the family. The temperamentally difficult child from toddler years has sleep problems, eating problems, and potty problems; is inflexible, avoidant, and distressed by new experiences; is slow to adapt to new situations; and has extreme moods of fussiness and crying.

If your son or daughter is temperamentally difficult, you have a greater challenge than the average mom and dad. You will be far more tempted to harm your child when you just don't know what to do anymore.

Parents should be mindful that temperamentally difficult children may be very gifted children but it may take a lot of time and patience to discover their gifts.

You may want to consult a family therapist for guidance on dealing with your difficult child so that you will all survive the growing-up years. Consult Appendix D for advice on finding a good therapist.

The Adopted Child

The adopted child can end up feeling like a fish swimming in the wrong school. You may feel that way also. Your own children take their personality traits from Mom and Dad. Both parents will be able to see what traits their child got and who they got them from. Parents are better equipped to deal with their natural-born children because their personalities will be familiar to them. You have learned to deal with these traits in yourself or your mate already.

The adopted child does not have either parent's personality traits; this child's genes came from a different pool. Neither you nor your spouse may know what to do with this child at times because the way he or she thinks, processes information, and behaves will be unfamiliar. Unfamiliar behavior is not necessarily a disciplinary issue, but some parents might see it this way if they are unenlightened. Your child is different, but that doesn't mean that child is bad or odd.

Get to know your adopted child. If you have difficulty dealing with him or her, consult a family therapist. It's better to develop a strategy now while the child is little rather than waiting until the teen years!

Use the charts above to discover your child's personality type, and if his or her traits are different from yours, pick up the book *Please Understand Me* (see Appendix E) and learn more about your child's unique temperament.

Word from the Wise

"O Lord, you have examined my heart and know everything about me. You know when I sit down or stand up. You know my every thought when far away." (Psalm 139:1–2)

Just as the father God knows us this well, as parents, we can also come to know our children this well. Discovering your little one's temperament is a joy and a challenge and is well worth the effort. When you know what makes your child tick, you are better positioned to live in harmony with that child. You can help your children live in harmony with the world, with themselves, and with others.

Maximizing Your Child's Potential

Everyone is born with gifts and deficits. While toddlers, our sons and daughters begin to exhibit signs that they are intellectually fast, intellectually slow, physically fast, physically slow, verbally advanced, or verbally regressed.

It's important to take our children as they are and work with what they have, not with what you wish they had.

One of my children thinks fast and moves fast. The other spends more time thinking before acting and can't do anything in a rush. Rushing him causes him to become mentally and physically stalled. Punishment is not the answer for the slower one; patient parenting and understanding how to work best with your child to maximize cooperation need to be the focus.

If we have a child of lesser intelligence, you have to modify your expectations of the child, or you will induce ongoing frustration and a sense that the child is never good enough.

The only fair and reasonable goal you can have for your children is that they work toward and strive to reach their potential. God doesn't expect the impossible from us. We shouldn't expect the impossible from our children.

If you begin to have concerns that your toddler isn't "in step" with his peers, seek out professional advice as soon as possible. If your child is developmentally delayed there is a lot you can do to lessen the effects of any disability on your child's life if you begin to address the concerns as early as possible.

Helping Your Toddler Manage Their Emotions

Everybody has emotions. Jesus had emotions, you have emotions, and your toddler has emotions. Emotions aren't right or wrong—they just *are*. Emotions have a function. They tell us something. Before our children can speak, they tell us how they are doing by displaying their emotions to us. We learn from their cry whether they are hungry, wet, or tired. We learn from the look in their eyes and the look on their face whether they are peaceful, happy, or excited.

Once our children begin to talk, we need to teach them not only language about the world and how to speak, but also how to identify and express and deal with their emotions.

When a child reacts emotionally to something, we should focus on what has caused the reaction rather than focusing on the reaction itself. We don't want to shut our children down—we all know what happens when people suppress their emotions. We begin to train our children with emotional skills as soon as they begin talking.

Focusing on a negative emotional reaction rather than what lies behind it may help us to see children's reactions as a disciplinary issue instead of helping them talk through the fact that someone has hurt them, that they are scared, or that they are hungry.

"Feeling" children may show their emotions more often, but "thinking" children still have the same emotions and the same intensity of emotions. Extraverts need to learn to process their emotions without hurting others, and introverts need to learn to express their feelings and come out of their inner world long enough to deal with the problem.

Safety and Sanity Tips

Scary teenagers develop from introverted toddlers and preschoolers who have never been socialized to talk constructively about their negative feelings and resolve their inner conflicts. If you have an introverted child, you must learn how to help him or her deal with emotions now.

Part 2

Development and Growth

During the toddler years, your son or daughter will go through developmental changes at lightning speed. As your child begins to acquire and use language, you will learn how to gain his or her cooperation and help them learn how to express their emotions. As a parent, your actions will help your little ones develop a sense of who they are as unique individuals and who they are before the Lord. Your toddler will develop an awareness of his or her genitals, and you will learn how to handle this discovery tactfully and in a healthy way. Play is an essential part of your toddler's development, and you will help your toddler develop physically, intellectually, and emotionally.

During the toddler years, most couples become pregnant or seek to adopt another child. You will learn how to make this transition as easy as possible for your toddler and help him or her receive a new brother or sister without retaliation.

Communicating with Your Toddler

The toddler years are fantastic. Your son or daughter was a babbling baby making no sense; now he or she is searching to learn your language to communicate with you. You are your children's first English teacher!

Here are some things you'll want to know about how children learn language and how you can help them to be successful in school in a few years.

Language Development

God programmed us as language learners. We have an inborn ability to learn verbal communication. All children of all cultures and languages learn language in the same way and at the same pace.

Children utter their first word sometime between 8 and 18 months. By first grade, they have about 8,000 to 14,000 words in their vocabulary. That's 5 to 8 new words per day!

Speech Production

To produce speech, we need to have control over our vocal cords, mouth, tongue, and lips. As our tots grow, they gain more control over their speech apparatus. It isn't until they approach one year in age that babbling decreases and true words are formed.

From the time of birth, our sons and daughters make sounds. They are trying out their vocal muscles just like they are trying out their other muscles. As our children babble, we let them know which sounds are important and which aren't. We guide them to pay attention to certain sounds that have meaning in our tongue.

Rules, Rules, Rules

Language is all about rules. To learn a language, you first must learn the rules of the language. As parents, we are the ones who teach our toddlers the rules of speech. We teach them through guiding them as they utter each sound.

Our children's ability to perceive speech sounds precedes their ability to purposefully produce speech. In other words, even if they can't make the sound correctly, they know what the correct sound is from listening to you. Children need to learn correct adult sounds in order to distinguish what is important in the language and what is not. Talking directly to children in adult words and phrases helps them master the language more quickly.

Words of Objects Precede Action Words

First children learn sounds; then they learn what meaning is attached to the sound. Words are just symbols that represent meaning. After they know the sound, we teach them the meaning of the sound.

The first thing you will be teaching your tot is the names of things in the everyday environment. Your child will learn these words faster if you repeat them more often. It's easier for children to learn objects first and then words for actions.

Singles, Then Doubles

First come the single-word utterances. Single words will be used between 10 and 18 months. After this period comes the two-word period and this will take them to about 24 months. Once your child moves from two words to three, there is a vocabulary explosion.

It's your job to correct children's language errors as they occur so that they can learn the language competently. Don't ignore speech errors—you will be doing your child a disservice.

For instance, if your child says "baba," hand him his bottle as you clearly say, "bottle." When he says the word correctly, praise him with the expression on your face and kind words. Reinforce correctly spoken words.

Story Books and Nursery Rhymes

On the other side of the equation, the more words you introduce your child to, and the greater complexity that the words have, the better. Your child will gain an advanced grasp of the language, and comprehension of the language will soar.

Do you want your children to enter school and be able to learn to read easily? Studies have shown that if you teach your children to recite nursery rhymes when they are three years old, you will cause them to have increased phonological knowledge and reading skills at age six.

Toddler Tales

Every night I had a bedtime routine of story reading with my tots—one book after another, one chapter of *The Picture Bible* after another. Interestingly, after getting into school, even though one of my children had a reading disability, they all scored years beyond their peers in reading comprehension. They have all become avid readers. It starts when they are two!

Children will more quickly learn how to read if they have preschool help from you. Learning nursery rhymes facilitates later reading. Read to your child every day, either during the day or at bedtime. Another great way to help your child's language development is to sing songs together.

Toddler Tales

One of my fondest memories of childhood is my mother singing songs with my sister and me. From the time my children were toddlers, I began singing songs to them and teaching them songs my mother taught me, as well as camp songs and choruses. We mostly sang in the car. Surprisingly, even though they are now all teenagers, when we take a long car trip, they ask if we can sing!

Making Conversation

Being able to initiate and maintain a conversation is a very important aspect of what it means to be human. When your toddler looks as if he or she is trying to communicate with you, respond with conversation. This will happen before the emergence of language. We can help preverbal children learn the nature of two-way communication.

Understanding

By 12 to 15 months, your child should understand simple directions. By age 2, he or she should understand concepts such as in, out, on, and off. Between two and three years, your child should understand when you tell him or her to put something somewhere or get something from somewhere.

Toddler Tales

One day my neighbor came to tell me that her daughter, Emelia, had asked her if she could have some "Emeliatards." Her mom didn't have the faintest idea of what she wanted. The little girl explained that her friend Leah had "leotards," and she wanted some for herself—you know, Emeliatards! How do they come up with this stuff? It's perfectly logical to a four-year-old!

Not only do you want to pay attention to whether your child can produce or imitate sounds, but you also want to know whether your child appears to comprehend what is being said. If your child doesn't seem to understand you or is having trouble following simple directions, seek an evaluation from a speech-language pathologist. Your child may need speech therapy, and you will be part of learning how to work with him or her.

Language Delays

If your child has no other words than perhaps *Mama* or *Dada* by 18 months of age and isn't pointing to objects, you should have your child's hearing tested. Hearing deficits may be the cause of the delayed language. If your child has a speech delay but is pointing to objects, you should see your pediatrician. Your child could have palate problems (which would also reveal itself in eating problems) or could have a developmental delay. Treat every ear infection promptly so that your child does not sustain hearing loss from an infection. The earlier you know whether any of these are affecting your toddler, the faster you can get help.

If there is a speech delay, ask yourself if the child has opportunities to verbally interact with adults in the environment (at home or at day care). Does your child get feedback as he or she speaks? Children need these interactions. They also need adult feedback. Often the younger children of a large family have far fewer opportunities for adult interaction than the first-borns. If you have a later-born child with delayed speech, you may need to spend some focused time verbally interacting with him or her. Spending time reading to your children, looking directly at them, and speaking with them gives them the opportunity to hear and produce language.

Sometimes children have speech delays for no apparent reason. Some three-year-olds have been silent and then speak in full sentences. But this is rare. Seek your pediatrician's advice. Don't presume that your child is the "wonder child" because you could lose valuable time with the speech therapist, and your child will be further behind and will take longer to catch up.

Word from the Wise

"But Moses pleaded with the Lord, 'O Lord, I'm just not a good speaker. I never have been, and I'm not now, even after you have spoken to me. I'm clumsy with words.'"

'Who makes mouths?' the Lord asked him. 'Who makes people so they can speak or not speak, hear or not hear, see or not see? Is it not I, the Lord? Now go, and do as I have told you. I will help you speak well, and I will tell you what to say.'" (Exodus 4:10–12)

If your son or daughter has any sort of disability, he or she needs to know that it is not a problem for the Lord. The Lord will use those whom he will choose. He chose Moses and made provision for his handicap. He will make provision for your son or daughter, too.

Dealing with "No"

As you teach your toddlers what they can and cannot touch, and what they can and cannot do, you will be saying "no" to them quite frequently. Your child learns quickly that *no* is a word of power.

After you say "no," you must show your child the appropriate way to do what he or she needs to be doing. Every "no" needs a redirection immediately thereafter. Children must know what the correct response is. They need to know the better way. You need to show this to them.

Gaining Cooperation

Your toddler will be more cooperative with you if you save your "no" for things that are important. Alternatively, you can say things like "We don't do things that way" or "Here is how you should do this" or "That could hurt you—you mustn't do that again."

When you say "no," it should be for important reasons associated with safety. Regardless of this, if you're like most parents, you will say "no" frequently to your toddler as he or she moves through the house exploring everything possible. Be forewarned that as much as you use this word in your vocabulary, your toddler will mimic you. For your child, it's how people communicate.

When They Say It

Some toddlers say "no" to their parents more than others. It's when they look you straight in the eyes and stand there with a firm stance and shout "no" at you that you will feel the hair stand up on the back of your neck. No parent likes outright defiance. In Chapter 15, we examine this more closely.

In terms of communication, your toddler will use the word "no" at times to establish that they are a separate person from you and to determine themselves. If you are put off by your toddler's "no," ask yourself if this situation requires you to assert limits on your child's behavior for the good of their development or if this is something that you need to let them maintain their stance on so that they can gain a sense of who they are.

Sometimes kids say "no" just to say something. There are many times when just ignoring their "no" will discourage them from overusing it.

Sidestepping

The best way to deal with most utterances of "no" is the classic sidestep. You can't presume that your short, tubby little two-year-old seriously thinks he or she can outpower you by saying "no." Not even a four-year-old can outpower a parent by saying "no."

First, what's the situation? Is it a "boundary" situation (see Chapter 5)? Tots are learning about themselves, where they end and where you begin. If you are laying out your toddler's clothes and you get a "no," ask what your child would prefer to wear. This actually will be helping your little one to make decisions that pertain to himself or herself and that don't really affect anybody else. If it's a "boundary" situation, let your child have input into what is happening.

Second, if your child is saying "no" just to get your goat, ignore it and continue on with whatever you are doing. If your child's voice is one of misery and command, simply say that you will be able to hear your little one only when he or she speaks to you using nice words. Then ignore your tot until you hear that.

Third, it takes two to tango and two to have a conflict. For example, if your daughter is saying "no" just to be oppositional, walk away. She won't make any headway with you if you aren't there. Most often she'll come running after you apologizing. Kids want to be in their parents' company and have their parents' attention. Removing yourself from their presence can often bring about the desired result: to not talk to you that way.

Fourth, make a conversation. You want your children to express themselves and learn to communicate well with you and others. If they say "no," ask them open-ended questions—that is, questions to which "no" cannot be an answer. For instance, "Suzie, put your shoes on." "No." "Will you be putting your shoes on by yourself or will you be needing Mother's help?"

Fifth, avoid eye contact. If your toddler is inappropriately saying "no" to you, look away and continue to talk, ignoring the "no." If he or she is trying to have a power trip, the plug is pulled if your eyes don't meet. There is power in direct eye contact, and no power for the child without it.

Sixth, children sometimes say "no" because it's the first word out of their mouths and they don't understand what you want from them. Describe what you see; describe the reason they need to do what they need to do. For instance, Johnny doesn't want to bathe and he's been playing out in the yard all day. He's being obstinate. Dad says, "Johnny, you've been in the dirt all day. If you go to bed like that, you will get the sheets all dirty. The dirt will rub off in your bed, and then you will be sleeping in it for days. We are not going to have you go to bed dirty and have to wash the sheets every time you sleep in them with a dirty body. Also, in the dirt there are little bugs and bug eggs. Some of those bug eggs may be in the dirt on your body or under your nails. Nobody wants bugs sleeping in their bed with them. You need to take your bath."

Seventh, nobody likes a command. Instead of commanding your children to do things, which creates resistance, you can engage their cooperation by simply telling them, in a few words, what they need to do next. Instead of "Get in that tub right now," try "It's time for your bath."

Dr. Mom Speaks

If you find yourself engaged in a power struggle with your toddler, you may need to ask yourself if you have power issues of your own. There are so many ways for us to gain the cooperation of our children; direct power battles should be few and far between. If your children sense that you are feeling out of control of yourself, if you are inconsistent or unpredictable, they will not know what to do with themselves, and one of their options is to react to you with obstinacy.

Eighth, sometimes one word is enough. Instead of a long-winded reason why your son needs to pick up his toys, just say "toys." Messy hair, say "hair." Your kids will come to know that when you say a word, that thing needs to be dealt with. This way you are not asking them or telling them to pick up their toys, to which they can say "no." If they say "no" with one word, say it once more and leave the room. See if they do the thing you told them to do.

One of the most detailed books written on communication with your children is titled *How to Talk So Kids Will Listen, and Listen So Kids Will Talk.* It's written by two moms, one with five children and one with six. Check out Appendix E for the details.

Raising Verbally and Emotionally Competent Children

Our sons and daughters need language, all sorts of language. First they learn objects, then they learn actions, and then they need to learn an emotional language. We must equip our children with words for emotional expression.

Emotional Intelligence

Emotional Intelligence was the title of a best-selling book. People are recognizing that there are many kinds of intelligence, including emotional intelligence. What does this mean?

Word from the Wise

"'Good Teacher, what should I do to get eternal life?' … Jesus (said) '… you know the commandments ….' 'Teacher,' the [rich] man replied, 'I've obeyed all these commandments since I was a child.' Jesus felt genuine love for this man as he looked at him. 'You lack only one thing,' he told him. 'Go and sell all you have and give the money to the poor, and you will have treasure in heaven. Then come, follow me.' (Mark 10:17–22)

Jesus "felt genuine love" for the man as he delivered the answer that he knew would be hard for the rich man to hear. This is emotional intelligence, of which Jesus is the master.

Emotional intelligence is all about a person being able to pay attention to his or her own emotions and those of others, and to use the information to guide thoughts and actions. It's all about …

- Recognizing your feelings as they occur (self-awareness)
- Dealing with those feelings appropriately and understanding why you feel the way you do
- Allowing yourself to feel the feeling, but restraining yourself from expressing the feeling because expression in that time and place may not be in your best interests
- Being sensitive to others' feelings, being concerned about them, understanding their perspective, and appreciating that different people feel differently about things
- Managing your own emotions in the context of relationships with other people

Step by Step

To teach emotional intelligence:

1. Teach your toddler a language for emotions.
2. Help your child identify his or her own feelings.
3. Help your child to see how his or her actions affect other people (if your child hurt someone else, make sure he or she has an opportunity to hear the other child tell about how they feel).

4. If you notice that your child looks sad upon seeing another child who is hurt-ing or sad or crying, ask your child how he or she feels and how the other child feels.

This will give your toddler a good start on developing emotional intelligence.

Extroverts and Introverts

Your little extrovert merely needs to be introduced to words and given the floor, and he or she will talk your head off! Give these children language and an audience, and away they go.

Your little introvert will wait until someone gives him or her the opportunity to speak and waits for a response. Your introvert won't necessarily be able to sponta-neously answer you when you ask a question; he or she will be thinking of an answer before he gives it to you. This must not be seen as resistance, but as a sign that you are raising an introvert.

An introvert's delayed responses can give parents the wrong impression that he or she is being obstinate. Just be patient, and the child will speak. (See Chapter 2 for more on recognizing and raising extroverts and introverts.)

Safety and Sanity Tips

Your sweet little introvert's communication style may really test your patience. You want an answer, and you want it now! Bury that thought! You won't get him or her to respond any faster than he is able. Pull up a chair, keep quiet, and wait. When your child's brain gathers all the information, he or she will report it to you. You have to wait "long enough" for your introvert to get it out. Remember, people waited for Moses.

Emotional Language

Just as language of things and actions fills your tot's head, language of feelings ought to do the same.

Often aggression in children is linked to lack of ability to express negative emo-tions. Kids feel all tied up inside and angry. They don't know what to do with their feelings, so they let them out on someone else. We need to help children learn to talk about things that are hurtful to them so that they won't be slugging their siblings, their neighbors, or the kids at school.

Give your children a feeling language, and then give them the opportunity to express themselves with the words they have. Some of the emotions you can help your child identify are sad, mad, glad, happy, hurt, proud, terrific, afraid, alone, disappointed, frustrated, envious, guilty, silly.

> ### Safety and Sanity Tips
>
> What do you do if you have a child who never stops talking? Of course, you'll be asking this if your child is an extrovert and you are an introvert. Now and then introverted parents have to tell their extroverted tot, "Daddy's ears are tired. They need a little rest. I'm going to put on the timer, and when it rings, Daddy's ears will be rested." Give your child something else to focus on before you start the timer. Don't set it for more than 15 minutes at a time.

Understanding Your Child

Toddlers are perhaps the funniest and most entertaining group of people. You can really bust a gut at some of the things they come up with.

Understanding these little ones comes through listening to them. They have to know that you want to hear their thoughts and ideas. It helps them process their inner workings and helps you know what makes them tick.

Out and About

Whether while shopping (a wonderful time to let Junior talk his head off), strolling, playing, reading, or driving in the car, initiate conversation with your children and ask them open-ended questions.

Sometimes you'll see a smile or a frown or fear come over your tot's face. Ask how your child is feeling. When you do this, you help your toddler to express an emotion as he or she feels it. It's especially pertinent that you do this when your kids have negative expressions on their faces. Children need to learn to identify and express their negative emotions as early as possible. They need emotional language to do this.

Bedtime

My favorite time of the day with my kids was bedtime. After reading stories, I'd ask them:

- What's the funniest thing that happened today?
- What was the saddest thing that happened today?
- What made you feel happy today? Or: Tell me one happy thing that happened today.
- What made you feel mad today? Or: Tell me one thing that made you feel mad today.

Asking open-ended questions invites a story. Based on your child's answers, you may find other open-ended questions to ask them.

Even with three children, I made it to everyone's bedside every night with stories, conversation, and prayers. Try a Bible or inspirational story that is comforting as your children approach sleep and are about to lose your company for the night.

Nighttime Prayers

Another way to understand your children is to invite them to pray alongside you. You can institute a very simple prayer regime for your toddler:

Mom or Dad prays: "Thank you, Lord, for ..."

Tot prays: "Thank you, Lord, for ..."

Mom or Dad prays: "Lord, could you please help (so and so) ..."

Tot prays: "Lord, could you please help (so and so) ..."

Mom or Dad prays: "Lord, could you please help me ..."

Tot prays: "Lord, could you please help me ..."

"Good night, Lord, see you in the morning."

As we lead our children into prayer, we also hear what is on their heart and what concerns they have for themselves and others.

Dr. Mom Speaks

The way for a mom and dad to understand their toddler is the same way that a psychologist comes to understand a new client: Give your undivided attention, listen, and observe.

Chapter 4

Developing a Sense of Self

Developing a strong sense of self is all about getting a good sense of who you are. Knowing "who you are" is part of your self-esteem, part of your feeling of security in life. It's about feeling strong inside and about feeling capable of dealing with the world and everything in it.

If our children are called into the world to minister the gospel, to win souls, and to give to others through teaching or nursing or volunteering, they first need to develop a sense of who they are in themselves and who they are in the Lord.

As parents, you start them on this journey. You are the first ones to make significant contributions to your child's sense of self.

The Importance of Secure Attachments

As your toddler walks out the next two to three years, they will have emotional needs and need to know that they can find refuge in you; it gives them the confidence they need as they work toward independence.

Parents who react negatively or dismissively when their toddler comes for hugs and cuddles leave their children to feel too insecure to leave or be apart from their parents.

If you have an insecure son or daughter read on! There may be ways you are interacting with your tot that are reinforcing your child's insecurity rather than promoting security.

When the First Year Is Disrupted

Secure attachments are important in the first year of life. Yet some children have their world disrupted during that first year (or after the first year, turning their established sense of security upside-down). Perhaps because of adoption, death of a parent, or family crisis you have received a child into your house during the critical years of development.

Can such children still form secure attachments? Yes, but you can't take them from where they are. You have to start with them right back at the beginning. When the quality of parental responses changes, secure attachments can be formed.

What does this mean? Simply put, if you receive a two-year-old into your home, you can't just deal with that child as a two-year-old. To become attached to a two-year-old, and for that child to become attached to you, a concerted effort must be made to hold him, look into his eyes, soothe him, and make a lot of physical contact (massage his back, legs, and feet, or put him in a backpack on your back or your chest). You need to work to establish what the child does not have: a secure attachment to a care-giver. This is a full-time job. You have to be there for the child. He first needs to attach securely to you before he will begin to manage well with others.

Your new two- or three-year-old would probably be helped by the suggested prayers of inner healing in Chapter 26. You will want to ask the Lord Jesus to repair the emotional damage to your little one that was caused by the change in care-givers.

Please be mindful that the suggestions here are cursory. You and your little one may need the help of a child development specialist to work through the effects of any abuse or neglect your little one has suffered. This is also true with regard to adopted children, foreign or local.

Foreign Adoptions

Adopting children from other cultures and languages is, of course, more successfully done when you can adopt a newborn. However, a lot of adoptions occur with older children. You must consider that these children have often been traumatized. They may have been traumatized by witnessing horrendous things or by having things done to them. They may have been abandoned. They may have been lying in an orphanage where they received inadequate human comfort and physical touch. You can't expect them to fit the "normal" developmental categories physically or emotionally. Refer to Chapter 26 to learn how to walk your child through inner healing exercises to help them heal from trauma.

When adopting children from anybody, foreign or local, parents ought to pray and ask the Lord to disconnect the child from the spiritual heritage of their biological family. Refer to Chapter 25 for a sample prayer. Your pastor may have suggestions for you as well.

Word from the Wise

"The Spirit of the sovereign Lord is upon me. ... He has sent me to comfort the brokenhearted. ... He has sent me to tell those who mourn that the time of the Lord's favor has come." (Isaiah 61:1, 2)

We can have confidence in the word of the Lord. He came for the brokenhearted. He is here for your little one, no matter what the history.

Awesome Lord—The Healer of the Soul

We have an awesome Lord! Jesus Christ, our Lord, loves little children so much that it is nearly unfathomable. If you are the parents of a child who has been hurt, abused, abandoned, or adopted and has had life disrupted in these formative years, you need to know that ...

- You now have spiritual authority over your child (presuming that you have become the legal guardian)
- You can beseech the Lord on behalf of your little one
- You can disconnect your little one from all connections to his past (parents, abuse, and so on)

- You can ask the Lord Jesus to heal the brokenness in your child's soul and spirit
- You can ask the Holy Spirit to fill your child's emptiness with his comfort and love
- You can ask the Lord to seal off your little one from his past
- You can ask the Lord for a fullness of his love as you work toward bonding with your little one
- You can ask the Lord to open your little one's heart to enable you to attach to him or her
- Your love can heal the broken or wounded heart of any child the Lord brings into your home

Separation Anxiety

Whether a child has had a stay-at-home parent or has been in day care full time has no bearing on separation anxiety in children.

Protestations over a parent leaving begin by about eight months of age and continue to be significantly high until after age two, when such protestations begin to wane. This remains true for children raised in different cultures as well.

Separation anxiety has nothing to do with whether your son or daughter is securely attached to you. It happens to the most securely attached children.

Growing out of separation anxiety is all about the cognitive-developmental timetable, which you have no control over. There is nothing you can do to "hurry" your child through this.

Making It as Easy as Possible

During this time span, consistency and predictability will make things easier on your tot. For instance, just because your tot has become accustomed to being dropped at day care each day doesn't mean he or she won't be distressed if left with other care-givers.

Toddlers have been shown to be more distressed if they come in one door with their moms and their moms leave through a different door, than if their moms leave through the same door they both came in.

The more predictable you can make your routine at this stage of their development, the better.

Don't Let Separation Anxiety Control You!

Just because your son or daughter goes through this very normal stage of development does not mean that you should stop your life, never leave the house, never go out, and never get a sitter. Of course not!

You and your spouse need time alone together, you both need to work, and you need to do the things necessary to keep your marriage healthy. But during this phase of your child's development, try to keep the sitter consistent, try to follow a routine when leaving the house, and try to come in and go out the same door!

When you go to leave and your little one screams, remember, as soon as you leave and close the door, your child will forget all about you. (Well, not really, but the tot will get distracted and not think much about you until you return. The longer you stay there while the child is screaming, the longer he or she will scream.)

Dr. Mom Speaks

Parents often have a worse time than their tots when separation anxiety rears its ugly head. Your tot will be fine when you leave, but you will probably be more twisted up inside as you stress over how your child is doing. Don't let this stop you from spending time alone with your spouse or by yourself.

Self-Recognition

By about 18 months of age, children are able to recognize their own image in a mirror. They know it is them. Children can have great fun with mirrors and images, but they don't know it is "them" in the mirror prior to this age.

When children can recognize themselves in a mirror, they come to understand what they look like and what their bodies look like. Coming to recognize themselves is part of their development and part of them developing an understanding of who they are: a distinct person different from all others.

Safety and Sanity Tips

Buy a big mirror and place it where you can keep an eye on your tot. You can get a nice break if your tot is occupied by significant periods of time in front of a mirror. Leave some toys there, and maybe hang something from the ceiling to dangle above. Your toddler will love it.

Self-Definition

In Chapter 4, you learned that your toddler will first learn words of *objects* before he learns words of *actions*. Objects are concrete and easily seen and touched. Actions involve conceptual thinking and are therefore harder to learn. Conceptual thinking is also necessary for your toddler to come to understand that he or she is a unique individual. Your toddler needs to learn three words that help him understand his separateness from others: *I*, *me*, and *you*.

These personal pronouns require that a person be able to take another person's perspective. For example, your daughter needs to learn that *you*, when she uses it, refers to someone who is not her, but that when her mom or dad addresses her as *you*, it refers to her.

By the age of three, children become aware that they have a "private self." That is, they have thoughts going on inside their heads that are their very own. What goes on in their minds is different from their body that everybody can see.

Between the ages of three and four, children make a verbal shift. Before the shift, children often talk out loud as they are playing. They verbally express the internal dialogue they are having. After the shift, their dialogue about their playing moves inside their minds and they talk far less as they play.

Dr. Mom Speaks

Toddlers' use of the word *no* is one thing that is part and parcel of their need to define themselves. It is their way of distinguishing between who you are and who they are. Saying "no" is about their little minds making a little decision. While you won't be giving in to their every "no," gently walking around it and side-stepping it (see Chapter 4) allows them their need for definition without your going along with the whims and fancies of a two-year-old.

Self-Esteem

Throughout your son or daughter's life, you will constantly be bolstering self-esteem. Believing in your children and their abilities will cause them to believe in themselves. When you intentionally bolster their self-esteem, they will …

- Learn to be confident in their perceptions and judgments, and believe their efforts will be met with favorable resolution
- Expect to succeed at new tasks
- Expect to be able to influence other people
- Have courage to express their opinions
- Approach tasks and people with the expectation that they will be well-received and successful
- Trust their reactions and conclusions
- Be more assertive and socially independent
- Participate more than listen in a group
- Make friends more easily
- Be able to consider what others say more openly

Not investing in your children's self-esteem encourages them to …

- Doubt themselves
- Doubt their abilities
- Fear the world
- Believe that they can't influence their own world
- Think that what they think doesn't matter
- Be more vulnerable to depression

A solid self-esteem begets selflessness and concern for others. Poor self-esteem leaves children open to being overly preoccupied with themselves and their personal problems, doubting themselves and questioning themselves.

It is errant thinking that it is possible to esteem your child too much in these years. Some people have been taught wrongly that if you pat children on the back too much, they will become selfish and self-absorbed. The opposite is actually the truth. The better they feel about who they are, the more energy they have to consider other people. Don't begrudge your child positive feedback.

Creating Good Self-Esteem in Your Tot

When you regard your children with respect, affection, and trust they come to believe they are worthy of respect, affection, and trust. All three help your child to develop self-esteem.

Self-esteem is also gained when your toddler develops a history of success and failure. Tots need to be challenged to grow and develop, but you must give them tasks that challenge them and that, at the same time, are within their reach. If you present them with a task they are unable to do today, it must be a task that they might reasonably be able to succeed at in a week or two. When they are presented with the task again and succeed, they will feel good about their accomplishment. This is esteem building.

Keep in mind that if your challenges to your child always produce failure, your child will feel terrible about himself and his abilities. He may move into the "learned helplessness" mode and stop trying altogether. When you do this to children, you are breaking their spirits. God forbid that anyone should inflict this cruelty on little ones.

In Chapter 15, you will learn more about how self-esteem is created and built through good discipline. Parents who are affectionate with their children, show acceptance of their children, give their children respect, are firm in enforcing rules, and have high expectations of their children create children who have good self-esteem.

Self-Esteem and Parental Messages

Successful people believe in themselves! Successful children believe in themselves! The messages you give to your toddlers begin the process. When parents believe in their children's ability to succeed, their children will take on that belief about themselves. Self-esteem is built.

If you tell your toddler "You are smart," "You are brave," "You are funny," "You can do it," "God loves you," and so on, your child will believe it. Your little ones believe what you tell them and incorporate these beliefs into who they think they are.

In the same way, if a person tells a toddler "You're stupid," "You'll never do it," or "You're a dummy," the child will live up to those expectations and not create any expectations for himself or herself. But also keep in mind that if you tell a toddler 10 times "You're smart" and once "You're stupid," the negative remark will weigh much heavier on the heart, will conflict with the positive things you've said, and will have an overall negative effect on the child.

Toddler Tales

"You are such a good boy," Dad often told his little guy. Then one day, his son picked up the spoon, scooped up some food from the baby jar, and offered it to his baby sister. He turned to his mom and said, "I'm a good boy, aren't I, Mommy?" "Yes, indeed."

Our words to our toddlers are incredibly powerful. When you are going to tell them what you think of them, think before you speak.

When Positive Reinforcement Has a Negative Effect

Remember that positive reinforcement sometimes has a negative effect on a child. By the age of about four, when your son spontaneously does something positive (like putting away his toys) and you give him positive comments, it can quash his motivation. Why? Because all of a sudden, he's doing it for you and not for himself. If you see your four-year-old doing something good on his own, save your praise for when he has completely finished the task. Then keep the praise quiet and small (for example, give a thumbs-up without saying a word, or say "great," or "good job"). In this way, he won't lose his internal motivation to do things on his own.

Parental Responsiveness

By the time children are 12 months old, they have a rudimentary understanding of cause and effect. They understand that they can make something happen and that they can stop something from happening. They affect their environment by responding or not responding.

Young children begin to learn about a sense of control when their parents are responsive to them.

Children tend to make all sorts of demands on their parents. Parental responsiveness doesn't mean giving your children everything they ask for or doing everything they want you to do for them. If you did this, you would be creating a selfish, spoiled little tyrant.

Parental responsiveness means dealing squarely with your children when they exhibit a need, even if it means saying "no." It's up to you to provide alternatives or options to your children that keep a balance in their lives and in yours.

Providing options to a child challenges him or her to think and find a solution independently, which encourages an internal center of control. Giving a child a specific directive all the time so that the child's thoughts are not engaged produces an externally controlled child.

Parents who provide suggestions and alternatives to their children produce children who are more able to shut out unnecessary distractions and focus better on tasks. Parents who tell their child precisely what to do produce children who become easily distracted by outside noises and who have a more difficult time when trying to learn.

What the Bible Says About Love for the Self

Our love for others comes out of the love that we have inside of us. The way that we share love occurs in three stages:

> ### Word from the Wise
> "Love your neighbor as yourself." (Leviticus 19:18, Matthew 19:19) Jesus reiterates the Old Testament prescription. Love for others springs out of our knowledge and ability to first love ourselves.

1. We receive love from a person or from God. We experience their love as that which takes care of us and our needs.

2. We learn to love ourselves by learning how to take care of ourselves and our needs.

3. We share what we have with others by caring for them and their needs.

It is errant teaching that loving ourselves is selfish. Those who don't love themselves become so self-absorbed that they can't think of others.

Along with our toddlers, we are vessels of the love of God. Love springs from a vessel that is full—not from a vessel that is empty.

Teaching our children to love what is inside of themselves, to be open to the love of others, and to be open to the love of God will make them healthy and strong and, most of all, competent servants of the Most High God!

Toddler Tales

One day the Sunday School teacher asked his class if anyone knew how a fountain pen was like God. He was stunned when out of a four-year-old's mouth came this reply: "The pen is us, the ink is the Holy Spirit, the ink jar is God. God pours his Holy Spirit into us and then as we do God's work, we use up the ink and have to keep going back to God for him to fill us again." The teacher's jaw dropped. His only question: "Who are this boy's parents?"

Who We Are in Christ

As parents, we are leading our children into life and into eternity. Giving our children a good, healthy knowledge of God and his love for his creation is part of our job.

Toddlers need to hear what God thinks of them. It's your job to tell them that they are ...

- Created in God's image and it is "good." (Genesis 1:27, 31)
- Made by God in Mommy's tummy. (Psalms 139:13)
- Accepted by God. (John 1:12, Ephesians 1:6)
- Complete in Christ. (Colossians 2:10)
- A child of God, and he is their Father. (1 John 3:1–3; Romans 8:14–15; Galatians 3:26, 4:6)
- Able to be content in all circumstances. (Philippians 4:1)
- Never alone, for he is with them. (Matthew 28:20; Hebrews 13:5; Psalms 23:4, 139:7)
- Guided by God. (Psalms 139:10)
- Able to do all things through Christ who strengthens them. (Philippians 4:13)

- "Chosen" in Christ before time began. (Ephesians 1:1–7)
- Chosen and dearly loved. (Colossians 3:12, 1 Thessalonians 1:4)
- Children of the kingdom of light. (1 Thessalonians 5:5)
- Blessed with every spiritual blessing. (Ephesians 1:3, Psalms 139:5)
- Recipients of wisdom. (1 Corinthians 1:30)
- Able to approach God with confidence and boldness. (Ephesians 3:12)
- Able to have all their needs met. (Philippians 4:19)
- Given magnificent and wonderful promises by God. (2 Peter 1:4)
- Given strength by him. (Psalms 23:3, 27:1, 139:10; Daniel 11:32)
- Recipients of power, love, and self-control. (2 Timothy 1:7)
- Never able to be separated from the love of God. (Romans 8:35)

Our precious tots need to know beyond a shadow of a doubt that they are loved by God the Father; his son, Jesus Christ; and the Holy Spirit.

Knowing who they are before almighty God, their maker, is critical to their identity and the security of their faith.

Cautions

Never, ever use threats of the wrath of God or judgment of God against your children! This will lead children to fear God and make them unable to come to him. Shame and condemnation are from the enemy, not from God the Father.

God has entrusted his children into your hands. It's your job to show them his love and introduce them to him. At this age, they are much too young to be accountable to God for their errors in life. You are the one who is accountable to God right now for how you are raising them. Raise them in God's love so that they will desire to do good with their lives, so that they will desire to serve the God who loves them beyond measure.

Chapter 5

Healthy Sexuality

Our sexuality is a gift from God. We don't become sexual people in our teen years or when we get married. We are sexual people from birth. In their preschool years, children discover that boys and girls are different, that their genitalia are different. In their preschool years, most children discover that their genitalia produce pleasant physical feelings when they are touched. In this chapter, you will learn how to help your child through these developmental issues. You will learn how to help your child value their genitals as a gift from God while at the same time learning the parameters around care and protection of them.

Healthy Sexuality Starts Young

When it comes to sexuality, we have two objectives as Christian parents: to instill in our children the value of sexual abstinence before marriage, and to teach our children that their sexuality is a gift to be fully shared with their future spouse. How do you teach kids to both stay away from sex and desire great marital sex?

Many Christian parents and pastors of old focused so much attention on sinful sexual practices that they preached a sort of "Eunuch Sermon": Avoid all sex—sex is bad, sex is evil, sex is sinful. Christians have been misled in the past to think that the way to teach kids to stay away from sex is to paint it as evil.

This sort of paranoia leaves children open to becoming sexually unfulfilled mates in marriage as they struggle to find sexual peace and fulfillment. If they don't start learning about healthy sexuality until they're married, we as parents have waited far too long.

Word from the Wise

"So God created people in his own image; God patterned them after himself; male and female he created them. ... Then God looked over all he had made, and he saw that it was excellent in every way." (Genesis 1:27, 31)

Our sexuality, being male and female, was an intentional act of God. We were created in his image. After God created us as he did, he said it was excellent! Let us affirm every part of who God created us to be to our children, including our sexuality.

The goal is to instill a value for abstinence while at the same time endorsing the gift that God gave us in our sexuality. But when do we start?

We don't start teaching our kids about healthy sexuality when they are teens— even that is too late. We don't start teaching them about healthy sex when the "good touch/bad touch" programs start in the elementary schools. No, we start teaching them healthy sexuality when they are yet toddlers.

We start when they are toddlers with age-appropriate information and messages, and we continue to provide age-appropriate information and messages throughout their growing years.

Children need to hear about God's creation of sexuality from their parents, where the biological information can be paired with the values of the faith. Our children want to know our values and why we hold them.

When your child first touches his or her penis or vagina, it's time to start talking!

Word from the Wise

"You made all the delicate, inner parts of my body and knit me together in my mother's womb. Thank you for making me so wonderfully complex!" (Psalm 139:13–14)

Every part of our children's bodies is created by God. Every part of our children's bodies is a gift from God. Our children need to have a positive view of their entire body, even their genitals. God created their genitals to have wonderful feelings. May our children never feel shame for what is natural and good.

Masturbation and Your Child

It doesn't take long for some children to notice that they have good feelings when they touch their genitals. Often boys notice this fact before girls. We may come across our sons fiddling with their penis. We may come across our daughters manipulating small objects against their vaginas.

Most often this is our first opportunity to teach our children a healthy attitude about their bodies and how God made them.

When we find our children playing with their genitals, we must not be stunned, shocked, or horrified. All they are doing is discovering the wonderful feelings that God created in their bodies.

Only two concerns arise when children touch their genitals: that they don't hurt themselves and that they don't become preoccupied with touching themselves.

Dr. Mom Speaks

When my daughter was a baby, I bought her a set of multicolored key blanks and put them on a chain for her. She was so proud and happy to have her very own set of adult keys. When she was two, I found her sitting cross-legged on the floor, without her diaper, digging around her vagina with those keys. I was completely unprepared for such a thing.

I asked her if what she was doing made her feel good. She said "Yes." I told her God made her body with nice feelings for her to enjoy, but that I didn't want her to hurt herself, that her skin down there was tender and could be hurt by the keys. I told her that if she wanted to have those nice feelings, she should touch herself only with her own fingers and not use any objects because she might hurt herself.

To ensure they don't hurt themselves, make sure your children know not to touch their genitals with objects.

The next issue of concern is preoccupation with one's own genitals. Extroverted children may be less likely than introverted children to become preoccupied with their genitals. The extrovert, remember, gets energy through interactions with other people, while the introvert is energized by his or her own inner workings. More often you will have to watch out for the introverts when it comes to genital preoccupation.

Your little introverts will be alone more with themselves and their genitals. Introverts will require more effort when it comes to teaching them how to express their emotions. Emotional distress or loneliness can produce genital preoccupation in preschoolers. If you find that your introverted son is spending too much time in his bed playing with himself, when you know he's heading to his room, call him to sit with you and read a book or play quietly with some of his toys with him. Ask him how he's feeling in his heart and what he's thinking, and invite him to talk.

If your little introvert is playing with himself in the living room, in front of or around other people, you need to talk with him. Tell him it's okay for him to touch himself but that it's something only for him (and when he gets married, something to share with his wife). This is not something to do around other people. It's a private event.

This type of guidance for children will not encourage them to touch themselves all the time, but it will validate the fact that their sexuality is a good thing. You will be teaching them that sexuality came from God when he created them, but there are appropriate and inappropriate times and places for enjoying these feelings.

Sexual Exploration with Peers

Around the ages of five to six years old, your sons and daughters begin to notice that boys and girls have many more differences than they might have thought. They want to know what those differences look like.

When there are both sons and daughters in a home and the kids sometimes bathe together or share a room, or see that their baby brother or sister has parts they don't have, they are unlikely to explore with other children. Once the curiosity is satisfied, the inquisitiveness ends.

The boys and girls who are more likely to explore sexual parts with playmates are those who are only children, those who have all female siblings, and those who have all male siblings. What they can't discover at home they'll look for elsewhere. This is perfectly normal, and you should expect that it will happen.

Healthy and Unhealthy Exploration

Normal sexual exploration of toddlers follows a basic pattern:

What is healthy:

- Exploration with age mates—that is, children within two years in age
- Exploration with kids about the same physical size

- Showing what you have
- Showing what I have

What is unhealthy and when alarm bells should go off:

- Exploration with those more than two years from your child's age
- Exploration with kids with large size differences
- Touching what you have
- Touching what I have
- Engaging in adult sexual behaviors

Children who have not been presexualized through sexual abuse will, of their own accord, limit themselves to what is normal and expected. They will seldom take more than one or two opportunities to "see" each other. Once the curiosity is ended, so is the behavior.

Keeping Your Cool

What if you come across your child and their friend with their pants down? First, don't panic, shout, or discipline. Keep your cool. Ask the children, "Did you see each other's privates?" When they say "Yes," tell them, "Well, you saw them once, you won't need to see them again." Tell them calmly to pull up their pants and go do something else (get a drink, have a snack—anything to get their mind going on something else). Later, when you have your own child alone, ask him or her to tell you exactly what happened between the two. As long as your child mentions only things on the first list presented earlier, don't worry. But reinforce that because the children have now seen what the opposite-sexed child's genitals look like, they shouldn't do that again because their privates are only for them and, when they get married, for them and their spouse. Also say that if the other child wants to show privates again, your child should say "no" and come straight to you. You should also let the other child's parent know what happened and how you handled it.

Our concerns begin when there is a spread in age between the children. Older and bigger kids shouldn't be doing this with kids who are younger and smaller because the younger or smaller kids don't feel an equal sense of power. They feel they have no choice to resist the other child's advances or invitations because they fear the other child might hurt them if they don't cooperate. The older child doesn't have to threaten outright—the age and size is threat enough. What happens then? Younger kids can feel victimized by the older kid's requests. This registers as sexual abuse in the soul of the younger child.

Children who have been presexualized through sexual abuse will introduce to their friends, cousins, and neighbors behaviors they have been exposed to. This is often the first indication that a young child has been abused or is being abused—the child has sexual knowledge beyond his or her years.

Toddler Tales

> One day a five-year-old daughter was caught in the basement grabbing at the nipples of her three-year-old brother. It was odd behavior. Where would she get the idea to do that? When the mother talked to her, she said that a man at the bus stop had grabbed her chest while she sat on the fence. Her behavior was the result of the fear, anger, and confusion over being touched inappropriately. She was doing to someone else what was done to her. This is one indication that something inappropriate has happened.

If you come upon your child showing his or her privates with another child who is older and bigger, first ask your child to tell you exactly what happened between them. Then go further:

- Ask your younger or smaller son or daughter specifically how he or she felt about what happened with the other child.

- Ask how your child felt in his or her heart and tummy. Children may not have enough words in their vocabulary to tell you many details, but they know if they felt bad in their guts.

Besides age and size, the next issue is whether there has been touching. You need to ask for all the details:

- Ask your son or daughter if the other child touched him or her, or made your child do the touching. If the answer is "no," don't go further unless you suspect your child isn't being straightforward.

- Ask your child who started the touching. Be aware that if your child has been presexualized by someone else, he or she might have motivated the touching.

- If your child was touched, ask him or her to show you every body part that was touched.

- If the other child did the touching, ask your child to show you everywhere on the other child's body where your child was asked to touch.

- If your child had bad feelings about what happened, he or she had the experience of being victimized. Walk with your child through the inner healing exercise in Chapter 26.

If you find that there was touching, you need to be suspicious about the safety of the child who initiated it. Reality is, there is incest and there are pedophiles. If you get disconcerting information from your child, think of whether you have any reason to suspect that your child or the other child might be getting abused within their own families. If you have any reason to suspect this, you should call the police or child protective services.

Sometimes parents find out from their five-year-old's exploration with their friend that they have been getting abused by their older brother or sister!

Safety and Sanity Tips

In the ordinary course of guiding your children in issues pertaining to their genitals, remember to keep calm and don't overreact to your children's behaviors. If they display any unusual behavior, something going on with them needs to be addressed. Discipline will bring shame and possibly close them up from sharing their bad feelings with your or from telling you that someone has hurt them. Our sexuality runs to the very depths of our souls. Tread carefully with your children's sexuality—affirm them and guide them.

The Limits of Physical Touch by Others

The basic message to your preschooler is this: Your privates are yours and nobody else's. They are for you to enjoy yourself and for you to share with your spouse when you get married. Nobody else has permission to touch your privates. Period.

Since toddlers are already starting into potty training, they are learning to wipe their own bottoms when they go to the bathroom. Whatever they don't wipe off properly will come off in a bathtub as they soak and play. If they want help wiping, help them. If they don't, put them in the tub later.

Children need to know that they have control over their own bodies, and this needs to be reinforced by their parents. They should not be "made" to kiss and hug every relative under the sun. Making children share their personal body space with others gives them the message that other people have permission to tell them what to do with their bodies. This is not the message they should get.

Toddler Tales

I had a grandmother who I felt was cold and mean. At the end of each annual visit, we were supposed to kiss Grandma goodbye. At the end of one visit, after Grandma had punished me for something I didn't do, I ran and hid. I did not want to kiss her! My parents called and called, but I wouldn't come. If I wasn't required to kiss her, I would have come out to say goodbye. Parents ought to be careful about requiring their children to kiss and hug relatives. If your tot shies away, let them have their personal space. This reinforces their right to not allow people to touch them. While our relatives may wish they could hug and kiss freely, this will help keep your children safe from unsafe people.

Parents can get a bit of a chuckle as they work toward reinforcing the limits of physical touch of their children. When your five-year-old son is walking naked from the bathtub to his room, and his two-year-old sister sees what he's got and then proceeds to walk up to him and cup his privates in her hands, you have to stop yourself from roaring with laughter (as he stands there totally stunned) and tell her she's not allowed to touch his privates. You can laugh your head off later, when your kids aren't around!

Dr. Mom Speaks

It's both cute and fun for your two-year-old and your four-year-old (or three- and five-year-olds) to bathe together and play with their tub toys and bubble bath. When your kids are put in the tub together, they need to know The Bathtub Rule: "No touching anybody else's privates." Every time they get in the tub together, ask them, "What's The Bathtub Rule?" and get them to repeat it to you.

The Little Bit That Preschoolers Need to Know About Sex

When your son and daughter are two and three years old, they need to know ...

- Their genitals and the nice feeling from their genitals were created by God for themselves and, when they get married, for them to share with their spouse.
- Before they are married, they are the only ones who can touch their genitals—nobody else.

When children get to be four to six years old, they begin to wonder where babies come from. Whether or not mom gets pregnant, children see other women with huge tummies, and their friends' parents will be having babies. The most basic information they need to know is this:

- Babies are grown inside their mommy's tummy.
- God created mommies to have one part of what creates a baby and daddies to have the other part of what creates a baby.
- Mommies and daddies have to share their privates with each other to make a baby.
- Mommy has a special place in her body where the baby can come out when it's big enough.

Preschoolers don't need detailed information about how babies are made at this stage—that's for later, the elementary school years.

Parents who have been sexually abused themselves tend to either blind their children from sexual realities, bring shame upon their children regarding their genitals, or give too much information to their children. As we read in Ecclesiastes, "The more words you speak, the less they mean. So why overdo it?" (6:11). Unless there is evidence that your children have had sexual contacts beyond their years, you shouldn't go any further than is necessary in focusing on this issue. Their sexual issues are very small in the preschool years if they have been in a normal environment without inappropriate sexual intrusions. Don't take this topic further with them unless there is some evidence that you need to for their sake. Then consult a professional or spiritual leader.

Chapter 6

Play for Your Toddler

Play is a primary learning mode for toddlers. Through play, toddlers …

- Develop physically. They learn balance, dexterity, and coordination. Their muscles and ligaments grow and develop through physical movement. Physical movement stimulates the development of neurons in the brain.

- Develop mentally. They learn to focus, concentrate, figure things out, develop creativity, use their imaginations, start to think for themselves, and solve problems.

- Develop emotionally. Children learn empathy and caring through play. Children learn about their own feelings and the feelings of others.

- Develop socially. Children learn social skills through play. They learn to share. They learn to cooperate. They learn how to resolve conflict. They learn altruism through role playing and putting themselves in other people's positions. Children refine their verbal skills through conversing with other children.

- Develop spiritually. Children learn that we live in a world that God created to be fun, relaxing, creative, and full of joy.

Play and the Brain

Your toddler's brain is exploding with activity. Those little neurons keep multiplying every time they are exposed to something new. Focusing on the idea that your little one is expanding his brain power when he is exposed to new things is quite important. Now is the time for the brain to grow! It grows through learning. Toddlers learn when they play.

Mom and Dad: Primary Playmates!

You're it! You're really it. Until your child gets to be about three, he won't be interested in playing with anybody but you. This is not because there is something wrong with him; it's because he's not developmentally ready yet to play with others. Two-year-olds who play together are merely in each other's presence—they don't actually play together.

Dr. Mom Speaks

Positive play with your child is an important way for bonding and attachment to continue and deepen between you and your son or daughter.

The parent-child relationship is the primary relationship of the preschool years. You are your child's world. Your tot's life revolves around you, and he's not yet sure where he ends and you begin.

Playing with toddlers helps their development. They will learn more from their parents in the next couple of years than you could ever imagine. For them, play is their job. For us, playing with them is our delight!

What are some of the areas that you should be aware that you are working on with them?

Coordination

Mom and Dad can help stimulate a tot's brain development by working together on coordination skills. The following activities will be fun for your son or daughter. Don't just set your toddler up with these activities—play them together.

- Playing with blocks
- Throwing balls
- Catching
- Stringing beads (or popcorn)

- Pounding with a hammer and pegs
- Kicking balls
- Playing T-Ball
- Dancing
- Riding tricycles and other things that peddle
- Walking backward

Physical, Then Mental

If you want your little ones to be able to concentrate on something or sit still for something, it's better to let them burn off some of their energy first. It's a mistake to make them sit still before they are allowed to play.

A toddler's ability to focus and concentrate and do peaceful things follows a period of physical activity.

Drawing

Drawing is a wonderful way for children to develop their ...

- Hand-eye coordination
- Fine motor skills
- Creativity and imagination

Additionally, if children are distressed, it will likely come out through their drawings.

While your two-year-old will mostly scribble and do hand painting, your three- or four-year-old will be able to draw distinct images. When these older children draw a person, they draw a circle with four lines coming out of it (two for the arms and two for the legs). These are known as tadpole people. This is how all children begin to draw people. Only when they grow a little older will they draw two circles (one for the head and one for the body) and have the arms and legs coming out of the lower circle.

After your tot draws a picture, use it as a springboard for conversation. Ask your tot these questions:

- Who are the people in your picture?
- What's happening in your picture?
- If the people in your picture could talk, what would they say?

If you're wondering how your three- or four-year-old is feeling about a particular person, first ask him or her to draw a boy or girl; then ask your child to draw himself or herself, then Mom or Dad, and then anybody else who seems to be significant. When toddlers are upset about somebody, they will distort the picture of the person they are upset with. (Have them draw a picture of their babysitter now and then, day care workers, grandparents, brothers and sisters, and so on.) Always remember to talk with them about their picture afterward, unless they really don't like to do that.

Sorting

Sorting is another neuron-building activity. It gets your toddler's mind thinking and putting things together. What can be sorted?

- Buttons
- Cards
- Toys (dolls, stuffed animals, by color or size)
- Tins and jars
- Yarn
- Socks
- Just about anything!

You can sort by ...

- Color
- Shape
- Size
- Order
- Number

Sorting gets the brain activated!

Repetition

Toddlers learn through repetition. A toddler might want a favorite nursery rhyme over and over again, or a favorite story over and over again. Ride with it, don't buck it—repetition is important for your toddler. Cheerfully do it again!

Word from the Wise

"This is what the Lord almighty says: Once again old men and women will walk Jerusalem's streets with a cane and sit together in the city squares. And the streets of the city will be filled with boys and girls at play." (Zechariah 8:4–5)

What a joy it is to the Lord to see children play! Provide creative opportunities for your child. It's a great way to learn and grow.

Plasticine, Clay, and Play Dough

Get out the rolling pin (you might want to buy one just for play), cookie cutters, and assorted gadgets for shapes and impressions, and be creative with your tot. Teach your child how to hand-roll the dough, how to use the rolling pin, and how to make a ball and other shapes.

An investment in play-dough accessories is well worth it (kids will use them far beyond the preschool years). Art supply stores sell all the equipment you'll need to shape, cut, and design clay. Clay can be purchased in solid pieces at an art supply store much more cheaply than at a toy store.

The Best Play Dough Recipe Ever

1 cup flour

1 cup water

1 tablespoon oil

½ cup salt

1 teaspoon cream of tartar

Food coloring

Mix thoroughly all ingredients in a medium-size sauce pan. Cook over medium heat until mixture pulls away from the sides of the pan and forms together. Take it out of the pan and knead it like bread until it cools. Make several batches, each batch a different color. This play dough will keep for three months, unrefrigerated, in a sealed plastic container.

Play, Bonding, and Discipline

Affection, love, and play are all foundational elements for a healthy family that honors God. Children who get such attention from their parents have little trouble when it comes to discipline. It's not far from the way our relationship is with our Heavenly Father. He offers us his love and shares with us his joy, and when it comes to discipline, we receive it because we know his heart for us. Our children learn what sort of heart we have for them by the moments we spend with them that are filled with joy and affection.

At Two, Together but Not Really

Two-year-olds don't play together. They may copy each other, follow each other, or try to boss each other around, but this is not playing together. They may play only next to each other. They can be nearly oblivious to the fact that another child is near. Unless both children jostle for one toy, they will be content in their own little worlds.

It's not possible to teach a two-year-old to be a sociable person with the two-year-old beside him. He's not capable of that yet. He can't think about others or their needs; he thinks only of himself. You can't make him do what he's not yet capable of doing.

It's fine to get together with other two-year-olds, and they may distract each other while they are together, but the social aspect of such visits won't contribute to their development just yet. Remember, right now, if they have only Mom and Dad and their siblings to interact with, it's enough.

Two-Year-Olds and Their Toys

Two-year-olds become very angry if someone encroaches on their toys, and they may become physically aggressive. This behavior is normal. They will grow out of it with your gentle response to the situation.

If your two-year-old is reacting to someone taking his or her toys, kindly approach the child (or baby) who took the toy, say that it is your child's toy, and give it back to your child. Not until they are past three years old will you be able to teach the kids about sharing. Let them have what is theirs. This contributes to their feeling of security in their world.

Don't forget the distractibility factor! Two-year-olds are easily distracted by nearly anything. If your child's toy is disturbed by another child, draw his or her attention to something else; a toddler will quickly forget all about what just happened (either forget or not care!).

If your two-year-old gets upset, he is not being bad; he's just being two! This is not a discipline issue, a resistance issue, or anything of the sort. This is a time to help your toddler calm down and feel your comfort.

If your two-year-old attacks the other child, you need to make it clear that your child can keep the toy but cannot be mean to the child who tried to take it. Even though your toddler's reaction was spontaneous and natural, you should model how to say "sorry." If your toddler can't handle the situation with the other kids around, remove him. He may be getting tired or hungry anyway.

Friends from Three: Socialization with Peers Begins

Toward the end of age three and into age four, you will see your toddler become quite capable of sharing; in fact, your child may be very happy to share. A spirit of generosity blooms. At this age, toddlers are not as possessive about their toys as they once were. They are looking now to cooperate with their playmates instead of dominating them. (If your child is into dominating them at this age, it will be necessary to try some behavior-modification strategies. See Chapters 14, 15, and 23 for further guidance on dealing with an aggressive or dominant child.)

Make-believe play starts in the third year. Dressing up in costumes, role playing, and using the imagination fill little ones' play lives. And they love to spend time with other children now.

Learning Routines the Fun Way

Age three is the time to start your child into routines of all sorts. Even though toddlers may become quite rigid if you've started a routine and they insist on completing it perfectly, it's your prime opportunity to introduce your child to playfully putting away toys and books and other things strewn around the room.

Now is the time to start learning habits for the future, from teeth brushing to bathing, to cleaning, to sorting, to eating, to reading, to putting clothes away, to straightening drawers. Three-year-olds are most conducive to this sort of learning.

Again, when you teach these routines to children in a fun way, they learn through playful activity. They can find joy and laughter in the ordinary and mundane.

Forever and Ever

At ages three and four, when your son or daughter finds a compatible playmate, they can literally play together for hours on end. Your child may develop a "best friend" he or she wants to be with all the time.

Silly Jokes

Be prepared to laugh. With such expansive language capabilities and a developing imagination, your three- or four-year-old will fill you full of imaginative tall tales and silly jokes.

Some of the jokes may seem a little funny, and most will just be silly, but your toddler will howl as he tells them. You'll have to howl, too. Everybody likes it when someone laughs at their jokes. Of course, now and then you'll have to tell them they are being a "little silly."

If you have a "silly joke" tot, get out the video camera. Your child will never believe this stuff later unless you have proof. And when your child is a teen, you can watch the videos together and laugh yourselves into hysteria!

Role Playing

As children approach four years of age, they start more active role playing. Role playing is very important to their development.

In role playing they …

- Practice being their same-sex parent in an adult role.
- Learn altruistic behavior if the role playing includes adults demonstrating kindness, concern, and positive actions toward others.
- Begin to gain a concept of what other people experience in life.

> **Safety and Sanity Tips**
> Role playing requires dress-up clothes. If you don't want your high heels and hats to mysteriously go missing, head to Goodwill or the next garage sale. Buy a large plastic bin and fill it with hats and old suit coats, shoes, purses, tops, pants, and belts. You can do this very cheaply. And buy lots of string bead necklaces and hair ware!

Fantasy vs. Reality

You may find that your four-year-old makes up stories that he or she is convinced are true. Sometimes there is a blurring of fantasy and reality at this age. This phase, too, shall pass. There is no need to "prove" or "disprove" most of their stories. For the most part, Mom and Dad need to just look interested and encourage the creative thinking. Who knows? These kids might become really good storytellers one day and write a novel! You wouldn't want to curb a potential Pulitzer Prize winner, now would you?

Pots, Pans, Computers, and Felt Pens

On one hand, today's technologies and inventions have created an endless supply of things parents can buy for their preschoolers. There is no end of it. On the other hand, you'll soon find out that your preschooler quickly tires of nearly every toy you buy. You don't have to keep up with the proverbial Joneses!

Clinical research has shown that the longest period of time a two-year-old will play with the same toy is 30 seconds. A two-and-a-half-year-old can maintain interest in a single toy for 42 seconds; a three-year-old's interest in a single toy rarely runs more than 55 seconds.

Wasted Money

You will look at all of the toys at Toyland and think your little ones need this and that, but they don't. Parents can easily overdo it in toy purchases. Not only do most children tire of toys quickly, but most toys are boring. Between toys that are not stimulating and kids with the attention span of a cricket, you will end up with many toys in the closet because your child isn't interested in them.

Wise Investments

Before you go hog wild buying toys for your kids, check out the Top 10 Toy List on websites like www.epinions.com and www.leapfrog.com. You will find toys that have been tested on kids and found to be of interest to children. Pick up the *Consumer's Guide* and get objective information. These websites and Consumer's Guide can also provide you with information on toys to avoid for safety reasons.

A good toy is worth the money you pay for it. It is an investment in your family's future. Not only will all of your children make use of it, but when they grow out of it, you can store it in the attic for your grandkids. If it's a good one, it'll have a timeless quality and be totally durable.

Toys in Every Cupboard

Parents on limited budgets, and parents who don't want to spoil their tots with everything imaginable, will find lots around the house that can easily hold the interest of their little ones.

Younger children like to scribble and bang and build. Old-fashioned wood blocks or big plastic building blocks are great. Basic crayons and paper, or chalkboard and chalk, or washable felts and paper, are great; so are the pots, pans, and bowls in your cupboard. If your two- or three-year-old is bored one day, get out a big mixing bowl, measuring spoons, measuring cups, a whisk, and some smaller plastic bowls, and pour some corn meal in the big bowl. Voilà—an indoor sand box. A sandbox in the winter!

Don't forget the homemade play dough we discussed earlier in this chapter. Real clay can be purchased by the block. You can cut off small pieces for your children, and they can make their own interesting projects.

Computers

We live in a world of computers. While your two-year-old isn't ready to engage others in play, she is able to enjoy children's games on the computer. There are fabulous programs out there teaching shapes and matching and numbers. There is no harm in getting your child on a computer at a very young age. Just never let them start it up, shut it down, or put discs in the drives. It's a little horrifying to find that your disk drives have been stuffed by your child trying to cram disk after disk into it. They do get stuck! Be forewarned.

Hide and Seek

You can play hide and seek with nearly anything. Put objects in things, under things, and behind things. It's cheap, yet fun!

Toddler Initiates

When you play with your toddler, allow for the development of your toddler's creativity. Allow your toddler to decide on what they would like to play when you play with them. Ask them what they would like to do. Follow their lead.

> **Safety and Sanity Tips**
>
> Does your toddler rock himself rhythmically or bang his head (other than on his pillow at bed time)? These are signs of disturbance within your little one. It's time to see your doctor. Head banging can indicate ear infections. Rhythmic rocking can indicate mental/emotional delays/ stressors.

Silliness

Toddlers can get to acting very silly very fast. It's funny at first, and your toddler may move on to something else before winding up out of control, but pay attention. If your toddler tends to get silly and goes so far as to hit or break things, throw a tantrum, or show any other bad behavior, you need to figure out what puts him or her over the edge (it may be as simple as being too tired and needing a nap).

There is usually a pattern to observe. Once you know the pattern, think backward in time and try to determine if it is a food, drink, or sleep issue. Consider whether some stress may be underlying your child's emotions. If your tot gets silly and out of control after a visit with certain people or at a certain place, perhaps he or she was overstimulated and is now finally unwinding. Try to get to the bottom of it. This may reduce the occurrence in the future of going from silly to catastrophe.

If silly-to-catastrophe is a behavioral pattern, make sure you interrupt the silliness with a distraction or a change of activity while your child is still being silly. Walk away and call your toddler to another room to do something else. Remove your attention so that the behavior won't continue. If there is no audience, there is no performance.

Playground Isolation and Rejection

Parents dread the thought, or reality, that nobody seems to want to play with their child. What a heartbreaker!

The first questions for a parent to ask are these:

- What is my child's temperament?
- How is it affecting my child's ability to connect with other children?

Children who have the most difficult time with peers are those at the more extreme ends of the temperament: the quiet introvert and the bossy, controlling extrovert.

Toddler Tales

At four, the little guy was found standing against a wall while other kids played. When asked why he didn't play with the other kids, his answer was simple: "I don't know their names." This little guy needed a formal introduction before friendship could begin. Find out what's inhibiting your little one, and take action.

These years are the years to start building on social skills. Helping your children now will spare them some grief when they get older.

The Quiet Introvert

You learned in Chapter 2 that the introvert needs time to think and can be slow to respond. Your little introvert may have difficulty initiating interactions but may, surprisingly, need less help than you think.

What happened to the four-year-old who didn't know the kids' names? The mom went to the teacher and let her know that the kids didn't know each other's names yet. The teacher made an extra effort to help the children learn each other's names. Additionally, when she became aware that a number of the shy introverts were wandering the playground alone, for two days, she paired them up by asking them if they would like to play together. After two days, they began looking to each other and asking each other if they'd like to play.

Toddler introverts do well with other introverts. They play quietly together. They get just enough connectedness.

Encouraging introverts to think about solutions to their problem is better than you just telling them what to do. Ask your tot, "How do you make a friend?" Let your child think about it a little. He or she may respond with the toddler's equivalent of "You have to be a friend to have a friend." Then you ask, "How do you be a friend?" Let your child think about what he or she needs to do to be a friend to another child. The more you can engage your child through his or her own thinking, the better.

The Bossy, Controlling Extrovert

Your child may be shunned because he or she is bossy. While the introvert may never mention isolation to his or her parents, the bossy child will complain about other children and how things aren't fair and what's wrong with all the other kids.

While the introvert is ignored, the bossy child is shunned. If your child is complaining about all the other kids, again, resist giving advice. Use the situation as an opportunity to get your child thinking about what to do differently to be more likeable. Ask your child to think about what he or she is doing that leaves the other kids not wanting to play.

An extroverted child who is not bossy but is kind and considerate of others is the one with the most friends. It's not extroversion that is the problem. The extroverts of the world are behind the church potlucks and social activities. We need them. Some, not all, extroverts have the tendency to dominate and control. This is what gets an extrovert into trouble.

Word from the Wise

"Others from Benjamin and Judah came to David at the stronghold. David went out to meet them and said, 'If you have come in peace to help me, we are friends.'" (1 Chronicles 12:16–17)

A friend is one who helps another. If your child has no friends, he or she needs to learn how to help other children. Explain some of the benefits of resulting friendship in order to motivate your child.

Do some role playing at home and have your child approach you the way he or she approaches kids at preschool. Ask your child to try another way. You may also want to take the opportunity to observe your little one and see how he or she interacts with other children. Your child will likely need help to understand how he or she affects other kids and makes other children feel.

Parents should focus on helping their three- or four-year-olds understand how they make other kids feel by what they do, and teach them other ways to behave that will help them get the friends they want.

Visits with Friends

When your toddler starts having friends over, it can seem like a blessing or a curse, depending on how it's planned or handled. There are so many variables. Here you are trying to socialize your toddler. You must choose who to have over, when to have them over, how long to have them over, and so on. You must also deal with any little scraps or fights they get into. Here are a few suggestions to help guide your decisions and your actions.

One at a Time

Toddlers need only one friend over at a time. Three is a crowd even when you're a toddler. Your toddler is used to having the whole house to himself, so another toddler in that space may feel like an intruder. You won't know how your child feels about it until you actually do it.

Similar Temperament

Try to choose a child who has a similar temperament as your child's. If your child is an introvert, try to invite another introvert. If your child is an extrovert, invite another extrovert. If your child is very verbal, invite a child who is equally verbal. You get the picture. Choosing playmates with incompatible temperaments has the potential to cause everyone a lot of grief.

Dr. Mom Speaks

One day I took two of my children to my good friend's to have tea. She had two preschoolers. In a short while, my children came to me showing me bite marks from her children with reports that her children were hitting them. In fact, she had two physical extroverts and I had two contemplative introverts. The children were incompatible. I learned a valuable lesson. As the apostles Peter and Paul had to agree to go their separate ways, such is the fact that we don't have to make our incompatible children spend time together!

Ask your child who they would like to have over. They will know who they like and don't like. This can prevent many problems between children. A convenient playmate may not make the best playmate. No playmate is better than an incompatible playmate!

There will be enough opportunities to teach our children about sharing, getting along, and resolving conflicts without the additional burden of dealing with mismatched temperaments.

When and How Long

Start off by arranging to have visiting children over for only an hour or so, to see how it goes. Arrange to get the kids together after they have eaten and had their naps. You want them to have the best possible experience together.

Plan a Little Snack

You can avoid the irritability associated with an empty tummy by planning for the children to have a little snack together. It also gives them a nice distraction. Kids love to eat. Make some fun food! Let them have a few laughs as they eat "ants on a log" (celery filled with peanut butter with raisins on top).

Put the Favorite Toys Away

If your child has toys that he or she will become possessive over, put them away before the playmate comes. This will help prevent tirades. Tell your child that these are the special toys and that you'll save them to play with later. Bring out toys that will not cause obvious conflict.

Cooperative Activities

Unless your toddler is a social butterfly, thinking ahead about setting up cooperative activities may help the visit go more smoothly. Do you have enough building blocks for each child to build something with? What about setting up the sprinkler in the backyard and putting them in their swimsuits? What about an indoor or outdoor jungle gym? A sandbox filled with utensils? Sidewalk chalk? Play dough?

Quit While You're Ahead

A retired military man who became the recreation director of my hometown once advised that the best time to end an activity with children is when everyone is at the peak of having the most fun. Never wait until the children become tired, miserable, and bored. Quit while you're ahead. This way, the final memory of the event is positive.

Pay attention to the kids. Are they tiring of each other, starting to pick at each other, rubbing their eyes, or getting too frustrated? Step in and get something else going with them, or call the friend's parents and ask them to come and get their child.

Your House

In your house, it's your rules. You're in charge, not just of your own child, but of all those under your roof. You must tell the visiting children what your "rules" are.

Socializing children requires that you concern yourself not just with your own children, but also with those with whom your child plays. If there are problems between the children, it's your job to show both children how to resolve their problem.

While it's your job to socialize your children along with their playmates, it is not your job to punish other children. If there is a serious problem, you need to tell the child's parents about it. They should deal with their own child.

If there are repeated problems with a particular child playing at your house, you have two options: First, don't continue to invite that child. Second, tell the child's parents how you would deal with your child behaving that way, and let them know that if their child comes to play again, you will treat their child like you would your own. Then they can decide whether they want to send their child back to your house.

Toddler Tales

One day my daughter's friend came over to play. They were playing tag in the yard. The next thing we knew, the friend was running straight through the house to avoid being tagged. I told her, "When children play tag at our house, they have to stay outside for the whole game." That was all that was necessary to say. It never happened again.

Accountability

Whether it's your children or their friends, they need to learn, no matter whose house they play at, that they are responsible for their actions. If one of the children breaks something or destroys another child's toy, that child must be called to account. While the children have no money to replace the item that was destroyed or damaged, mom and dad need to walk them through it to provide the example. For instance, if your child destroys another child's doll, you should take your child to the store with you, buy a replacement doll, and then have your child take the new doll and give it to the friend. This teaches a very important lesson to children. You don't want children to get the idea that they can damage other people's property without consequence. When they start getting an allowance, it will be their money that pays for damaged items.

Clean-Up

It's a good idea to insist that all the children who played together clean up together before the friends go home. Try to make an agreement about this with the other parents. Even if the other parents won't do this, you should. If you know the friend's parents are on the way, start the clean-up. If the parent arrives at the door, tell the kids to clean up so that the friend can go home with his or her parent.

This is especially important if your child's friend is the equivalent of a human cyclone. Your child will start getting resentful if he or she has to pick up after the friend after each visit. Pretty soon your child may not want the friend to come over again because he or she will start having a bad feeling about it all.

Introducing Your Toddler to Your Newborn

Put some thought and planning into bringing home a new baby when there is a toddler in the house. Not to do so can bring some very unpleasant consequences for your newborn.

Preparing for the New Baby

First-time pregnant is very different than second-time pregnant. When the first baby came home, there was only baby and Mom and Dad. When any other baby comes home, that baby comes home to a fuller house!

The first child had no competition. Every other child brought into the house has the potential to be seen as competition. What Mom and Dad do to prepare for their additional children can pave the way for a harmonious family or can create years of rifts.

What can you do to set the stage for a smooth transition in your family? Let's take a look.

Announcing the Pregnancy to Your Toddler

Once you know you're pregnant, you need to consider when and how to deliver the news to your children. Here are some tips.

One-Year-Olds. Your one-year-old is too little to have any clue that he's about to be joined by another baby in the house. You can tell your one-year-old about a new baby coming but he is not old enough to comprehend what it means.

Two-Year-Olds. Your two-year-old does not need to be told about your pregnancy until you're beginning to really show. Two-year-olds have no concept of time. Telling them eight months ahead that they are going to have a new brother or sister won't mean much to them. When your belly is obviously "full," then it's time to start talking about babies.

Your two-year-old should be told that Mommy has a baby in her belly and that soon that baby will come out of her belly and be part of the family. Take opportunities to show your toddler other people's babies and say that soon your family will have one, too.

Three- and Four-Year-Olds. You can tell your three- or four-year-old that Mommy is going to have a baby before it becomes obvious that you are pregnant.

Keep in mind, though, that, like any pregnancy, there is always the risk of miscarriage, which is higher in the first three months than later in the pregnancy. If you miscarry in the first trimester and have already told your toddler that he or she is going to have a baby brother or sister, you are left having to explain what happened to the baby.

According to WebMd.com, 50 percent of fertilized eggs miscarry before the mother knows she's pregnant. Of pregnancies in which the mom knows she's pregnant, 10–20 percent of pregnancies will not survive the first 20 weeks of gestation. If you've told your three- or four-year-old that you're pregnant and then lose the baby, you can give the following explanation: "Sometimes when babies are growing in their mommy's tummy, they don't grow quite right. When that happens, God takes those babies right from their Mommy's tummy to heaven to be with him. When we get to heaven, we will see the baby that was in Mommy's tummy."

While your two-year-old may not wonder how the baby will come out of your belly, your three- or four-year-old might ask. Simply tell them that God created all people with two openings in their private area—one is to let out poop and the other is to let out pee. God made girls and women different from boys and men. God made women to be able to have babies. There is a special place in Mommy's belly where a baby can grow. There is a passageway from where the baby grows to the outside world. God made women with a third opening in their privates to let babies come out. Most of the time babies come out of their mommy's belly that way.

The Newborn's Bedroom

It would be wise not to outdo yourself in decorating a room for your second baby. Your firstborn has been the only star in your eyes for a couple of years already and has been used to being the center of the universe. You shouldn't kick him or her out of that position too quickly or harshly. Bringing the new baby into the family in a quiet and sure way is better than all the fanfare. You don't want to induce your toddler into jealousy. This won't be good or safe for your baby.

Your newborn isn't going to care what the room looks like. Decorating the newborn's bedroom is more about Mom and Dad than about their new baby.

The Toddler's Crib

Perhaps your newborn isn't getting her own room just yet. Maybe you're putting up a crib in your toddler's bedroom. Perhaps you've just moved your toddler out of the crib and into a bed to prepare for the new brother or sister.

Most families don't want to have to purchase two cribs if they don't have to. If you're moving your toddler to a bed, it's a good idea to start doing this a couple of months before the newborn arrives. You want your toddler to get adjusted to a new sleeping routine, to take ownership of the new bed.

When you put up a bed for your toddler, take down the crib and put it away for a few months. You want your toddler's mind to say, "I'm a big boy. I have a big-boy bed. The crib is no longer here because I'm not a baby anymore." You want your toddler's ownership over the crib to be gone when the baby arrives.

If your child goes straight from the crib to a bed, and the crib stays in the room and all of a sudden someone else moves into it, he or she may become jealous. The tot may think you are giving away that bed to someone else. You don't want your toddler to get mad over something like this because that anger will come out in some vengeful way against your baby.

The Baby Doll

Before your newborn arrives, you can buy your toddler a baby doll or a special stuffed animal and begin to talk about taking care of babies, loving babies, holding babies, and so on. Set your toddler's mind in the direction of loving care.

Not a Baby Doll

Don't talk to your toddler in such a way that you send the message that the baby actually *is* a doll. You should refer to the newborn as "your brother" or "your sister," not "the baby." When your baby is born, refer to him or her by name.

Avoid talking about "the baby" to other people, too. When talking with others, talk about your son or daughter by name. The newborn must be viewed as a human being, not an inanimate object. Your language helps to set the stage.

Not a Plaything

Don't set your toddler up to think he or she is going to get a playmate! The new brother or sister won't be capable of playing for a long time.

One way to avoid frustration on the part of your toddler is not to get expectations up. Any frustration between your toddler and your newborn can leave your newborn vulnerable to misbehavior from your toddler.

Our Baby

Talk about the new baby coming as "our baby," a baby that belongs to the whole family, that the whole family can love, and that your toddler can love. Don't refer to "Mommy's new baby" or "Mommy's baby"—refer to "our baby."

Let Your Toddler Decide

When your toddler is invited into making decisions that involve the baby, the probability increases that the newborn will be welcomed, not rejected.

Take your toddler with you to look at new cribs (if you're buying a new crib). Include your toddler (if three or four) in naming the new baby. Include your toddler in deciding where the crib should go in the new room (or the room they will now be sharing), where the brother or sister's dresser should go, and so on.

Find ways to include your toddler so that he or she feels more ownership and investment in your new family member.

Tour the Hospital

You may want to take your toddler for a tour of the maternity ward or birthing center and show where mommy will be going to have the baby. Let your toddler know if Daddy or Grandma will bring him or her to the hospital to visit after the new brother or sister is born. Show your tot the waiting rooms, the nursery with all the new babies, the cafeteria, the chapel, and so on. Make it interesting.

Visit the Doctor

You may want to take your three- or four-year-old with you on a visit to your obstetrician for a brief introduction and to offer the opportunity to ask the doctor any questions he or she might have.

Word from the Wise

"A relaxed attitude lengthens life; jealousy rots it away." (Proverbs 14:30)

Jealousy is a normal reaction on the part of an older sibling toward a coming newborn. If you take the advice in this chapter, it will help to create a relaxed attitude in your older child, which will make life a whole lot easier for all of you.

Introductions Start at the Hospital

There you are with your new baby. Is it Dad or someone else who will be bringing your toddler and other siblings to the hospital to see Mom and the new baby? Plan this ahead.

Home Delivery

Sometimes new babies are born at home. This is an incredible and exciting event for the family. Having had two hospital deliveries and one home delivery, I can appreciate both.

Depending on the ages of your children at home, you need to decide whether to allow them to watch the delivery. I assure you, preschool children age five and under should *not* witness their mother giving birth. This is simply too much for them to take in. They become afraid for their mother, see all the parts of their mother that they have no need to see, and see their baby brother or sister all bloodied. This can be a traumatic event for the very young!

Plan for your young children to stay with someone else when you go into labor. They should be brought back home after the baby and Mom are all cleaned up and, hopefully, after Mom has had a day or two alone with the new baby.

Bring your toddler and other children home after the baby is fed and sleeping. Set up a bassinet or basket for baby. Surround the basket with gifts for your other children. When your children come home, spend a few minutes of relaxing time with them and then let them go from room to room looking for the baby. Come in the room after the new baby has been found. Let the children open their presents "from our new baby."

As friends and relatives come to visit, encourage them to first greet and acknowledge your toddler before attending to the newborn. Also, if they would bring a little something for your toddler along with the baby gift this will help your toddler not to be jealous. You may want to keep some small gifts on hand in case your visitors don't bring a gift.

Hospital Delivery

Place gifts for your toddler and siblings in the bassinet in the hospital nursery. Have Dad (or grandparents, or whoever) take your children to the nursery to look at all the babies and see if they can find their new baby. Of course, their baby's bassinet will have the preplanted gifts within. They will want that baby to be theirs! After they spot their baby, dress them up in the hospital garb (if required by hospital staff) and let them go in and get the baby's bassinet. Let them touch and talk to the baby. Then ask them if they would like to take the baby to go see Mommy.

Let them introduce their new baby to Mommy!

Dr. Mom Speaks

Your toddler will be feeling very vulnerable when the new baby finally arrives. Be proactive and check in every few days for the first little while. Ask your tot how he's feeling and what he's thinking about his new brother or sister. Let him know you are there for him and that he is very, very precious to Mom and Dad.

Issues When the Newborn Comes Home

When everybody gets home from the hospital, the reality of the new addition hits hard and fast. You're back to taking care of a baby but, unlike the firstborn, the new one is not the sole focus of your attention. Here are some tips to help the transition of the new addition go smoother.

Safety and Sanity Tips

When you let your toddler sit and hold your newborn, make sure they are both propped up and secure.

Private Time with Your Toddler

When your baby naps, you may see that as a time to get stuff done around the house. The cobwebs can wait—your toddler can't. Especially during the first few weeks or month after you bring home the newborn, when baby sleeps you must spend focused time with your toddler.

Your toddler must know that he or she still has a significant place in your heart. Your tot will come to know this with the time and attention that you give. In the first few weeks, your newborn is pretty much just eating and sleeping, so you will have lots of time to hang out with your toddler.

Consider hiring a babysitter (or Grandma or Grandpa) to come over and sit at the house while your newborn sleeps so that you can get out to the playground, the toboggan hill, or the mall with your toddler. Get away from baby now and then, just to be one-on-one with Junior. Both Mom and Dad have to do this with Junior.

Your newborn won't notice if you're not in the room every minute of the day, but your toddler will.

Sending Baby Back

Your toddler may ask you or tell you to send the baby back! There is a two-step response:

1. Help your toddler deal with these feelings about the baby and how he or she feels put off by the baby's presence in the home. Listen, hear him out, comfort him, and assure him of your love for him.

2. Junior needs to be lovingly told that your family doesn't send anybody back—not the new baby and not kids already there! You are a family, and families love each other and stay together.

Toddler Doesn't Sleep with Baby

Your toddler may surprise you by requesting to climb into the crib and sleep with the new little brother or sister. Your toddler needs to know that everybody has their own bed and that everybody has to sleep in their own beds.

Let your child know that it is not good for the baby to have anybody sleep with him or her because the baby is so small and everybody else is so big. Sometimes big people roll around in their beds and can bump babies and hurt them. Say that you don't want this to happen to your baby, so it's safer if the baby sleeps alone.

You might tell your older daughter that it's really sweet that she loves her little sibling so much that she wants to cuddle up and sleep together. Instead, encourage her to reach in and rub the baby's tummy or hold baby's hand.

Toddler Tales

> When I was only four or five years old, my mom's friend came over with her newborn baby. She placed the baby on a child's table in my bedroom for me to watch or play with. Before I knew it the baby had flipped onto the floor and was crying. What was that mother thinking? No four- or five-year-old is competent to be responsible for a baby!

Helping Take Care of Baby

Your toddler may love to help take care of the baby. Encourage this altruism! Your child can feel really good about being Mommy's helper.

Recognize your toddler's limits. Never leave a toddler alone to care for baby. Accidents can happen too quickly, babies can flip or flop unexpectedly, and your toddler will feel miserably responsible if anything should happen to the new little one.

Toddlers drop babies all the time. Even four- and five-year-olds can easily drop babies. My pastor's one-year-old has been dropped on his head more than once by children in the church who pick him up while he's crawling around. Please be careful with your newborn around *all* preschool children.

Tips for Avoiding Hostility and Jealousy

If a toddler becomes jealous of a baby, he or she can be quite mean.

My Own Stuff

Your toddler needs to be able to have ownership over his or her own toys and belongings. When the baby tries to keep holding on to the big sibling's stuff, you need to give your toddler back that stuff and distract baby with something else.

Your child needs to know that the little sibling isn't getting to "take" his or her stuff. Allowing the baby to take over your toddler's stuff will cause jealousy, resentment, and retaliation. The retaliation will come, whether you witness it or not.

This is not the time to teach your children about sharing. It's inappropriate to expect your toddler to share with a baby. You will be teaching your toddler to share with age-mates, playmates, and others. This is not the venue.

The baby needs her own toys!

My Own Space

Make sure your toddler has his or her own space if both are sharing a room. Section off the room and keep the baby's stuff on the baby's side, and protect your toddler's side from the baby's incursion.

Just because your toddler needs to share space doesn't mean he or she should have to lose it all.

Baby Can Wait

Sometimes you will have to decide between meeting your baby's needs and meeting your toddler's needs.

While it's true that babies need Mom and Dad to be responsive to them and to develop a solid attachment to them, the concern for the baby's long-term safety is

> **Toddler Tales**
>
> While the parents' backs were turned, the four-year-old son grabbed his baby sister's arm and bit her. She began to scream. When the parents looked over, their son acted like he had no clue what had happened. If your baby begins to cry, don't presume your angelic toddler hasn't participated in their pain, no matter how sweet and innocent they look. Keep an eye on baby!

also at issue. Toddlers will react against their competition if the baby is seen as competition. They will retaliate. Don't let the baby be competition for your toddler. This sets up a dangerous and unpredictable situation for your baby.

Once in a while, you can ask your toddler to wait and let the baby take priority, but don't let the tables turn that way most of the time. There will come a time to even out this situation, but not now, when the baby is still really helpless. Your toddler needs to be about four or five years old before he begins to develop the concept of sharing, waiting for his turn, and so on. He can't learn everything when he's two or three.

Reward Kindness and Helpfulness

Mom and Dad need to express their pleasure with their children when they act kindly towards their little sibling. Showing admiration for positive behaviors will produce more positive behaviors.

Let your toddlers know that when they treat the baby well that it is just like they are being kind to the Lord Jesus himself.

Word from the Wise

"'Lord, when did we ever see you hungry and feed you? Or thirsty and give you something to drink? … Or naked and give you clothing? When did we ever see you sick … and visit you?' And the King will tell them, 'I assure you, when you did it to one of the least of these, my brothers and sisters, you were doing it to me!'" (Matthew 25:37–40)

As we teach our toddlers about Jesus Christ, this is a beautiful lesson to impart. Let them know that when they do nice things for their baby siblings, it is like they are doing nice things for the Lord.

Expressing Frustrations and Jealousy

Take the time to listen to your toddler and allow them to express any feelings of frustration and jealousy they have. Lovingly assure them of your love for them.

Include Your Toddler in Feedings

The time when your toddler may feel the most jealous is when you are nursing your baby. At the same time that you may want this just to be a bonding time between you and your baby, your toddler must be considered.

When your toddler is in bed sleeping, you get to have exclusive time alone with your baby to nurse. Planning an afternoon nap for your toddler can create at least one time during the day when you can nurse alone. At other times when your husband is home, he can take your toddler for some one-on-one time and you can nurse the baby.

When your toddler is there, invite him or her to come close to you and experience your love while you are nursing. While nursing the baby, cuddle your toddler. You can have your toddler hold a book and read to him or her while nursing. Or have your tot get out a book with many objects in it, and ask him or her to identify objects. During this, you can sneak in those all-important eye contacts with your newborn. Looking into your baby's eyes while nursing is important; do it as much as possible when your toddler is with you.

Toddler Is Not Responsible for Baby

By all means, invite your toddler to help you get diapers, bottles, blankets, or whatever, but don't demand it. Let your child make a choice. Then be sure you offer praise when he or she decides to help. Remain silent if your toddler goes off on his or her merry way. Don't punish or scold. This can cause resentment.

Your toddler may want to help diaper the baby. It is never his job to do the diapering; it's your job! This should never become one of his assignments.

It is also not your toddler's responsibility to …

- Feed.
- Entertain.
- "Watch."
- Otherwise care for the baby.

Making your toddler responsible for care for your newborn can easily breed discontent in your toddler. Along with discontent comes potential aggression.

Never Alone

Never, ever leave your toddler alone with your newborn. Your toddler has no idea what to do with this little thing and shouldn't be left to guess or become creative!

> **Dr. Mom Speaks**
>
> Don't feel guilty if you forget that you have a baby in the house! Many parents have stories in which they get busy with their toddlers and completely forget that they have a baby in another room. This isn't uncommon because a family is usually in a good routine by the time the second or third child is born. Once we were pulling away from the house with our three-year-old son and five-year-old daughter when we realized that our newborn baby was still asleep in the crib!

Special Privileges

One way to let your toddler know that he or she has not been displaced by the baby is to give a few more privileges. This sends toddlers the message that you recognize them as more grown-up. It's a way to make them feel special. Perhaps they get to stay up a little later, have a friend over for a sleepover, or have a little pet.

Regression

Expect it! Your toddler is no longer the center of your life. Even if your toddler receives the newborn well, his or her world has still changed. Any kind of stress can cause regression in your toddler, including the addition of a new brother or sister.

Your toddler may return to …

- Wetting the bed.
- Thumb sucking.
- Having toilet-training accidents.
- Waking in the night.
- Demanding a pacifier or bottle.
- Resisting the bedtime routine.
- Returning to baby talk.
- Wanting to be carried.
- Wanting to sleep with Mom and Dad.

Tips for Dealing with Aggression and Regression

Seeing aggression or regression in your toddler should cause you to react with love, patience, and kindness. Your toddler is troubled and needs your help.

Never allow a comment by your toddler about unhappiness with the baby go by the wayside. Make sure you talk together about it.

All About Feelings

If your toddler shows any aggressive or hostile signs, these are telling you that your child is mad, jealous, and resentful of that little bundle that came home with you and won't go away.

Emotionally pent-up toddlers act out because they can't express how they feel about what's happening around them.

Your toddler needs to know how special he or she is to you, that you love him or her just as much now as you ever did. Your tot also needs to have you draw out his or her feelings about what is happening. Help your little one open up and express those feelings with you.

Let Junior know that he can come to you like he always did for hugs and cuddles and stories and playing. Let Junior know that he can come to you when he's feeling lonely or sad or wishes he was a baby again. Ask for ideas of things he'd like to do with Mom and Dad to make him feel better.

Be prepared to make some changes. Don't just expect toddlers to "deal with it." Toddlers are not mature enough to deal with it like adults. They'll deal with it by doing things to the baby behind your back!

Explain Baby's Needs

Talk with your toddler about when he or she was a baby. Show pictures of him or her as a younger and much more helpless child. Remind your tot how much more he or she can do now than as a baby. Just as Mommy and Daddy had to take care of the older kids, they need to take care of the new baby—with Junior's help.

Help your tot understand that the new brother or sister won't be a baby forever—only for a little while. Then that baby will get bigger, like your older child, and won't need everybody's help as much.

Not Hurting Baby

Your toddler needs to know that the baby needs to be loved just like he or she does. Your family is a family that doesn't hurt each other. You all have to be careful not to hurt each other.

If your toddler ever feels like hurting the baby, it's important to come to Mommy or Daddy right away and get a hug and a kiss. Say that if he or feels like that, it's because he or she needs a little more loving and should just come and ask for it. Better to get love from Mom and Dad than to get trouble!

Bad Attention

If your toddler is acting out over and over toward your newborn, you have to ask yourself what sort of relationship you have with your toddler. Why must he or she misbehave to get your attention?

Not giving toddlers sufficient attention sets them up for a cycle of misbehavior and punishment that leaves them more distant from you and more resentful of the love you're giving the baby. This aggression will increase. Don't get into this cycle with your toddler.

If you're already in the bad attention cycle, turn it around. Start off tomorrow with a good attitude toward your toddler, arrange babysitting for the baby, and spend time talking with your toddler, playing games, and reading books. Get a schedule going with your toddler that is positive and rewarding.

Pray for Your Toddler

Your children will always need your prayers, even when they grow up and leave home. It's the parents' job to pray for their children.

If your toddler is having a tough time in spite of all of your valiant efforts, he or she needs your prayers.

If your prayers and efforts don't stop Junior from hurting your baby, go to your pastor for prayer, or find a family therapist or other counselor. It's possible that Junior is expressing anger against the baby when other things are bothering him or her. Stress in the family, being hurt by someone else, and not sleeping or eating well can all cause your toddler to act out. The new baby may not be the root of the problem—only the visible evidence that there is a problem.

Part
3

Everyday Routines
with Your Child

Here is where most of your parenting will be done—in the everyday, mundane things of life. From eating to bathing, to potty training, to bed wetting, to making your house safe, to putting your little bundle to bed, you'll discover ways to make everything go as smoothly as possible.

Chapter 8

Eating Healthy, Getting Clean

As toddlers begin to assert themselves and use their new vocabulary to their best advantage, they will likely try to assert themselves at the table or in the bathroom. Here are some ideas to help gain their cooperation.

Good Eating Starts with Baby Food

Children develop a sweet tooth in their preschool years, but only with their parents' help and indulgence.

You've just been through the first year of life and are starting into baby foods. You may have started your child on baby food around six months of age. By the time kids are one, their bodies are finally mature enough to digest cow's milk, and you can stop buying formula or begin to wean your baby if you haven't already done so.

Cow's Milk and Supplements

Cow's milk can't compare to mother's milk and formula. It does not contain all of the vitamins and minerals children need. By the time your toddler is on cow's milk, at about 12 months old, you need to make sure your little one is eating a well-balanced diet so that he or she is nutritionally well-rounded. Consider children's vitamins for a consistent daily intake, since kids don't always eat consistently at this stage of life.

Toddlers can drink too much milk. Those who drink too much are getting their hunger needs met through milk, not through food. Drinking 1½ to 2 cups (12–16 oz.) of milk a day is enough.

Get a Grip on Fruit Juice

The American Academy of Pediatrics says that parents need to cut back on how much juice their infants, toddlers, and young children—even older children—are drinking. Too much fruit juice gives too many sweet carbohydrates, and kids aren't as hungry for other foods, can become malnourished, can suffer tooth decay, can become obese, or can suffer from diarrhea.

In other words, if they feel full all the time from milk and juice, they won't have an appetite for meat and vegetables.

If you give your kids fruit juices, citrus juices are recommended over other juices. Also, give them the real thing! Pure, unsweetened frozen orange juice is great. You can even make frozen pops out of it by just adding one can of water instead of three. Don't give more than 4 to 6 oz. of juice per day.

Buy the juice with the fiber in. Strained fruit juice is just sugar and water!

Avoid anything with high-fructose corn syrup.

Of course, if you can get your kids interested in vegetable juice or carrot juice, you'll make their pediatrician really happy!

Water, Plain and Simple

Besides needing milk for calcium and some protein, the only thing we really need to drink is water. Our bodies need water all the time—pure water, not soda, not juices. Water is readily available and cheap!

Lack of water can cause headaches, dehydration, nausea, and emotional misery for your toddler. Consider keeping a cup or bottle filled with water. Adding a little lemon juice with a little honey or sugar is far better than offering a soft drink or all the sugar in fruit juices.

Brain Food

Protein, protein, protein. When we have enough protein in our bodies, our brains are better able to learn, remember, think, and process information. Keep a couple of things in mind about feeding your child's brain:

- **Make sure choline is part of their diet.** No choline, no memory. Choline is an essential nutrient. It's found in egg yolks and organ meats. It's also present in spinach and cauliflower. Nuts and wheat germ contain good quantities of it.

- **Give them more than food.** Besides actual "food," kids' brains develop through reading, playing and listening to music, engaging in conversation (talking and listening), writing, being taught how to count and recite ABC's, imagining, visualizing, drawing, doing rhythmic activity with music, humming or singing a melody, listening to new sounds, dancing, touching new textures, moving the body, and role-playing.

Dr. Mom Speaks

Seeking to raise healthy kids, I never gave my children soda, desserts (other than real fruit), or packaged foods. One Christmas we were at a family party and I saw my four-year-old son's reflection in the living room window. He was sneaking over to the food table (filled with sweet treats, chocolates, and other desserts). He looked around to make sure no one was looking and reached up to the table to sneak—a carrot stick! I could hardly stop laughing! He's now 19 and snacks on red peppers, tomatoes, and cucumbers. He has little interest in sweets, chips, or soda.

Hunger Impulses

In God's great plan, he designed us with a digestive system. The digestive system tells us when we are and aren't hungry. It is your job to teach your toddler how to pay attention to hunger pangs and how to pay attention to the signals that he or she has had enough to eat.

They Won't Finish It All—Don't Make Them

Toddlers have very small stomachs. They can't eat as much as an adult, and they shouldn't.

Expect food left on the plate. Don't scoop a lot of food on your toddler's plate, and don't expect your child to finish all you have scooped. You don't know how hungry your tot is at any given time, and neither does your tot. Let your kids know that when they're full, they can stop eating.

One Big Stretchable Balloon

The stomach is stretchable, like a balloon. It starts out about the size of your two fists put together. If we eat as much as we need, it stays about the same size. When people overeat, their stomachs stretch out to accommodate the extra volume. The problem is, if you repeatedly overeat, the stomach doesn't stretch back to its normal size—it stays bigger. Then you have to eat more food to make it feel full. The vicious cycle begins.

Toddler Tales

At four years old, my son didn't want to waste too much time eating his porridge for breakfast. It was Saturday morning, and he wanted to rush to his cartoons. He woofed down a ton of food in record time, jumped up from his chair, and crossed from the kitchen to the dining room—and up came all his porridge all over the carpet. Eating too fast? Risk loosing your cookies! Or porridge!

If the stomach is made to expand too much too fast, it sometimes reacts with one huge contraction! Everything comes out immediately. Plop!

The Toddler Appetite Ebbs and Flows

After the first year, a child's growth slows considerably. Your toddler needs fewer daily calories now. These little ones' bodies become leaner, and they start to lose their baby fat.

Your toddler will eat voraciously for a few days or weeks and then pick for a few weeks. Eating ebbs and flows with body growth. Sometimes toddlers' bodies are going through a tremendous growth spurt, and sometimes their bodies are resting.

This is why you can't expect them to eat three balanced meals per day. This does not give their bodies what they need. They need to eat when they need to eat.

Healthful Snacks Are a Must

Have toddlers? Must have snacks! You can't predict when they will be hungry and how hungry they will be, but you do know that they will get hungry. When they do, you need to put good things in their bodies.

Healthful snacks will keep your tots' energy levels up and those tantrums down.

Chips or other little food treats come after a healthful meal, not before it or in place of it.

Early Bird Special

You may find your tot is hungrier in the morning and less hungry at night. That's not unusual. Don't forget that when kids graze every two to three hours during the day and go all night without eating, they need a morning jolt of calories to get them going. After they are up and running, they can cruise.

As adults, aren't we reminded constantly that breakfast is the most important meal of the day?

Avoiding Obesity

Avoiding obesity means that toddlers needs to learn to pay attention to their tummies to know when they are hungry and when they are full. If kids eat only when they are hungry and stop eating when they're full, they'll avoid obesity.

Obesity starts when people eat for the sake of eating and keep eating even though their bodies don't need any more.

Here are some guidelines to keep in mind:

- **Know that TV and eating don't mix.** When kids are watching TV, they can get so engrossed in it that they don't sense that their tummies are full. They keep eating. Constant overeating stretches out the stomach so that, over time, they'll feel like they need to eat more to fill up the stomach. Keep out of this terrible cycle. Feed your children in the kitchen!

- **Keep it fresh.** Avoid prepackaged foods. A fresh slice of red pepper, a carrot, a slice of cucumber, a piece of cold chicken, and a cup of frozen blueberries or raspberries have good calories. Prepared foods are loaded in sugar, fillers, and bad carbohydrates. All they do is fill up children so they aren't hungry for the good calories.

- **Don't give desserts.** Nobody needs them! Children shouldn't have a sweet dessert as an enticement to eat an entire meal. Desserts should be reserved for special occasions and should seldom enter a child's mouth. The more sweets you eat, the more you crave. You can turn your child into a sugar addict before you know it.

- **Skip the whole milk.** Kids don't need fat calories from whole milk. Use 2 percent, 1 percent, or skim milk. Whatever you give them they will grow to like.

- **Avoid deep-fried foods.** This is a nation of deep-fried fatty foods. These are just empty carbohydrates. Take deep-fried coatings off of food before giving it to your toddler. Better yet, don't buy or order these foods to begin with.

- **Get them moving.** Kids who aren't losing their baby fat, or who are acquiring more fat, aren't moving enough. They should be constantly burning off calories. Everybody needs 30 minutes a day of physical activity, and toddlers are no exception. If you're a sedentary type of parent, enroll your children in a kids' gym class, swim class, or other activity, and keep them moving.

- **Avoid the white stuff.** White bread and sugar may be toddlers' worst enemies. They need whole grains, and they get enough natural sugar in their fruit. If they are getting overweight, leave out the potatoes, rice, and pasta, too. These are fat producers. If your child is active enough, he or she can eat these last three without gaining weight, but an inactive child will gain weight with these three.

- **Encourage slow eating.** When people eat slowly, they are more able to discern when they are full. Don't rush toddlers when they are eating. If they eat too fast, encourage them to slow down. Put on some boring music to help everyone wind down. When we're more excited or agitated, we tend to eat faster.

- **Watch for overeating.** Experts estimate that 75 percent of overeating is emotional eating. That means eating because you feel bad or sad, depressed, lonely, bored, angry, frustrated, or anxious. If your child is overeating, in your opinion, talk together. You may find out that your child is upset about something that is causing a lot of stress. Help your toddler deal with those stressors. Children need emotional skills, not food, to deal with stress!

- **Don't put cereal in the bottle.** Putting rice cereal in your toddler's bottle is known to put children at a higher risk for obesity. Some parents give this to toddlers when they put them down to sleep. There are so many calories in the bottle, and the child is getting nuzzled to sleep and is not able to pay attention to natural feedback mechanisms that he or she is full. Also, the child could choke on this while lying down. Don't do this.

If your child is already obese, consult your pediatrician for healthy ways to help him or her trim down.

The Perils of Forcing Food

Making your children eat after they are full can have messy consequences. Just because they can get it in doesn't mean it will stay in.

Toddler Tales

My mom tells me she learned really fast about making a toddler eat all the food on the plate. She insisted that my sister eat the entire bowl of porridge. She was full partway through. Mom made her eat it anyway. She did. When she got up from the table, she threw it up all over the floor. Mom had to clean it up. That was the end of Mom's "force-feeding" attempts.

The Old Standby—PBJ

No parent can completely cater to a toddler's tastes. You will want to cook a variety of things, especially if you have older children. For any one meal, one of your children may not want to eat what you've cooked, so don't send the idea that this is a restaurant. If your kids really think they hate what is on their plate, tell them this:

> If you don't want to eat what is on the table, you may go to the kitchen and make yourself a peanut butter and jelly sandwich. After you make it, you will have to bring it to the table and eat with the family." (Sandwich ingredients are optional.)

Through all of the spicy East Indian cooking I do and the interesting sampling into Chinese food, Ukrainian food, and all sorts of homemade experiments, with three kids growing up in my house, only once or twice did any of them ever take me up on the sandwich offer. Whenever they complained, I just told them to go and make their own sandwich if they didn't want to eat what I had cooked. And no matter what sort of concoction I came up with for supper, I made them try one spoonful.

No matter how bad they said it smelled or how terrible they said it looked, I required them to put one spoonful in their mouths before they were allowed to go and make their sandwich. The result: culinary adventurists!

The Pleasant Family Meal

Mealtimes should not be used to scold or discipline children or for people to raise contentious issues. If there is conflict at the table, your child may eat too quickly or may get too stressed to eat. Family stress at the table could leave a toddler reacting to his parents, not eating himself, then having his parents mad at him for not eating, and having his food taken away, all because he's reacting to Mom and Dad's problem. Try to avoid these scenarios. A child's reaction to his parents' conflict should result not in discipline, but in understanding.

Mealtimes should be a time to talk about things you've done and things you're going to do, and to just connect through conversation.

Toddler Tales

One day my three-year-old daughter was seen holding a ladybug in her fingers. In a flash, she popped it in her mouth, crunched it up, and swallowed it. We think she thought it was an M&M! Mmm, protein!

New Foods

Introduce new foods slowly, not more than one or two per week. The way to do it is to offer a food the kids like "just as soon as they try the new food" and swallow it.

The new food may need to be "tasted" many times (8–12 times) before your toddler acquires a taste for it. A bite a day for 10 days to 2 weeks can help your toddler acquire a taste for nearly anything!

Don't make your kids eat more than a bite or two of a new food. A taste is a taste.

Food Fights

It might be part of your son's natural development to refuse everything! It might be part of him establishing his own sense of self, part of defining himself. Saying "no" to food is going to happen.

This shouldn't cause great worry, especially in the food department, for one very good reason: Hunger is an innate drive! Your toddler will get hungry and will need to eat.

He can decide "when" and "how much"—that's up to him—but you decide "what" (make sure it's healthful). If he insists that he wants only desserts, or soda or chips, or other non-nutritious stuff, you can wait him out. Eventually, he'll have to settle for that piece of banana or chicken!

If your son gets miserable at the table, take his food away. If he wants to get fed, he must behave at the table. This means no whining, fussing, playing with food, etc. If he starts into these behaviors, take his plate away and say, "I guess you've had enough to eat—off you go." Let him sit there for 10 to 15 seconds of silence if he wants a second chance. Always allow a second chance.

If he leaves the table and later comes back because he's hungry, sit him at the table and offer him his dinner, as long as he behaves.

Refusal to Eat

Don't worry—hunger will drive toddlers to eat. You can outwait them. Make sure while you're waiting that the kids aren't filling up on juice or milk. Perhaps they'll have to be happy with water while they're waiting for food because it gives no calories to keep them satisfied.

If you get upset because of a child's refusal to eat, your little one will find you very entertaining and will make sure to keep up the shenanigans. If a toddler sees that a refusal to eat will leave both parents at odds with each other, that might be entertaining, too. Don't indulge your tot. Keep calm, deal with these things matter-of-factly, and stay on track.

Force-Feeding

This should never happen! If you find yourself force-feeding your child, it is not because your toddler has a problem. Please seek your pastor's or counselor's assistance because you're probably overly stressed or overwhelmed, or could be becoming depressed.

Charting Growth

It's a good idea to chart your toddler's growth. Ask your doctor for a growth chart—they are usually given free to your doctor by drug companies. If your daughter's weight curve falls below her height curve, it is a signal that she's not absorbing her calories, is not getting enough, is burning off too many, etc. See your pediatrician if this happens. If the body doesn't absorb enough calories, growth and development can be stunted.

Bathing, Washing, Scrubbing, and Brushing

Get out your camera. There are a lot of fun pictures to take as your toddler begins to really make a splash! Bubbles that tower over the tub by a couple of feet, games of volleyball bubbles, the sight of your toddler making a long beard with the bubbles— these are Kodak moments you won't want to miss.

Your goal is to get your children clean in a fun way and to avoid unnecessary battles and power struggles. Don't ask "How can I make my son do this?" but rather "How can I help my son want to do this?" One way to engage cooperation is to get kids to use their imaginations. Make it fun!

Bathing Is a Blast

Scrub-a-dub-dub! These days, there are so many cute little knickknacks to make bathing more fun than ever. Bubble bath is always fun for kids and is a sure way to get them into the tub.

Most kids love their bath. For those who love it, only a few tips are needed:

- **Never leave them unattended.** When you are bathing your toddler, everybody else in the world can just wait! A slip and fall or a head bump is all it takes to submerge your toddler. If a little one goes under, he or she will panic and be afraid, and could swallow enough water to drown. (In lifeguarding class, they taught us that a person can drown in a teaspoon of water!) You have to be able to respond quickly. People can phone back or come back later. If you must run for the door, grab your toddler, wrap him or her in a huge beach towel, and go to the door together. If you use a cordless phone, don't leave the bathroom to talk. Get call display and take only what appear to be important calls.

- **Find bath toys on a tight budget.** Throw in your plastic measuring cups, some plastic storage containers, a sponge, a rotary egg beater, a wire whisk, plastic egg shells from Easter, and a rubber ball.

For those who are tub-troubled, keep the following in mind:

- **Don't bathe every day.** Daily bathing is not necessary! Every mother who has taken a child to the pediatrician because of eczema has been told this. In fact, kids with sensitive skin are encouraged to sponge off obvious dirt or spills as needed and bathe with soap once a week. If your toddler has tub aversion, to start, reduce the trips to the tub. Put bath day on the calendar and make it a predictable weekly event.

- **Offer enticements.** Consider a small amount of water and lots of toys, bathtub finger paints, favorite music, bubble-blowing stuff, bubble bath, washcloth puppets, sponges, etc.

- **Get a baby tub.** A large bathtub can cause fright in a little tot. Try using the baby tub on the floor of the bathroom, or buy one of those huge plastic wash tubs from the hardware store. After a few weeks, move the small tub into the big bathtub, if it will fit.

- **Give sponge baths.** Kids don't have to get into the bathtub to get clean. What about a sponge bath? Put a big towel on the floor of the bathroom, and help your toddler learn to wash down with a wet facecloth with a little soap on it. Remind your tot once in a while that being in a tub of water will be warmer than the sponge bath. To wash hair, your child will have to kneel on the floor facing a baby tub of water or lay on his or her back, head leaning backward over the edge of the tub.

- **Bathe with your toddler.** Either naked or with a bathing suit on, get in and play together. Make it fun.

- **Change your schedule.** Have the bath at a different time of day.

- **Be prepared.** Have the tub ready when your toddler gets there, and drain it after he or she leaves—the noise could scare her.

- **Give your tot some control.** Encourage your child to round up favorite bath toys. Let kids squirt the bubble bath under the running water themselves.

- **Take advantage of summer.** In the summer, let your toddler bathe in the out-door pool. Fill it with warm water, use the squirt soap and a hand puppet washcloth, and throw in all the toys, weather permitting.

- **You bathe.** Take your own bubble bath, and let your child stand at the side of the tub and play with the bubbles. Put some kiddie toys in your bath and play with them together as your child stands outside of the tub. Each time, invite your tot to come and join you. Eventually, it will happen.

Sidestepping Bathing Resistance

As with other issues when your toddler might offer resistance, you need to think about how to sidestep from a power struggle.

"Johnny, it's time for your bath." "No, I don't want to take a bath." "Will you be taking your bath while the water is still warm or after it has gotten cool?"

"Do you need me to scrub you down, or are you a big enough girl to do it yourself?"

Hair Washing

Some kids have no problem having their hair washed. For those who have trouble, try these ideas.

With "tearless" shampoo, use as little water and as much shampoo as is necessary to be able to sculpt the hair. Get out a mirror and let your tot look at all the funny things you can do: Put plastic toys in the hair, insert chop sticks, etc. Make it fun.

Wash each other's hair!

When it comes to rinsing (the worst part of the hair washing), fold up an adult face cloth and have your child hold it tight against the eyes. Use a big juice jug to pour the warm water to get out the bubbles. Pause between refills and check with your toddler to make sure she's okay and that her eyes are still dry.

Tell your daughter exactly how many jugs will be poured, count them off, and stop when you get to the number you said, whether there are still bubbles in their hair or not. You'll get them next time. It's important that your child can trust you to keep your word. If you tell her four jugs, it's four jugs. Next time, tell her five.

Use spray hair detangler instead of putting kids through the conditioner cycle. Towel dry, spray on, and comb carefully and slowly. Don't let the comb-out hurt.

Combing Away Cradle Cap

Your kids may not like having their hair brushed. It may take some time to work with them on this routine. Meanwhile, you might notice that your tot is developing cradle cap. Cradle cap develops when your child's dead skin accumulates and sticks to the top of their head. A thick layer of scaly dead skin develops. It can turn yellow and crusty. If left untreated it can spread to the face and neck. It takes a good regular hair brushing to prevent cradle cap. What to do? What to do?

Comb through kids' hair when they are napping. If you put a little baby oil on their scalp and let it sit there a few minutes, the dead skin will come off their head fairly easily with a baby comb. Gently comb through their hair to remove cradle cap. You can wash out the baby oil with the next hair washing. Alternatively, you can put a little shampoo on their hair, let it sit for a few minutes, comb out the cradle cap, and then have a bath later and wash it all out.

Gleaming Teeth

Parents should start introducing toddlers to brushing their own teeth when they are two. By the time they are three, they should be able to manage fairly well on their own.

Only a small pearl-size bit of toothpaste is needed for daily teeth brushing (for adults and kids).

Tips for fun teeth brushing:

- Buy three or more flavors of toothpaste.
- Let your toddler help pick out the toothbrush.
- Buy your toddler at least three different, fun toothbrushes.
- Buy a puppet (that you hold), and let the puppet help brush Junior's teeth (or use a favorite stuffed animal).
- Make a game of it; keep it light.
- Make the chipmunk face (toothbrush in closed mouth brushing under cheeks).
- Make the bunny face (toothbrush in closed mouth brushing front teeth).
- Make the whale mouth (wide open for the molars).
- Avoid regular mint toothpaste because it can start to burn the mouth if left in too long.

> **Word from the Wise**
>
> "Comb your hair and wash your face." (Matthew 16:17)
>
> Jesus tells people when they fast that they should keep doing the regular daily things so others won't notice them fasting. God expects us to keep up our toddlers' appearance for his glory.

- Brush softly, quickly, and precisely (brush teeth, gums, and tongue). Have Junior stick out his tongue and make a face for the tongue brush, and brush in a circular motion around each tooth.
- Brush each other's teeth!

Toothbrush hygiene:

- Replace the toothbrush every three months.
- Replace the toothbrush after recovery from sickness.

Lots of parents like Tom's of Maine toothpaste, which comes in tons of flavors. It's available at the website www.tomsofmaine.com and from Trader Joe's and Wild Oats.

Take your toddler to the dentist before the age of two for a first visit. It will just be a little look and see. The purpose of the visit should be to desensitize your toddler to the office and the dentist. This little visit will pay off next year.

Bottle to bed. Don't give your toddler a bottle to take to bed. In particular, don't give milk in a bottle. Kids end up with a pool of milk in their mouths that will rot their teeth. Having to sit with a toddler having a pulpotomy (baby form of a root canal) is such a waste and can be completely avoided. Wean your child to some other security item for naps and for bedtime.

Toothpaste eaters. Brushing with water can be just as effective as brushing with paste. To get the fluoride for your toddler, ask your doctor for fluoride tablets that you can give to your toddler daily. Tell Junior that if he eats the toothpaste this time, he can't have toothpaste on his brush next time.

Mundane Yet Meaningful

Eating and getting clean, these are daily activities with your toddlers that give you many opportunities not only to take care of the necessities of life, but also to bring the Lord into your child's life. Help your little one learn how to give thanks to the Lord as they enjoy their snacks and meals. Talk with them about God's creation of the animals and plants and how they are provided to us by God for our nourishment and health. Talk with your child about God's creation of the heavens, from the sunshine that helps plants grow, to the rain that gives us the water to bathe in.

Chapter 9

Making Your Home a Safe Place to Live

When you are the parents of toddlers you know that you can't let them out of your sight. They find every possible danger just through their normal and natural desire to explore their environment. They are truly the "Great Explorers!" Your toddler is too young and immature to know what is harmful and what is not. What is dangerous is taught through experience over the course of years. While you are in the process of teaching your toddler what is and is not dangerous, you must protect them from the dangers that exist. You must make your home a safe place. In this chapter you will learn how.

Childproofing the House

Most accidents at home occur when you go to answer the door or the phone. Get a cordless phone or phone headset and an intercom for the front door. If you have to go to the phone or door, pop your child into the playpen or crib first, or take Junior with you.

Word from the Wise

"Set boundary lines that the people may not pass. Warn them, 'Be careful! Do not go up on the mountain or even touch its boundaries. Those who do will certainly die!'" (Exodus 19:12)

Just as the Lord set boundaries to keep us safe, we must set boundaries to keep our children safe.

Safety and Sanity Tips

Get down on your hands and knees and see what you can find; then protect your toddler from it.

Today we can do better than the parents of the past. Far more safety devices and gadgets are available today. No matter how careful you are, it's a miracle if your toddlers get to first grade completely unscathed by some kind of accident. You can only do your best to look out for your toddlers. Here are some things you can do to make your home as safe as possible for your little sweethearts.

Doors, Drawers, and Drops

Now is the time to install safety latches and locks, safety gates, doorknob covers/locks, a Lazy Susan door latch, bedside rails, cupboard door latches, drawer latches, security latches or barriers for sliding doors and windows, and window guards.

Can your toddler open the bedroom window? How far down is the fall?

It's a terrible day when your child's dresser topples because your tot opened the top drawers. Get some furniture safety straps and secure chests of drawers, bookcases, file cabinets, big-screen TVs, and other tall cabinets. Toddlers can climb up on nearly anything when you aren't looking. They can do it very quickly.

Light switch extensions will deter your toddler from dragging something across the floor to climb up on to turn the light on.

Heat, Smoke, Fumes, and Electricity

Make sure you have a shower head heat control, turn down the temperature on the hot water heater for a few years, make sure your smoke detectors are working, and install a carbon monoxide detector in the hallway in front of your child's bedroom door or above an air vent.

Plug all electrical outlets. You can buy covers for power strips, PC tower protectors, VCR locks and guards, computer straps, fireplace gas valve covers, stove knob covers, dishwasher covers, fridge guards, stovetop shields and guards, appliance locks and straps, and soft spout covers. A nonslip mat in the tub is also a good idea.

Safety Nets

Many toddlers can slip between handrails, railings, and banisters inside and outside the house (including apartment balcony railings). Think about your outdoor deck, playhouse, pool enclosure, and so on. Toddlers have the ability to slip under and through railings. You can now get clear plastic panels to put around these railings, but if you're broke, cheap chicken wire is worth a consideration.

Toddler Tales

In the days before plastic plugs, my toddling daughter had a twist tie in her hands. She happened to poke it into an electrical outlet. The result: a small, thin red burn mark across the inside of her hand, along with an electric jolt.

Edges

Soften the blow on sharp corners. Get corner guards and table edge guards.

Strings and Things

Kids can get themselves tangled up in cords and strings very quickly. You can get blind cord winders and electric cord shorteners. Cords on all vertical and Venetian blinds, drapery cords, phone cords, and telephone lines for computers should be assessed. Perhaps it's time for a cordless phone if you don't already have one.

Dreadful Dieffenbachia

Did you know that your dieffenbachia (dumb cane), elephant's ear, angel wings, philodendron, candelabra cactus, snow-on-the-mountain, poinsettia, calla lily, amaryllis, aloe vera, cyclamen, English ivy, hydrangea, azalea, and Jerusalem cherry plants are poisonous plants?

Among other things, chewing or swallowing parts of these plants can cause …

- Painful burning sensation of the lips, mouth, tongue, and throat.
- Contact dermatitis when touched.

- Diarrhea upon ingestion.
- Temporary blindness.
- Vomiting.
- Stomach pain.

Some kids are plant chewers; others have no interest in plants. If you have a plant chewer, you need to put these plants out of reach.

Dr. Mom Speaks

I love dieffenbachia. When my kids were young, I had them all over my house. Accidentally, when cutting down my dieffenbachia, I got some of the milk on my skin, and some ended up in my mouth. It felt like pieces of poisoned glass chips cutting into my mouth and tongue. I would never wish this on any child.

Toxic Matters

There is no such thing as a childproof bottle. "Childproof" bottles will slow down children, but if they're intent enough, they'll bite through the plastic! Vitamins with iron and Vitamin A are a danger to your children. Tylenol (acetaminophen) must be taken only as directed, not one bit more and not more often than directed. The levels between helpful and toxic are very close, and toxic doses can cause liver damage.

Keep your pills in a locked cabinet. Don't take your medications in front of a toddler; your child may think you're eating candy and try some when you aren't looking! When visitors come to your house (or you go to theirs), be aware of how medications are stored.

Toddler Tales

When Auntie Effie was a toddler, she grabbed a bottle from under Grandma's sink. It had lye in it. The lye burned her throat. Many times as an adult, she had to have a steel ball lowered down her throat to open it up as much as possible and had to chew all of her medicines because she couldn't swallow them whole. Grandma never forgave herself.

If your son or daughter appears to have swallowed something toxic, don't try to make him or her throw up. Whatever was swallowed may do more damage coming up (burn the throat) than being flushed out the other end. Keep ipecac syrup in your house at all times, but don't use it unless instructed to by the Poison Control Center. Ipecac syrup will cause your child to vomit. Before you take action, call your local poison hotline for advice (enter your ZIP code at the American Association of Poison Control website [www.aapcc.org], and find the number of the poison control center nearest your home—or call 1-800-222-1222).

Most poisonings occur when the product is in use—because you left it unattended for a moment!

Pesticides absorb through the skin. Don't let your child play on grass that has been sprayed for bugs!

Fireplace

Fireplace latches and fireplace gates are now available. If you have a fireplace, make sure your child can't get in it when cold and doesn't get burned by it if hot.

Other Safety Issues of Note

Here are a few other things you may want to think about.

Where's the Cereal?

For a time, let your cereals and your household cleaners trade places. Put your cereals in a cupboard under the sink or other lower cupboard, and put your cleaning solutions up high. In fact, why not buy a small lockable storage cabinet just for all of your cleaning solutions?

Backyard Pools

Drowning is the fourth leading cause of death of children under five in the United States, according to the U.S. Product Safety Commission. Every summer, we hear it on the news: one more toddler drowned in a backyard pool.

One thing about toddlers is, they toddle. They wander all over the place. Once they discover mobility, they have a greater desire to explore the world around them. You can't let your toddler out of your view for even a moment; a moment is all it takes.

Safety and Sanity Tips

Tips from a former lifeguard: Never take your eyes off your child in the water. Don't even turn your head away from your child. If someone comes to speak with you, keep your eyes on the pool while talking with the person. Sit in an upright position without crossing your legs. Be attentive. If your child goes under, you have to be ready to respond immediately.

Is it your pool? Put a motion detector or alarm on any door that leads to the backyard. Make sure you have a high fence around the pool with a locked gate. Make sure there aren't any chairs or boxes or other climbing things that a toddler could push up against the fence in order to climb over it. Don't leave objects in the pool that could tempt your child to want to go in after them. Never let your toddler out in the backyard without an adult present (and take a phone with you, and put a note on the front door for people to come around to the back). Don't leave open the opportunity to tempt yourself to run into the house for anything, or to the front door and leave your toddler by the pool alone. Don't feel safe because your toddler is wearing those blow-up water wings on his arms—they can come off or pop. Also, it takes only a teaspoon of water to drown in, so even if your toddler puts his face in the water and it goes down the wrong way, your child could panic and be in trouble. No floating devices are safe for your toddler. Even adults slip off of floating devices.

If your children are going to be in the water, they have to learn how to swim. Take them to parent and tot lessons ASAP. Take a CPR course.

Drain all wading pools when not in use. Fill them up fresh each day.

You are not only liable for the blame if your child has an accident in your pool, but you are also liable if someone else's child has an accident in your pool! It is your job to protect all children from being harmed in your pool.

Make sure you have rescue equipment within arm's reach of the pool.

If you are at a public swimming pool, remember that the lifeguard has many children to watch. Toddlers should never be in the water without Mom or Dad within arm's reach of them. Not all lifeguards are as vigilant as they should be. Watch your own child, and don't let your guard down even if there is a lifeguard on duty.

Backyard Plants

Check your shrubs. Berries on shrubs may look inviting to a toddler. Are yours safe? Check the U.S. Army Center for Health Promotion and Preventive Medicine website, at chppm-www.apgea.army.mil/ento/PLANT.HTM, to see if they are safe, or talk with your local nursery.

Sand and Other Fine Delicacies

You may have a toddler who puts everything in the mouth. At the beach, these kids have to try eating sand. They play in the dirt and chew their nails.

While a little dirt or sand or chewed grass won't really hurt your toddler (and playing in the dirt actually helps your child to develop the immune system), there comes the risk of worms. Your toddler may wake up screaming in the night because his or her bottom is sore. It can be disconcerting to take a peek and see the little worms scurrying back into the rectum. A round of worm medication from your doctor will kill the nasties.

Car Seats

Of course, you will have a car seat for your toddler, and it will be an "approved" car seat. The question is, will you take the time to install it properly? The car seat you buy will not be safe unless the manufacturer's instructions for installation are followed. Many health departments, police departments, emergency medical services departments, and the Red Cross will inspect the installation of your car seat for free. Make some calls in your community to see where you can have your car seat checked.

Animals—Friend or Foe

Do not trust your cats or dogs around your toddler, no matter how well you think you know your pet.

Children see pets as toys. Toddlers are notorious for poking, prodding, slapping, dragging, and biting their pets. Eventually, your animal will get fed up with the irritation. Your pet can react by scratching, biting, barking, or hissing.

Dogs are very territorial and are pack animals. Dogs respect those who have authority over them. Your toddler does not have authority over your dog. Your dog may think it's his job to dominate the underling in the pack: your toddler. This can be very dangerous for your toddler.

Keep your cat out of the children's bedrooms during all naps and at night. A cat could conceivably smother a child by cuddling close to his face.

Teach your toddler to have a healthy respect for animals so that the risk of injury is reduced. Your child's fear of animals isn't a bad thing at this stage. Remember, your toddler is no match for a quick-to-react animal.

Helmets

Whether on a tricycle or another pedal-powered contraption, you owe it to your kids to put a helmet on their heads.

Presuming that you have a helmet for your toddler, ensure that it is positioned correctly on the head and that the strap is adequately secured. Check the directions that come with the helmet, to learn the proper way to wear it.

It's amazing to see children with helmets on that are tipped up at the forehead (leaving the forehead exposed to fracture) or with a strap so loose that, if an accident occurred, it would hurt the child's neck and allow damage to the head as well. There's no sense in having a helmet if it isn't worn properly. It gives a false sense of security.

Living Life Without Regrets

Nobody likes to have regrets. Regrets are those things that you could have and should have done differently. You want your toddler to grow up healthy and happy just like every other parent. Take the precautions necessary to do everything you can to ensure the safety of your toddler.

Chapter
10

Potty Training

Diapering nursing babies isn't too bad. Their yellowish liquid poop has a bit of a sweet smell, doesn't it? It's when the little rascals start eating real food (or formula) that those diapers start to get disgusting. Vomit control, here we come! Yes, it doesn't take long before parents are itching to get their toddlers out of diapers and onto the toilet. How do you go from "we wipe" to "they wipe"?

From Diapers to Underwear

The first thing to know about potty training is that your toddler has to be ready for it. If you are ready before your daughter and you push potty training on her, you're in for a battle. And let me tell you, it's not worth it.

It will probably take your toddler two to three months to master potty training. Relax, take it easy, and be prepared for lots of accidents before it's over. If you can stay loose about this journey you're on with your toddler, it will be much easier on both of you.

Self-Control and Will Power

The development issues of "autonomy" and "self-definition" are wrapped up tightly in a child's ability to learn to control his or her own body. This is why potty training can't be "all about you." It has to be "all about them." Parents need to see themselves as their children's guide, helping them do something they need to learn to do. Being a guide means showing the way, not commanding the way.

Parents who try to "make" their children use the potty whether they are ready or not will emotionally damage their toddlers, the consequences of which are far reaching. Potty training is one area of parenting in which any form of force, punishment, or pressure will backfire. The only way to successfully potty-train and not cause your children to need future therapy is to engage their cooperation and work with them when they are ready. Like the saying goes, you can lead a horse to water, but you can't make him drink. He'll drink only if he's thirsty.

If your toddler doesn't show signs of readiness, wait. Keep changing diapers until Junior starts figuring out that this whole diaper thing is for the birds.

Signs of Readiness

All kids have a drive and desire to grow up. No kid wants to go to play school or kindergarten in diapers. Your kids want to become more like you. You sit on the toilet. One day, they will want to sit on it, too.

Children are ready to toilet train when they …

- Want to sit on the toilet.
- Want to wear underpants.
- Wiggle out of a wet diaper—don't want it on after it's soaked.
- Wake up from naps with a dry diaper.
- Get upset when the diaper is full.
- Can put pants on and take them off without assistance.
- Can walk to and from the bathroom.
- Show interest in using the toilet.
- Have predictable bowel movements.
- Have the comprehension to follow simple instructions.
- Make a face before peeing or pooping.

Kids are not ready if they …

- Are resistant when taken to the toilet.
- Poop or pee right after being taken to the toilet—not enough control of sphincter muscles yet, or too uptight about it at this time.
- Wet a diaper in less than two hours.

Normal Development

Your son or daughter will start showing these signs at anywhere from 18 to 24 months. When you see a number of readiness signs, you can begin testing the waters to see if your child is really ready. Remember, don't push it; delaying this whole process six months wouldn't be the end of the world. By about age three, potty training will be over for most, but a lot of three-year-olds are still in diapers.

The American Academy of Pediatrics reports that kids who start potty training at 18 months may not be fully trained (day and night) until after age 4, while children who start after age 2 are often done by age 3. In other words, you aren't ahead of the game by pushing it.

Begin Preparations

You'll want to consider the following when preparing to toilet train your child.

Potty. Once you see some of the readiness signs, it's time to go shopping for a little plastic child's toilet or a child cover to put over the regular toilet.

Using a toilet is a learned behavior. Most children learn about the use of the toilet by seeing a parent on the toilet. It's best that this be the same-sex parent, if possible, because the differences in gender will be more easily worked through.

Training pants. Whether you choose to use cloth training pants or "pull-ups," it's time to make those purchases. Some parents say that disposable training pants are not an incentive for their children to use the toilet. They are so absorbent that the kids aren't bothered by the pee in them like they are with cloth training pants.

Clothing. To potty train, kids need pants that they can easily pull down and up. Zippered pants take too long to undo. Put away the overalls, and pull out the sweatpants. Make sure the elastic has enough give for easy removal of the pants by your toddler. The fewer the clothes, the better! Some parents potty train their kids by keeping their bums naked. It makes them more aware of when they need to pee, and they feel it if they have a pee accident because it runs down the leg. This gives them a chance after the first little dribble to head to the potty. Summer is a great time to potty train because of better weather and lighter clothes. Can you wait until summer? It's a consideration.

Doll. You may want to buy a doll that pees and comes with a doll toilet. Teach your toddler to feed the doll her bottle and put her on her potty to see her "pee" come out.

Book. You can also buy one of the many children's story books about learning to go to the potty, and start reading about potty training with your toddler. Try Taro Gomi's *Everyone Poops* (Kane/Miller, 1993), Alona Frankel's *Once Upon a Potty* (HarperCollins, 1999), and *What to Expect When You Use the Potty*, by Heidi Murkoff and Laura Rader (HarperCollins, 2000).

Stepping stool. Whether you start out on the big toilet or on the child-size potty, eventually your toddler will be using the big toilet. You will need a stepping stool to help your child up and down. Make sure you buy one of sturdy construction. Your toddler has to be able to plant both feet firmly to effectively push during pooping.

Word from the Wise

"Again and again they tested God's patience and frustrated the Holy One of Israel. ... But he led his own people like a flock of sheep, guiding them safely through the wilderness. He kept them safe so they were not afraid." (Psalm 78:41, 52–53, 56, 72)

You must do for your toddlers what God the Father does for his people when they test his patience and frustrate him: Lead them, guide them, keep them safe, care for them, and remain patient.

"Bye, Bye, Poo Poo": Saying Good-bye to Part of Me

Many children see the departure of their poop as the departure of part of their self. Some children think this is an adventure, laugh, wave at their poop as they flush, and say "Bye, bye, poo poo." Go ahead, indulge yourself and your daughter, wave along with her, and have a little laugh.

Other children can have the opposite reaction and become frightened that part of their self is leaving them. This is when you have to tell your child that God made our bodies in a really wonderful and unique way:

> God made our bodies really special. Our bodies need food so we eat. While the food is inside of us, our bodies take all of the good things about our food and use them to help us grow and get bigger. Our bodies need to get rid of all the stuff that we don't need to grow, so our bodies "poop it out" and "pee it out!" This is a good thing because we wouldn't want our bodies to get filled up with things that aren't good for us because it could make us sick. Peeing and pooping keep us feeling good.

Fear of the Flush

Some toddlers are freaked out by the flushing toilet. They fear they'll get sucked down with their poop. If your son has this fear, let him wipe his bum and get off the toilet before flushing.

Explain to your son that there is a hole at the bottom of the toilet that is "this small." Show him that the hole is too small for his body to go through and that he can't possibly go down all the way with the poop.

Dr. Mom Speaks

Becoming potty-trained is an emotionally critical task for toddlers. They begin to learn a sense of themselves through this task. This is why kids must be ready, and you must wait for your toddler to be ready. If it's "all about you getting your way," it will be detrimental to your little one.

M&Ms and Behavioral Reinforcement in Potty Training

Many years ago, psychologists did research into ways to teach desired behaviors. They found that if a reward was given each time the new behavior was attempted or successfully completed, the new behavior could be learned fairly quickly.

Knowing this, the psychologist mother tries to train her daughter:

The big jar of M&Ms sits high up in the bathroom, beyond her reach but within full view. Tell her, "Sweetheart, when you start sitting on the potty and peeing and pooping in the potty, you're going to get M&Ms." The daughter …

- Pulls down her own pants—one M&M and praise ("Good girl!").
- Sits on the potty—one M&M, plus lots of verbal praise ("Good job!", "Good girl!" "Wow, what a big girl you are!", etc.).
- Pees while on the potty—two M&Ms (maybe three) plus lots of verbal praise
- Poops while on the potty—four M&Ms, plus lots of verbal praise.
- Wipes her own bottom—two M&Ms, plus lots of verbal praise.
- Flushes the toilet (or dumps the contents of the child's potty into the adult toilet and flushes)—one M&M, plus lots of verbal praise.
- Pulls up her own pants—one M&M and praise ("Good girl!").

This reward method of potty training works well!

Trips to the toilet have to be a positive, fun, rewarding experience. If she sits on the potty but doesn't pee, she gets only one M&M. One is never enough, is it? So, she'll want to keep going into that bathroom to try to perform!

Save It for the Bathroom!

If you want this tasty incentive to work in the bathroom, you can't be giving your child sweet treats all day long. Why would a child care about getting a measly little piece of candy on the toilet when you'll just hand out a candy bar or bag of chips upon demand?

Diabetic? Diet Restrictions?

Pick one of the dietetic candies or bars that your toddler likes. Make sure they are in little pieces. Another option is to save your son's daily fruit portion for use in the bathroom. If he likes fruit, during potty training, tell Junior he'll get his bite of apple if he sits on the potty; if he pees, he gets another bite (cut up into bite-size pieces).

If he's ready for potty training, great. If not, put it off for a week, let him have his fruit during the day, and try again another day.

Always remember to give the verbal praise with the treat every time.

If food incentives are completely out for your toddler, think of something else that he or she really likes or might get interested in that would be an incentive to be interested in potty training. Perhaps it's collecting marbles and getting one marble for each successive accomplishment in the potty routine.

Weaning Off the Tasty Rewards

For the first couple of weeks, be steady about both a tasty reward and verbal praise. You wean off the candy by starting to forget about it, by waiting for your toddler to remind you that he or she needs the treat for being good. And give only one M&M for the pee and poop instead of four. If your child notices you giving less, give what you did before.

Continue to praise your child. Don't reduce the praise along with the treat.

Then one day, you run out of M&Ms and can't give any until you pick up some more at the store. After you get some more, your child will get treats again for going on the potty.

After a while, you'll notice that your tot doesn't need all those rewards and reinforcements: He or she just wants to get in there, take care of business, and get back to playing.

If your toddler regresses after being fully trained, you may want to reintroduce the treats to get focused on doing business again.

Accidents

Don't sweat the small stuff. Accidents are the small stuff. They are going to happen. You will end up with pee on the floor or in the carpet. That's one reason some parents choose not to buy good furniture until all of their children are finished with potty training. Don't get angry at an accident; just clean it up. Trial and error—it's one of the ways we learn in life. None of us wants to be punished for all our errors. The Lord is gracious to us; we need to be gracious to our children.

Safety and Sanity Tips

Learning to pee standing up can be quite a balancing act when standing on a small stool. You may want to consider waiting to teach your son about that when he's tall enough for his penis to be above the edge of the toilet!

Boys—Sitting or Standing?

Most often, people start training their sons to pee sitting down on the potty. As the little guy gets a bit older, Dad teaches him how to stand and pee, but not always.

Many families are deciding to continue to have their sons pee sitting down. One advantage they cite is that it keeps the bathroom much cleaner.

There is no right or wrong. Your son might even prefer to stay sitting. Don't make issues out of nonissues!

When Potty Training Is a Power Struggle

If you've been caught up in power struggles with your toddler, stop potty training for a few weeks and go back to diapers. Spend the next couple of weeks doing fun things with your toddler—play games, go swimming, read books. Work on positive bonding with your tot. After all the stress and strain of the previous potty training attempt has dissipated, try again, but this time, go slower and be more patient.

Baby Steps

Throughout the day, encourage your toddler simply to come into the bathroom and be there with you. Offer an M&M for coming into the bathroom. Get your child used to coming in there with you without any demand or expectation, only a little treat.

Word from the Wise

"Patience can persuade a prince, and soft speech can crush strong opposition." (Proverbs 25:15)

Patience, gentleness, and encouragement are the keys to successful potty training.

When you sit on the toilet, invite your child to sit on her potty beside you. Even if it's with all clothes on, give an M&M. Don't give more than one M&M unless your toddler does another potty-training step. The next step is pulling down the pants.

If you and your tot have already had a bad time training, you will want to go a lot slower the second time around.

"Yuck. It's Another Wet Bed!"

Of school-age children in the United States, more than five million suffer from primary nocturnal enuresis (PNE or "pee, any?"). PNE isn't about emotional stress or dysfunction, emotional immaturity, or low self-esteem. If your child isn't dry through the night on the timeline of "normal" development, he or she probably has PNE. Make sure you check with the doctor to see if your child has a chronic urinary tract infection. Forty percent of children under three wet at night. From there, as they get older, fewer wet at night, but some go on for years.

It Runs in the Family, Literally!

Do you have a bed wetter? My dad wet the bed until he was about 12, I wet the bed until I was 11, my son wet the bed until he was 12, and I'm pretty sure at least one or more of my grandchildren will wet the bed for several years past the norm. Oh, well—some people's bodies just don't work like others'. We just have to deal with it. If you have a bed-wetter, you probably have other family members who were also bed-wetters.

The Two Problems

Essentially, the child who wets the bed has two problems:

1. Needs to pee in the night (like a lot of people)
2. Doesn't wake up to go pee (not like most people)

Children who wet the bed sleep so soundly that they don't sense when they have to pee. They are nearly comatose!

Medical Stuff

Low levels of antidiuretic hormone at night might be the cause of (or a contributing factor to) bed wetting. For most people, levels of this hormone rise at night (to prevent us from peeing), but levels in bed-wetters remain at the low, daytime level. The doctor can try a run of ADH medicine. The idea is, if you add some of this hormone into your child's body, the body will then give the signal not to pee at night. The medication comes in tablets and nasal spray. It works for some but not for others. If it doesn't work for your child, don't blame your child.

There are theories on smaller bladders, imbalances between bladder muscles and sphincter muscles, and the possibility that bed-wetters may produce more urine than the average person.

Studies show that these kids don't sleep more soundly than others, but their brain doesn't signal them to wake up when they have to pee. Parents insist that their bed-wetters sleep like logs.

No matter what the medical reason, you have a situation to deal with.

Alarms

Bed-wetting alarms have been around for a long time. In essence, you clip a little electrode to your child's underwear and, at the first drop of moisture, the alarm goes off. The alarm wakes up your child, who can then run to the toilet.

Alarms work for some kids, but not all. Some kids don't hear the alarm. If it works, it works; if it doesn't, don't blame your child.

Dr. Mom Speaks

If you can't keep a grip on your anger dealing with your bed-wetter, ask your spouse to take over dealing with this. It's most likely that one of you has been through this personally or someone in your family has gone through it. The one with the most patience should deal with the bed-wetter. The other one may have to stay out of it completely.

Vinyl Mattress Covers

You can buy full vinyl mattress covers that zip at one end. You will need to replace the cover when it wears out. It may not last as long as you need it. Check it well.

If it doesn't wear out, it might start stinking you out. You can wipe it down with bleach now and then, but be prepared to replace it if the smells can't be removed.

Mattress

You may want to consider buying an inexpensive mattress for your child's first bed. Wait to see whether your toddler has a bed-wetting problem. When Junior is consistently dry through the night, invest in a decent mattress. (Pass on the cheap mattress to the next child.)

If your child wets the bed until the age of 12, you may have to replace the mattress more than once. Vinyl mattress covers are great, but they do tear, and your mattress will see its share of urine. When the mattress starts smelling, it's time to throw it out, or you can try pressure-spraying it and putting it in the sun to dry (summer only).

Safety and Sanity Tips

Don't deprive your child of a new mattress cover or mattress when it's needed. Urine crystallizes when it dries and embeds itself in both. If you don't change them regularly, your child will get rashes on his or her body.

Toddler Tales

I've tried it all—using a bed-wetting alarm, giving ADH medicine, and waking up my son in the night. He never heard the alarm (although it woke us up in another room), the medicine didn't work, and waking him up only left me with a lack of sleep. Bottom line—lots of laundry until he grows out of it.

Drinks Before Bed

After supper, limit fluid intakes. If your child is really thirsty, don't refuse him or her anything, but give just a few sips. Make those sips of water, milk, or juice—no sodas because they can have a diuretic effect (especially colas).

Make sure your child goes to the bathroom right before bed. You nighttime routine may look like this:

1. Bath
2. Teeth brushing
3. Potty
4. Pajamas
5. Stories
6. Prayers
7. Lights out

When your toddler has nighttime enuresis problems, he will need to pee before stories and try again after prayers.

Clean Up

While your child is still a toddler, you'll be responsible for doing all his laundry. Keep him in "pull-ups" at night as long as you can (until he won't wear them anymore or they don't make them big enough for him). Plan on it. If he doesn't grow out of it by the time he starts school, start teaching him to put his sheets in the laundry when he gets up.

Guilt and Discipline

No amount of guilt or discipline will cause your toddler to stop wetting the bed sooner than his or her body is ready. Also, don't try to give rewards for waking up with a dry bed because your child will only feel defeated failing day after day. Bed wetting ends when it ends.

The Pee Dream

One thing you can tell your son is to pay attention, if he is able, to his dreams. If he starts to dream about going to the bathroom, it's a signal that he has to pee. Encourage him to try to wake himself up and run to the toilet if he has such a dream. Keep a night light on in the hall and the bathroom for him, just in case.

Normal Regression

After children successfully conquer a developmental stage (like sleeping through the night or graduating to the cup), it's possible for them to regress if they come under stress. This can happen if a family moves to a new house, a baby is born, someone in the family dies, and so on.

If your child has faced a stressor (likely the whole family has), talk about how he or she feels about what has happened. If your toddler has regressed because of stress, talking with you may help him or her get back to normal faster by providing a means of letting out stress.

Expect regression when there is change. Don't discipline children when they regress. They need more love and patience than they did before the stress entered their life.

Let them be in their regression for a few days before encouraging them back to more mature behaviors. Do so gently.

When They "Go" for Other Reasons

Unfortunately, because peeing and pooping are all about control of the body, for some children, they become all about controlling you or resisting your control attempts! And sometimes defecating is just about curiosity.

Fascination

Some children become so fascinated with this stuff coming out of their bodies that they want to play with it. It's just experimental. Don't overreact. Do the following:

1. Lead your child to the bathroom.
2. Wipe off her hands and put the tissue in the toilet.
3. Tell her poop goes in the potty.
4. Tell her that people don't touch their poop—it's like garbage that has to go in the garbage can.

Controlling You

People are people, and kids are kids. It's human nature to push people to see where their limits are. Your toddler has already been pushing you in other areas (like eating and bathing) and may push you in potty training.

Don't engage in a power battle with your tot over the bathroom. If Junior is defiant over toilet training, he isn't ready. Engaging in power struggles over potty training is no good for you and is detrimental to his emotional and psychological development.

If there is opposition, go back to diapers and wait another week before trying again. If the opposition is still there, wait another week. Sooner or later, your child will cooperate. Remember, kids want to grow up. They want to learn to do things the way big people do. When they are ready, they will cooperate.

Anger and Retaliation

Sometimes a potty-trained tot will use defecating skills to give you a message: "I'm mad at you! I don't like how you treated me!" Of course, kids won't say that outright—they'll poop or pee somewhere they aren't supposed to.

If your daughter does this, before you explode, get a grip on yourself. In as calm a fashion as you can, sit down with her and ask if something is bothering her. Is she angry about something or at someone? Let her talk. After she has told you what was bothering her, tell her it's time for her to clean up her mess (give her a little help, if she needs it). Get out the paper towels and have her pick up her poop, take it to the toilet, put it in, wipe her bottom, and flush. Then tell her, "Next time you're mad, just come and talk to Mom. You don't need to do this anymore."

Sadness and Other Emotional Distress

Tots are disadvantaged emotionally because they often don't have the language to express how they feel or what they think. When they feel bad and don't know how to let it out, they do things they shouldn't do. Sometimes that involves poop and pee.

Toddler Tales

Many times my three-year-old son came up from the basement with his pants wet. He was toilet-trained. One day I asked him, "What are you feeling when you're downstairs and you pee your pants?" "Lonely," was his reply. Next time I saw him head downstairs, I asked him to come and read a book with me.

Before getting angry when your toilet-trained child poops or pees somewhere other than the toilet, ask about his or her emotional state. Sometimes kids just can't express themselves. Once that door is opened and they see that you can help them talk about what's bothering them, these behaviors usually stop.

Chapter

11

Shopping with Your Preschoolers

While parents of toddlers know that shopping alone is so much easier than shopping with little ones, sometimes it's unavoidable. Special accommodations need to be made and much patience is required. Accidents and incidents can happen anywhere, any time. Here are some tips for making shopping with toddlers as pleasant as possible and how to deal with those difficult situations that will inevitably occur.

Safety When Out and About

From the car to the shopping cart to germs, your goal is to bring everyone home healthy, uninjured, and unharmed.

Never Leave Your Children in the Car

Leaving your children in a vehicle is not just about weather. The weather is a no-brainer. If it's too hot, your kids could die from heat exhaustion. If it's too cold, your kids could freeze.

The main reason you don't leave your toddlers and preschoolers in vehicles is that they should never be left unattended, not even for a moment. It takes only a moment for a disaster to happen to your child.

How often on the news do you hear of people who get their cars stolen with kids in the back seat? Do you want to risk a child abduction to spare yourself the added work of taking your kids in and out of the store? That may be a decision you regret for the rest of your life!

What if your child begins to choke? What if one of your kids starts hurting the other one? What if one of the kids puts the car in gear? Falls out of a window? Wakes up to find Mommy or Daddy missing and gets scared?

What if something happens to you in a store while your kids are out in the car? What if you collapse? How will people know you have kids unattended in a car outside? Parents are now being charged by the police for leaving their children unattended in vehicles.

Don't do it. Just when you think nothing will happen, something will. A momentary lapse of judgment could become a lifelong sorrow. It's not worth it.

The Shopping Cart

According to the U.S. Consumer Product Safety Commission, approximately 12,800 children 5 years and under are admitted to hospital emergency rooms because of head trauma from falling out of shopping carts. Need more be said? About one quarter of those produced concussions and fractures.

Protect your child by using the seat belt restraints in shopping carts, not allowing your child to ride inside the basket (only in the designated sitting area), not allowing your child to ride on the front of the cart or outsides of the cart, and not allowing older kids to push other kids in carts.

Many of you will not take the advice about keeping kids out of the cart. People put their kids in the carts every day without a thought of the danger. If you do put your child in the cart, make sure he or she sits down and stays seated. Never allow a child to stand inside the cart. Children tend to want to reach out to the grocery shelves. That's when they lose their balance and topple down on their heads. That's how they end up at the emergency room.

The Tether

In the olden days, parents could buy tethers for their kids. However, they were leather and looked like dog leashes. Today you can get those things that look like telephone cords that connect your child's wrist with yours.

It's important while you're out shopping that your toddlers don't get away from you. In fact, they should never leave your side or your sight.

Toddler Tales

One Christmas a dad had his preschoolers out shopping at the mall. He was trying to keep good track of them. One was in the stroller and the other was by his side. The child that was walking went around the other side of a clothing rack. He was gone! A man walking briskly by grabbed the toddler and ran. There was a large crowd in the mall because it was Christmas. The father yelled out and started running. Then the child in the stroller was left unattended. He caught up with the man and ripped his kid out of his arms. His other child was unharmed.

The moral of the story: Keep physical connection with your preschoolers while shopping, by having them either in a stroller or strapped on your back or chest or arm. Don't lose physical contact.

Two- or three-year-olds should be in a stroller, in the seat in a shopping cart, or on a tether while out. Four- and five-year-olds can easily walk. The danger for them has to do with the parent giving in and letting them ride on the outside, sides, or front of the cart. It's not safe to let them do that, either. They can slip and fall off, get their feet and ankles run over, or fall and hit their heads on the ground. The safest place for them is to walk behind you or beside you.

A four- or five-year-old can be easily entertained by pushing one of those child carts and can become their parent's helper. Have your child put nonbreakable, easily reached items in the cart. It's better to have the child follow behind your cart. Other shoppers will not see the child as easily as they will see you when you're rounding the ends of the aisles. You don't want your little one to get run into. If your child's cart gets hit, it will knock him or her over—another possible head injury. While it is safer for your little one to follow behind you from this standpoint, keep in mind that you can't see them as well. Be mindful of them, keep a little conversation going, and be attuned to who is around them.

Keep Their Hands Off the Merchandise

Don't let your preschoolers touch things in the store. There is the risk of things falling on them. Even small kids can have a strong grip. They could topple a rack or a stack very quickly.

Preschoolers don't have the insight to see the consequences of all their actions. When they grab a can of peas at the bottom of the stack, they won't be able to make the logical deduction that the whole stack will come down. This is also a reason you shouldn't scold your toddler if this happens. You are the one who has the insight for these consequences; your toddler doesn't. If your child does something like this, it's an opportunity to instruct, not punish.

If you're having your toddler help you shop by picking things off the shelf, say he or she can't take anything off the shelf until asking Mommy or Daddy first. Make sure you offer verbal rewards when your child asks you.

Remember, you are responsible for your child. Don't let your toddler touch things in a store. If your kids' hands are mucky, get out the baby wipes and wipe them off. Don't let them get their mucky hands on clothes hanging from racks as you push the stroller around.

Some children want to grab and touch everything. A small toy that fits in their hand can do the trick. Make sure to tether it to their shirt or the waist of their pants so they don't lose it. A little stuffed animal works well.

Germs and Other Things You Don't Want to Bring Home

You can pick up nearly anything at the mall—including sickness and disease.

Toddlers are notorious for putting things in their mouths. If your toddler is orally fixated, try to provide something for him or her to fixate on that is healthy instead of filthy. Kids who tend to pick things up off the ground and put them in their mouths are better off staying in their strollers and being handed their bag of Cheerios.

It's a good practice, either before you leave the mall or right when you get home, to wash everybody's hands well with lots of soap and water. Another option is to keep wet wipes in the car and clean everybody's hands in the car.

The Public Bathroom

Parents these days are fortunate. Many malls and stores have family bathrooms where parents can take all their kids together, boys and girls. But what if one is not available?

If you are a mom, never let your preschool sons go into the men's room alone. Take them into the women's. This is not your child's decision. Make sure your five-year-old son doesn't make you change your mind.

What about dads out with their little girls? Are women's bathrooms any safer? Yes, they are. However, you may not want your three-year-old daughter to wander off into a public bathroom by herself, no matter how safe it is. Even if there aren't child predators there, she could get hurt. What will you do then?

Dads shopping with their daughters have two options. First, if your daughter can hold it long enough until a mom with children comes out of or goes into the women's room, you could ask her if she could help your daughter. If she's there with her kids, she's probably a safe bet for your daughter. Other moms out shopping would be happy to help a dad in this situation. Even moms with teens with them or grandmotherly women would help out a dad in this situation.

Sometimes dads have to take their daughters to the men's room. Peek your head in first to make sure no one is standing at the urinals, and then sneak her into a stall with you. Another option is to cover her eyes so that she doesn't see any men standing at the urinals. Before you come out, you can make an announcement that you're bringing your daughter out to wash her hands and would appreciate it if any men needing to use the urinals could wait until you and your daughter leave. Then pray they respect your request.

Why So Ornery *Now?*

Kids get miserable just like adults. They get miserable for the same reasons as adults, and more. Like us, they get tired, hungry, thirsty, and overstimulated.

Tired. We all get miserable when we are overly tired and are trying to keep going when we really need to rest. Make sure your children are rested before you go out. Make sure *you* are rested before you go out. Don't push yourself or your children beyond your physical and emotional limits. Go home before you both get miserable.

Hungry. Feed your child and yourself before you go out, or plan to stop for a meal as part of your outing. Take healthful snacks for both of you with you when you go out. Take zipped baggies with raisins, Cheerios, cheese cubes, or pieces of fruit. Don't allow the shopping trip to become the sugar trip. Giving your little tike sugar snacks (like cookies and candy) or high-carbohydrate snacks (like chips and cheese puffs) will cause their blood sugar to spike and then drop. The result: hyperactivity followed by misery. Protein and slow-acting carbohydrates are better snacks.

Thirsty. While out, keep yourselves (parents and tots) hydrated. Dehydration can cause headaches, crankiness, and nausea. Milk, water, and vegetable juices are the best options for drinks—not just for shopping, but all the time. There is no need to ever feed your preschoolers soda. That is a shopping mom's nightmare; it's terrible for their teeth, it causes a huge sugar spike and crash, and it can create a sugar-craving child (who turns into a sugar-craving adult, who turns into an obese adult).

Word from the Wise

"For I was hungry, and you fed me. I was thirsty, and you gave me a drink. ... Then these righteous ones will reply, 'Lord, when did we ever see you hungry and feed you? Or thirsty and give you something to drink?' ... And the King will tell them, 'I assure you, when you did it to one of the least of these my brothers and sisters, you were doing it to me!'" (Matthew 25:35,37,40)

Overstimulated. Both parents and tots can become ornery when they are overstimulated. Too much activity, too many visual cues, too much noise, too much motion, too much temptation. Shopping trips with preschoolers need to be as short and sweet as possible.

The tired, hungry, thirsty, overstimulated child and parent become the ones the store employees remember for all the wrong reasons.

Be realistic. The day you take your preschoolers out shopping is not the day to make returns on purchases, read all the labels, or dig through coupons. Of course, many parents have no choice but to take their preschoolers on every shopping trip because they have no one else to watch their kids. As parents, just try to do your best in whatever circumstances you find yourselves.

Keeping Control of the Situation and Your Sanity

Of course, the only way to be in complete control of your shopping expedition is to go alone. Leave the kids with Mom or Dad. If you want a family outing, one of you should focus on entertaining the tots while the other quickly picks up what you need. Remember, you can pay babysitters just so that you can go shopping alone.

No matter how well you prepare for your shopping trip, sooner or later you'll have one of those experiences that all parents dread. Junior makes a scene in public. "Please, Lord, don't let it be me!"

Junior's behavior doesn't determine *your* behavior. As parents, you have to choose your behavior and your actions toward your children. As stated before, if you're not tired, hungry, thirsty, or overstimulated you'll have a much better chance of doing a good job. Even if you're completely exhausted and frazzled, if you know a good option, choose to do it rather than lose it!

The out-of-control parent helps a child learn that people don't need to control themselves. As a Christian, you know that one of the fruits of the Spirit is "self-control" (Galatians 5:22). As they say, the gifts are given, but the fruit is grown. You are teaching your children every day about developing self-control by showing them that you are able to control yourself and that they need to control themselves.

Here are your options when your kids act up at the store:

- **Distraction.** Sometimes kids act up because they're bored. They may start to whine or fuss. Stop for a minute. Talk to them. Let them hear your soothing voice. Show them something interesting in the store. Ask them to hold something for you. Give them a job. Ask them to count something.

- **Food and water.** Sometimes kids get fussy because their stomachs hurt. They may be hungry without realizing it. Having healthful snacks on hand is a good idea. Ask them if they are hungry. Dehydrated tots can start to feel miserable and sick. If they get fussy, offer them a drink of water or milk.

- **Potty break.** Sometimes kids have to go to the potty and start to feel uncomfortable. They may not realize that they are uncomfortable because they have to pee. How many kids have wet their pants while playing because they were having so much fun they didn't want to stop? Once toddlers learn how to go to the bathroom, they can develop an abhorrence for going in their pants and get anxious until they get to a bathroom. A trip to the bathroom gives them an opportunity to get out of the hustle and bustle of the store for a few moments, even if they don't actually use it. The bathroom is quiet. Some bathrooms have chairs to sit on. Take a break, if you need to.

- **Conversation.** Sometimes kids settle down when you talk with them, interact with them, and otherwise make them part of the outing. Having Junior face you while sitting in the child seat of a shopping cart gives you an opportunity to smile at him, kiss him, blow in his face, tease him, and so on. Having direct interaction can settle him down. The bored and ignored prince acts up for attention.

- **Cuddle.** Sometimes preschoolers just get overwhelmed and overstimulated, and start to feel like they're falling apart inside. Mom and Dad are focused on the task of shopping. Junior is no longer their primary focus. If your toddler is fussing, stop everything, take him or her out of the stroller or strapped-in seat, and just hug and hold him or her. Everything else in the world can wait for a few moments. Kiss your child. Say that you love your tot and that you'll be going home soon. Then go home soon. If your child has gotten to the breaking point and is overwhelmed, it's best to go home and put your little one to bed, and finish your shopping later.

- **Reward.** If it looks like your child is reaching the shopping limit, reward continued good behavior. Get a little egg timer/hourglass (plastic, of course). Ask your preschooler to hold it until all the sand runs out. If your little one can be good and quiet until the last bit of sand falls, you will give him or her a treat. Make the treat something small, like an M&M, Smartie, or gummy bear (of course, nothing a kid could choke on). Give only one. Turn the timer the other way. If your child can be good and quiet until all the sand falls again, hand out another M&M. Preschoolers can't wait long to get a reward; it has to be quick. Promising go somewhere after shopping or when you get home might curb bad behavior for a minute or two, but toddlers won't be able to maintain it. If you're in the checkout line, say that you will buy your toddler a treat at the food service area if he or she will keep quiet and well behaved until you get through the line.

- **Ignore.** Sometimes kids just do something to see if they can get a reaction out of you. Sometimes if parents ignore it, a child will get distracted and move on to something else. Sometimes reacting to the child's misbehavior is exactly what feeds it. There is a limit to ignoring misbehavior—that is, if it doesn't stop fairly quickly.

- **Command and count down.** Sometimes little ones are just being little brats. They need to stop their behavior, and they need to stop it right now. You command them to stop. How? By looking them straight in the eye and saying, "Stop it!" If they continue, make them look you in the eye again and say, "Stop it! Now!"

  Using the countdown as a disciplinary technique is useful when out shopping. The countdown is something to be taught at home, not in public. The parent counts down from 10 to 1 or from 5 to 1. The child is warned to stop the behavior before you get to "one." For toddlers, you should hold up your hand and count off your fingers so they understand the idea of the countdown. If the child has not adjusted the behavior before you get to one, he or she should know that it will result in a small infliction of physical pain (a flick on the hand, a slap on the hand, or a slap on the thigh). It takes only a few demonstrations of the countdown with preschoolers to produce successful results. Once the kids are responding at home, you can do it out shopping, but you must be prepared to follow through. Even if your toddler is not yet speaking, he is still capable of understanding what you are saying.

- **Go home!** If your preschooler just can't settle down, he or she is probably at their wit's end with exhaustion and overstimulation. Don't try to push your child. If you've been out too long or your little one didn't sleep that well the night before, go home and put him or her to bed.

Do not …

- **Threaten to leave your child.** Do not tell your child that if he or she doesn't smarten up, you're going to leave your child at the store. This strategy instills terror and insecurity in children. They need to know that no matter what they do, you will love them and stand by them. This is God's love for his people that you need to show to your children. You are also telling children that *their* behavior is determining *your* behavior. That is not correct. No matter how badly your child is behaving, you are the adult, and you choose your own behavior. You don't want to give children the message that if they are bad enough, they can make you do something rash. A child ought not to feel the burden of this power over a parent.

- **Humiliate or shame your child.** In Psalm 25:20, David asks the Lord to guard his life, to deliver him, and not let him be put to shame because he takes refuge in him. Your children take refuge in you. They need you to guard them and protect them. If parents shame or humiliate their children in public, they are not guarding and protecting them. It is your job to develop a solid inner core in your children. This solid inner core is developed when children feel safe and secure with their parents. Humiliating and shaming a child leaves them feeling unsafe and insecure.

- **Slap your child.** Slapping a child on the face is a no-no. This is instant humiliation and shame for every human being, child or adult. Please, don't ever slap your child on the face, not in public, not at home, never.

- **Ignore your child.** Ignoring a child has limited use as a parental tactic. If the child's behavior doesn't shift quickly, you must still deal with your child. Sometimes your child just needs to know that you'll drop everything and attend to him or her. Once that brief moment has occurred, your tot might be satisfied and you can carry on with your shopping. However, if your child has completely lost it, don't act as if it isn't happening and let him or her scream, yell, run, destroy, etc. To ignore a child's bad behavior is to not be in control of the situation. Your job is to be in control. If your child is uncontrollable, go home. Tomorrow will probably be a better day. Don't you have days where you just can't bear to shop? Your children can have these sorts of days also.

The Risk of Indulging and Rewarding Their Behavior

Ask yourself this: "Is God the Father a good father?" Of course, he is. Next, ask yourself, "Does God the Father reward bad behavior?" No, of course, he doesn't. The sum of both equations: Good parents don't reward bad behavior.

One reason it's dangerous to give a child candy when misbehaving is because it rewards bad behavior. Another danger with giving candy is that you will put your child on a sugar high (more bad behavior) and then a sugar crash (more bad behavior). Parents add to their grief when they do this. Also, you're setting up your child to combine rotten feelings with ingestion of sugar. There are obesity concerns here.

Some parents inadvertently indulge their children by threatening that if they don't smarten up, you'll go straight home. This may seem like punishment to you, but Junior might want to go home. Your child may just keep acting up so that you'll leave the store and go home. You don't want to give your child cause to defy you and get his way. If you begin to notice a pattern with your toddler acting up to get you to go home, talk with them about it. Encourage your child to tell you, while shopping, if they are hungry, thirsty, or tired; also, when they think they've had enough. Perhaps you're pushing Junior too hard and too long in the shopping excursions. You may need to shorten the errand list or leave Junior at home. Make sure your child has a way to tell you, in a reasonable way, that they are tired and played out. Encourage them to ask you nicely if you might go home now. Then let your child know whether or not that is possible. If there is one more thing to get or one more errand, tell your child and encourage them to hang in there until you're done, and sometimes, forfeit the other errands and take your little one home.

Remember, if Junior can get you to crack through misdeeds, Junior holds way too much power! It can become a challenge for Junior to see just how far you can be pushed. You need to get a handle on shopping misbehavior as quickly as possible, and from there on you have to be consistent.

Safety and Sanity Tips

The key to having the greatest amount of fun shopping with your preschoolers is not buying a thing! Now and then, just go to the mall to have fun. Window shop, buy ice cream, and run with the stroller down the concourse until they howl with laughter.

Think of one fun thing you can do at the end of each shopping trip, and do it. Create a routine that ends in fun and a stress release.

What if you just have a child who is a squirmer or a talker? Some kids just can't sit still, and some seem to never stop jabbering. This has to do with the personality of your child and has nothing to do with being tired, hungry, thirsty, or overstimulated. Depending on the personality of your child, you will be making more or less effort to arrange child care so that you can go shopping alone.

More Than One? Divide and Conquer

If you have two or three preschoolers at the same time and one or more acts up, you need to divide and conquer. When the first one acts up, try to work with that child first to settle him or her down. Don't let a second child interfere. If that happens, turn to the second child quickly, tell him or her to stop, and turn back to the first one. If that child doesn't stop, ignore him or her completely and continue to deal with the first one who needed your attention.

If you attend to the one who interrupts, you are rewarding the interruption. Kids need to learn to keep their noses out of it when a parent is dealing with one of their siblings. Also, if you are dealing with one child and the other two start squabbling, try to finish what you started first. If the other two get out of hand, turn and give them a directive, and then turn back to the first one.

If your child don't respond and you have chaos on your hands, pack them up and go home. Even if your cart is full, you don't have to try to get it through the checkout counter. Just leave it, if you have to. If your preschoolers have all "had it," don't fight it. It's a difficult task to take three preschoolers shopping. If it's a bad day, it's a bad day.

> ### Word from the Wise
>
> "To discipline and reprimand a child produces wisdom, but a mother is disgraced by an undisciplined child." (Proverbs 29:15)
>
> When you take the easy road as parents and withhold discipline, you encourage your children to be unruly. Their misbehavior and how you deal with it is a public reflection on your parenting. Godly discipline and reprimand will be seen by all and admired.

Shopping as an Adventure, Not Just a Job!

Shopping can be a lot of fun for parents and little ones—learning to play along the way, learning to sing, learning to laugh and be silly. If you play while you shop, you can all have fun.

It's quite possible to spend several hours at a big mall and have a great afternoon with three preschoolers. It's all about planning and attitude. Yes, things can go wrong because we're all human, but a lot can go right.

Be well rested, be fed, have water, have treats, have hand toys, have a great attitude, plan to play, and plan to laugh, and you can create a good memory for yourself and your children.

Putting Junior to Bed

Bedtime with your toddler can be a very pleasant or very unpleasant event. Of course, you would prefer to have many more pleasant "nite-nites" with your tot. To tip the balance in favor of pleasant bedtimes, you need to plan.

The Basic Plan

Your basic plan should include ...

1. A routine.
2. A "key phrase."
3. A determination to go slowly.

First Things First: Create a Routine

Think about how you would like bedtime to go in your house. How would you like to remember your evenings with your toddler? What would you like your toddler to remember about being put to bed?

Options:

Toddler goes and gets his own pajamas.

Parent gets toddler's pajamas.

Take off dirty clothes.

Put away toys.

Make a puzzle.

Take dirty clothes to laundry basket.

Put on pajamas.

Have a snack.

Brush hair.

Bathe.

Brush teeth.

Sing a song.

Mom reads a story.

Dad reads a story.

Junior gets to pick the books.

Mom prays.

Dad prays.

Toddler prays.

Hug.

Listen to soft instrumental music.

Toddler Tales

The routine of Dad praying and Mom praying for our daughter was so established that she lay there and refused to go to sleep until both parents had done their job. Then she was fine.

Kiss Mommy goodnight.

Kiss Daddy goodnight.

Rub on the lotion after the bath.

Recite nursery rhymes.

Talk about the day, joys and sorrows.

Take a trip to the potty.

Say "I love you."

Turn out the light.

These are all ideas for you to use. Choose which of these you would like to put into your household routine, order them, and then do the routine consistently, every night. Don't forget that the most important one is prayer, regardless of who does it.

Dr. Mom Speaks

Learning to deal with life's little frustrations is part of children's growth and development. They can't always get what they want, and bedtime is no exception. As parents, it's your job to decide on the nighttime routine and carry it out, no matter how much they complain. Eventually, they will get into the routine and flow with it.

Parental Agreement

Mom and Dad should talk about their family nighttime routine. It's not for Mom to tell Dad how it's going to be. Both of you need to discuss the routine thoroughly and agree on it, because both of you will be walking your toddler through it at different times. For your toddler's sake, the routine should remain the same, no matter who carries it out.

Word from the Wise

"The Lord himself watches over you! The Lord stands beside you as your protective shade. The sun will not hurt you by day, nor the moon at night. The Lord keeps you from all evil and preserves your life. The Lord keeps watch over you as you come and go, both now and forever." (Psalm 121:5–8)

David writes a beautiful prayer for you to pray with your little ones at night.

Remove the Element of Surprise

You create a routine to remove the element of surprise. Children need to know what to expect and how things are going to go. When there is routine, you will find that kids know what's next and they walk in it with you.

Word from the Wise

"I think of the good old days, long since ended, when my nights were filled with joyful songs." (Psalm 77:5–6)

Singing songs that bring peaceful joy may help your toddler shift from anger and frustration to peace.

Set the Time—Time for Yourself!

Decide on a bedtime, and be consistent with it. Keep in mind that you and your spouse need some time alone and some time together after Junior goes to bed. It may be easier to keep Junior up with you until he falls asleep, but this won't help your marriage and won't give you any personal rest or free time.

Word from the Wise

"One day soon afterward, Jesus went to a mountain to pray, and he prayed to God all night." (Luke 6:12)

Jesus needed time alone to pray. He needed to rejuvenate himself by spending time with his father. Parents, no less than he, need time alone to rejuvenate. The demands on both of you will always be there. You must plan to make this happen for your own well-being.

The bedtime routine takes time. It may take an hour from start to finish! If you want to start "your" time at 8 P.M., you need to start the bed time routine at 7:00 P.M. Your toddler needs 10–12 hours of sleep to function well and not be miserable all day. If children are asleep by 8 P.M., they will wake up between 6 A.M. and 8 A.M. the next day. If you go to bed at 10:00 P.M. and they wake up at 6:00 A.M., you'll have had eight hours of sleep. You need your sleep, too!

Don't Wait Until You're Exhausted!

Start the kids to bed when you still have energy. Don't wait until you're exhausted. You will be less patient, your toddler will pick up on it, and his or her resistance may be a reaction to your emotional or physical state. Start the kids to bed when you're still in good shape; crash after they crash.

When Bathing Shouldn't Be Part of the Bedtime Routine

For some families, the toddler bath is part of the bedtime routine and works well. However, it won't work for those whose children can't bathe every day because of eczema.

If your toddler has skin sensitivities and can't bathe every night, don't make the bath part of the bedtime routine. Let your toddler bathe during the day.

If your tot just doesn't like baths, bathing shouldn't be part of the bedtime routine. In these situations, you should bathe your toddler during the day.

The Key Phrase or Sound

It's a good idea to use a "key phrase" that will signal to your toddler that it's time to start your evening routine. Your key phrase could be ...

"Time for jammies."

"Where's that toothbrush?"

"Time for bed, sleepy head."

"Bed bunny is looking for his friend."

"Time for nitey nites."

"Where's your favorite blanket?"

Sound of the 8 o'clock chime.

Playing the bedtime song.

Singing the bedtime song.

A verbal or tonal cue will help your toddler make the mental shift between day-time activities and nighttime activities.

Slow and Steady Wins the Race

Telling your toddler to "hurry up and get to bed right now" won't create a pleasant evening for you or your tot. Going to bed is all about winding the body down until it falls asleep. It takes time for this to happen.

Think about your bedtime routine. You go through many steps between deciding to go to bed and actually falling asleep. Your toddler needs lots of steps, too. You have a routine. Everybody pretty much does the same things every night on the way to bed. As they say, we are creatures of habit.

Nobody can tell you just to get into bed and go to sleep! You can't expect this of your toddlers, either.

Don't Wind Them Up

If you want your toddler to start the bedtime routine at 7 P.M., you won't want to start rough-housing at 6:45 P.M. How long does it take you to wind down from vig-orous activity?

The worst thing is when friends and relatives come over and want to play with toddlers, tickle them, laugh with them, and get them all stirred up in the evening. You'll have to tell them that if they want to play like that with your toddler, they'll have to come before dinner!

After supper, a quiet evening will help your toddler with the routine. Having a little fun isn't a big deal, but all-out physical activity should be avoided. If you want to tucker out the kids so they'll sleep well, it's better to do it before dinner.

Bedtime and Hunger

Children usually need to eat something every two to three hours. Going from bedtime to morning is a big stretch for them. You need to find ways to tide them over until morning without their teeth rotting. Here are a couple of ideas.

Warm Milk and Turkey

Yes, it's true, warm milk has medicinal qualities! Tryptophan is a natural protein in milk (also found in some cheeses and in turkey). It is known to help people stay in deep sleep longer (it also helps with memory and learning). Around Thanksgiving, there are usually news reports about the tryptophan in turkey and how it produces that "afternoon nap" on Thanksgiving Day. Warm milk and a little turkey sandwich is a good idea for a bedtime snack.

If your daughter wakes up hungry in the middle of the night, warm her a little cup of milk in the microwave. Have her drink it and go back to sleep. Don't engage her in conversation, and don't stay at her bedside longer than necessary.

The only time you should talk a little with your children at night is if they wake up afraid. You need to do a little interview with them to find out what is bothering them. Pray and then tell them they need to go back to sleep. See Chapter 16 for dealing with nightmares and monsters.

Bottles and Bed

Don't put your toddler to bed with a bottle. Give a pacifier instead, or just remove it completely. Your tot will fuss about the bottle for a few nights but will get over it. Don't cave in to a little person who doesn't know what's best. You are the one who knows this! No bottle of milk in bed (or after teeth are brushed at night).

You can wean your toddler off the bottle at night by reducing the milk by half an ounce or an ounce every night. But if your little one is hungry at night, it's better just to provide a real-food snack to fill up that tummy before Junior goes to bed. Turkey, turkey, turkey!

Daytime Naps: Needs of Parents and Children

Worn-out parents get just as cranky and impatient as worn-out kids. Whether or not toddlers think they need a nap, if you need one, they need one. You just need to make it happen.

Toddlers show signs of fatigue when they need a nap. They rub their eyes, start drooping their heads, suck their thumbs, rub their ears, or start getting really cranky. If you think your tot needs a nap, put him or her down for one. Every toddler ever asked "Are you tired?" will answer "No!" The only thing toddlers know is that they don't want to miss any action. That's why they don't want to have a nap or go to bed at night. They want to see it all and be a part of it all.

You know when your kids need a nap. You don't need to ask your son; just pick him up, hug him, and tell him it's time to lie down. One little trick, since kids want to do what you're doing, is to lie down yourself and fake sleeping. They are up only because they are hoping you'll entertain them and be busy with them. If they see there is no hope that you'll be getting busy with them, they will have nothing better to do than to lie down beside you. After they fall asleep, you can either sleep, too, or go have some time to yourself (or tend to other children).

If your toddler is nap-resistant, try this. Buy a beanbag chair. Put a blanket on it. Pull it up alongside the sofa. Tell your tot that you're taking a nap. Lie down and keep one eye partly opened to see what your tot is up to. You can put up baby gates around the room you're in, to keep it contained, if you like, but odds are, your little one will want to stay near you. More than likely, within 10 minutes Junior will crawl up on the beanbag chair and go to sleep.

As with the nighttime routine, you can create a daytime napping routine. If kids know that after lunch each day they will be taking a nap, they'll come to anticipate it. Schedule appointments first thing in the morning or later in the afternoon (same with shopping) so that your toddler will be rested when you go out.

Not all kids need daytime naps. Some kids are just little live wires, and they go all day like an adult. If your child isn't tired and you need a nap, put him in a play pen (contain him, keep him safe) and tell him he can play quietly there while you nap. Nap on the couch where he can see you.

Nighttime Comfort and Warmth

Children won't sleep well if their pajamas are too tight or uncomfortable. It's worth asking your toddlers if they like their pajamas or if their pajamas hurt them anywhere.

Like adults, children won't sleep well if they are too cold. They will shiver all night, will not sleep well, and then be miserable the next day from lack of sleep.

 **Word from the Wise**

"I will lie down in peace and sleep, for you alone, O Lord, will keep me safe." (Psalm 4:8)

Pray for your little ones as they lie down to sleep. Let them know that they have a mighty God who watches over them at night and keeps them safe.

Ask your kids if they feel chilly in bed. They may not think to tell you they are chilly at night. You should ask them directly. Consider flannel sheets, polar fleece sheets, and those hotel room blankets that are so warm. (On the cheap, I custom-made polar fleece sheets for two of my children's twin beds by simply buying 60-inch-wide fleece and sewing up the corners. They are always warm.)

Check to see if the wall by your child's bed is warm or cold. If it's an older house, the insulation may be thin or may have settled. A bed against a cold wall will make the entire mattress cold. Is the bed under a drafty window?

When You've Simply Had It!

Let's be real here for a minute. Sometimes you and your spouse are simply too exhausted to handle walking Junior through his nighttime routine. As much as your child needs routine, some days neither parent can do it. Life is life. Sometimes stressors just leave us without any reserves. In this type of situation you may choose to abbreviate your routine, keep the order, but leave out some of the activities.

In a situation like this, if you will just be miserable, short-tempered, or mean while putting your son to bed, just get him in his pajamas, put him in bed, and say "Sweetheart, Mommy and Daddy are too pooped to put you to bed tonight the way we usually do. We love you. You have to go to sleep on your own. Good night." Kiss him, close the door, and walk away. He might start crying and screaming, but he'll fall asleep on his own. If he comes to the door to run out of the room, put him back to bed, say good night, tell him to stay in bed, and leave his room. He will be mad; he will cry and scream. Tell him you love him and that he has to go to bed. When he sees that he's not going to get you involved with him, he'll give up and go to bed.

No, this isn't the ideal. But sometimes it's all you can do.

If you are feeling like this nearly every night, some family adjustments are probably necessary. You must be under unbearable stress, and you probably need some help. Look into some professional counseling, make an appointment with your pastor, ask a friend to care for your toddler, or consider putting Junior in day care for a few months. Get yourself well. Only a well Mom and Dad can be effective, loving parents.

Nighttime Ordeals

You have to give toddlers a lot of credit. It's amazing the kinds of things they can come up with to stall going to bed, staying in bed, or keeping you with them.

Remember, you are their world. They want to be with you all the time, including at night. Part of their successful development includes their coming to understand that you are separate people. One of the ways they learn this is by starting to sleep in their own bed by themselves. In their little hearts and minds, they will be happy only if they are with you. This isn't true, but they will try everything to convince you that it is.

Nonstop Requests and Demands

Once your bed time routine is over, it's over. Your toddler should be fed and watered, should be emptied of poop and pee, and should have a dry diaper (if he or she is still wearing one). Be consistent and firm. If you start catering to your toddlers' requests for this and that at the end of the bedtime routine, you essentially tell them that there is no routine and that they call the shots. There will be no end to it. Don't give in.

Dr. Mom Speaks

So many bedtime troubles arise because loving parents have a tough time "ending" the nighttime routine. Their hearts are too easily tugged by the whimpers of their tots. Don't let their requests for additional attention stop you from doing the right thing. Get them to bed on time.

Fears

Chapter 17 addresses many fears a child may have of the night through various prayers. Aside from the kinds of things mentioned ahead, you child may be afraid of the noise of thunderstorms or the crackle of lightning, or of being alone.

The Awesome Wonder of God: Thunder and Lightning

Parents create either a fear of thunder and lightning or an excitement for thunder and lightning. While there may be a natural tendency for that noise to induce a little fear, when Mom and Dad run to the window with their tot and say with excitement, "Wow, look at that beautiful lightning! Isn't this exciting?", they teach their kids not to be afraid.

My mom would sit us kids in front of the big living room window, and we'd watch every storm. "Did you see that?" "Wow, let's count seconds between the lightning and thunder to see how far away the storm is." Watching a storm was like a free movie at our house. When my kids were little, I wanted them to love storms, too. We had a house with a glassed-in veranda. We'd all sit out there on a sofa and watch the night sky together.

Unfortunately, some parents teach their children fear of storms. One person I knew said her mom hid under the bed during such storms. Of course, this person was terrified of storms, just like her mom.

Fear of Being Alone

Fear of being alone can't be cured at night. It is cured during the day by developing a secure attachment with your toddler. See Chapter 5 for further information.

Meanwhile, your child needs a security object. Be it a special blanket, a favorite teddy bear, or a favorite doll, toddlers needs something to cuddle at night so that they don't feel alone. You may want to get a "life-size" stuffed animal that your child can tuck under the sheets as a "nighttime buddy."

Kids afraid of being alone at night may need their bed covered with their "friends" (all their dolls and stuffed animals) to keep them company.

Safety and Sanity Tips

Sometimes little ones wake up in the night with fear. Make sure they have a night light. Buy them a kids' flashlight, too, and leave it beside their bed. This will help them get to your bedroom if they are really scared, or to the bathroom, if necessary.

Stay in Your Own Bed—All of You

If your toddler comes into your room at night, go back together and put your child in his or her bed. You can stay for a minute, say a little prayer, and tell your tot to stay in bed and go back to sleep. Don't sleep with your kids through the night, even if they are afraid, or they will expect it every night.

Don't Let Them Sleep Between Mom and Dad

Everybody needs to learn to sleep in their own bed. There is no healthy reason for a child to sleep between parents.

All the couples I have known who let a child sleep between them had marital dysfunction. One of the spouses "needed" the child to provide a barrier against the spouse. In one case, the mom insisted that the son sleep between her and her husband. Eventually, she had her husband on the couch. Soon he was out the door!

Healthy couples with a healthy sex life don't want their kids in bed with them. If your spouse insists that your child has to sleep between you, it's time to see a marriage therapist and have a little talk with your pastor.

> **Toddler Tales**
>
> One morning I woke up and couldn't roll over. My little girl had come into my bedroom in the night, had crawled on top of me, and was sleeping on my back. I had no idea she was there until I woke up in the morning.

Don't Lie with Her Until She Falls Asleep

If you lie with your toddler until he or she falls asleep, you are sending the subtle message that the child can't fall asleep on his or her own. This promotes the idea that kids can't be safe if not attached to you at all times.

Letting kids fall asleep on their own tells them that everything is okay, that they are getting bigger, and that they can handle it.

You can lie down beside your daughter to read stories together and pray, but after prayers and maybe a few quiet minutes, it's time to get up off her bed, say good night, turn off the light, and leave.

Bedtime Is Not Playtime

Toddlers need to learn that there is a time for playing and a time for sleeping. Don't let them think they can sit up in bed and play for hours. Their job at bedtime is to sleep. They need to focus on settling down, not getting more excited.

If your toddler won't lie down and insists on playing with toys, you may have to add the activity of putting all the toys in a big box or bag each night and removing it from the room. Your message needs to be consistent.

The Nighttime Drink

Your toddler will probably be a little thirsty at bedtime. Milk, water, or vegetable juices are probably best because they are not loaded with sugar or stimulants (like fruit juices, sodas, and chocolate milk). The goal is to wind down, not up.

Don't cave in to kids' demands for other drinks. Stick to your guns—you will survive their antics over this, and so will they.

Waking Up in the Night

Like everyone else, sometimes your toddlers will wake up in the night. When they wake up, they are likely to come to your bedroom. They can't read a clock. They may think that if they wake up, it's time for everyone to wake up. You need to teach them that this is not so. Take them back to bed, tell them it's not time to get up yet, tuck them in, and tell them that they need to go back to sleep.

One mom I knew was complaining about being up every night at 3:00 A.M. with her three-year-old daughter. Further inquiry uncovered the fact that her daughter came to her, they went to the kitchen together, she made her daughter a little snack, they had a little talk, and then she put her daughter back to bed. She also mentioned that with being a graduate student and studying, she had her daughter in day care and hardly saw her. I responded, "Well, then, I guess it's really a treat for you and her to spend some time alone together in the middle of the night. You need to do that with her, don't you?" Yes, indeed. Being up in the night served a purpose for their relationship. Unfortunately, as much as it might have served a purpose for the mom, the little girl was the loser the next day, trying to survive day care with a ton of kids and lack of sleep.

The Value of a Delayed Response

Sometimes little ones squawk at night for no good reason. A delayed response can help them learn to settle themselves. Try the following:

- First, wait a few moments to see if your child settles on his own. If he doesn't settle …

- Call to him as softly as possible and tell him everything is okay and to go back to sleep. If he doesn't settle …

- Stand at his door and tell him softly that everything is okay and to go back to sleep. If he doesn't settle …

- Stand by his bed and talk with him softly. If he doesn't settle …

- Put your hand gently on his back, rub his back a little, and tell him you love him. He should settle by now.

- Always try the least amount of contact and intervention first when responding to cries or complaints at night.

- Don't get into any discussions, arguments, or issues at bedtime.

- Less is more. Your child can't talk if you don't respond.

Emotional Stressors and Sickness Cause Regression

Just when you think you've got things running smoothly, something upsets the apple cart. Like my little niece's bib says, "Spit happens."

Stressors that hit your family or your toddler will cause internal disturbance. When kids are disturbed inside, they lose their grip on themselves. They regress from their developmental accomplishments.

When kids are sick, they get special attention from Mom and Dad. They have to get this additional attention. They need you to take care of them. But this also becomes a time for them to be babies again. They are helpless, but as they get better, they are not so helpless anymore. When they start to get well, having enjoyed so much additional attention and care, they may want to continue their dependence instead of moving ahead. When this happens, you need to be patient but firm. They need to know that it's time to get back up to speed—time to sleep through the night again! You may have to just let them cry themselves to sleep for a couple of nights for them to know that Mom and Dad won't be running in there now since they aren't sick anymore. Two nights usually does it.

Signs of regression (from stress or illness) include these:

- Not sleeping through the night
- Wetting the bed again
- Wetting their pants again during the day

Signs of stress include these:

- Having nightmares
- Being miserable for no visible reason (not hungry, dehydrated, or tired)
- Showing aggression toward people or animals
- Having a preoccupation with touching their genitals
- Exhibiting outright defiance

When your little ones are stressed, you need to help them talk about the things that are bothering them. Cuddle your tot and ask open-ended questions to try to get to the bottom of the unhappiness. Try to just listen to what's on kids' little hearts.

Part 4

Spiritual Development of Your Child

You can give your child no greater gift than your faith in God. In this part, you will learn how to help your toddler be sensitive to the Holy Spirit and how to help him or her develop self-control and a sense of morality and altruism.

Essential to all children's development is setting limits and establishing consequences when they go beyond those limits. The Lord disciplines those he loves, and there are times when you must discipline your children, in love and within limits.

For some children, nighttime is a scary time. Learn how to pray for your little ones so that they may be restful and calm through the night.

Chapter 13

Training Your Toddler to Discern the Holy Spirit

Throughout history, almighty God has spoken to his people, even to children. What an exciting opportunity we have as Christian parents to guide our children in hearing the voice of God! Only when our children know how to listen to the Lord can they effectively become his servants. It is one thing to know who God is and yet another to know him so personally that we recognize when he is speaking to us, guiding us, and leading us. As young as three years old, children can be mentored to come to know the presence of God in a very real way.

The Spirit Within: God Speaks to Kids

Does God speak to kids before they accept Jesus Christ as their Lord and Savior? Yes, of course he does. Almighty God has been speaking to his children since he talked with Adam in the Garden of Eden. He speaks to whom he pleases, unbelievers included. Remember that God spoke to Abimelech (Genesis 20). God's communication with his people occurs in many different ways.

Our job as Christian parents is to teach our children the different ways God speaks to people so that they will begin to recognize when he's speaking to them.

How does God speak to kids?

- Through his written word, the Bible
- During prayer
- Through their spirit
- Through dreams and visions
- With his audible voice
- Through their conscience

Through the Bible

Our preschoolers begin learning about the Spirit of God speaking to them when we start reading Bible stories to them. Buy *The Picture Bible* for each of your tots. It is truly the most exciting way to introduce your children to the word of God. *The Picture Bible* emphasizes the miracles of God and God speaking to his people. At the end of each section, you will want to tell your children that just as God talked with Abraham, Moses, Noah, Elijah, Elizabeth, Mary, and Jesus, he seeks to talk to them, too.

Sometimes we read the Bible and know that God is speaking to us through his word. He uses his word to encourage us, teach us, soothe us, and train us. Helping our children to develop a desire to read the Word of God starts when they are just tots. They need to see that we want to read the Word of God. There are enough adventure stories in the Bible to fill many years of bedtime reading.

During Prayer

You need to build a framework for your children to want to pray—that is, converse with God. Prayer is not a one-way street. We sell our kids short if we just teach them to fold their hands, thank God for stuff, ask him for stuff, and say "Amen." When we teach our children to pray, we teach them both to talk with God and to listen to God. Time should be allowed at the end of prayer time for us to ask God to tell us anything he may want to tell us. Then you and your children should be still for a moment. Ask your little tikes if they felt God speak to them about anything. Tell them if you think God spoke to you about anything. Talk about it.

You are setting the stage for them. One day, they will be praying alone, and they will ask God a question and he will answer them.

Prayer is a relational event.

Through the Spirit

Sometimes the Spirit of God speaks directly to our spirit. We just know that God is telling us something. Jesus perceived in his spirit what the scribes were thinking in their hearts (Mark 2:8). The Holy Spirit spoke to Jesus' spirit and told him what he needed to know for that situation. In the same way, the Spirit of God can speak to our spirits and tell us what we need to know.

Toddler Tales

One day eight families gathered to praise and worship God together. As everybody was praising God, a woman's four-year-old son began to weep. The mom took her son aside and asked him what was wrong. He said that nothing was wrong but that the Lord was speaking to him. The mom inquired further. The boy said, "Mom, the Lord is telling me that we are in the heart of God!" God speaks to preschoolers.

Through Dreams and Visions

God speaks to his people in dreams and visions. God came to Abimelech and spoke to him in a dream (Genesis 20:3). An angel of the Lord came in a dream to Jacob and spoke to him (Genesis 31:11). God appeared to Laban in a dream (Genesis 31:24). The Lord told Miriam and Aaron that he communicates with people by visions and dreams even though that was not the way he communicated with Moses (Numbers 12:6).

Job writes in 33:14–17 …

> But God speaks again and again, though people do not recognize it. He speaks in dreams, in visions of the night when deep sleep falls on people as they lie in bed. He whispers in their ear and terrifies them with his warning. He causes them to change their minds; he keeps them from pride.

> ### Word from the Wise
>
> "Then after I have poured out my rains again, I will pour out my Spirit upon all people. Your sons and daughters will prophesy. Your old men will dream dreams. Your young men will see visions." (Joel 2:28)
>
> Joel's prophecy is reiterated in Acts 2:17 as something we are to anticipate. Let's prepare our children for this now.

When our children tell us about their visions, we need to gently affirm their reality. We do not want to quench the Spirit of God or grieve him by trying to convince our children that it's all in their imagination. At times children may hear something that may contradict the Word of God because none of us, even adults, always hears what God is saying. Our own spirits can get mixed in. Don't use it to squelch the child's listening ability. Rather, use it as a teachable moment to better understand what the Word of God says in reference to what your child hears.

We need to let our children see what they see and not pass judgment on it.

Toddler Tales

> One day a four-and-a-half-year-old boy was having lunch with his mom. Out of the blue he said to his mom, "Mom, I'm seeing a bright light inside of me. Mom, it's the Lord—he's blessing me. Mom, now I see a whole bunch of little lights going around the world. It's the Lord—he's blessing the whole world." God speaks to us in mysterious ways, even through our preschoolers!

With His Audible Voice

Samuel was a small boy when God chose to speak to him in an audible voice:

> Meanwhile, the boy Samuel was serving the Lord by assisting Eli. Now in those days messages from the Lord were very rare, and visions were quite uncommon.
>
> One night Eli … had just gone to bed. … Samuel was sleeping. … Suddenly, the Lord called out, "Samuel! Samuel!" "Yes?" Samuel replied. "What is it?" He jumped up and ran to Eli. "Here I am. What do you need?" "I didn't call you," Eli replied. "Go on back to bed." So he did.

Then the Lord called out again, "Samuel!" Again Samuel jumped up and ran to Eli. "Here I am," he said. "What do you need?" "I didn't call you, my son," Eli said. "Go on back to bed."

Samuel did not yet know the Lord because he had never had a message from the Lord before. So now the Lord called a third time, and once more Samuel jumped up and ran to Eli. "Here I am," he said. "What do you need?"

Then Eli realized it was the Lord who was calling the boy. So he said to Samuel, "Go and lie down again, and if someone calls again, say, 'Yes, Lord, your servant is listening.'" So Samuel went back to bed. And the Lord came and called as before, "Samuel! Samuel!" And Samuel replied, "Yes, Lord, your servant is listening." (1 Samuel 3:1–10)

How many people would love to hear God speak to them in an audible voice? Almighty God is almighty God. He can speak to people however he chooses. Our children should know this. The story of Samuel is a wonderful story for us to share with our little ones.

In Samuel's days, as these days, messages and visions from the Lord were rare. But they do occur, and they can come to our children. We need to pay attention to what our children tell us and be ready to acknowledge that the Lord himself is speaking to our little ones.

Share the story of Samuel with your children and tell them that if God ever speaks to them like this, they should do as Samuel did and answer, "Yes, Lord, your servant is listening."

Our little ones need to know that God can and does speak to children and always has.

Through Our Conscience

God gave us our conscience. It exists to tell us right from wrong. People who are in touch with their conscience have a gut feeling when something is right or wrong, good or bad, true or false. This can be called "God in your guts!"

Paul says that some people have violated their consciences, and as a result their faith became shipwrecked. In Jeremiah 31:33, the Lord says that he will put his law within people, that he will write his law on their hearts. No matter where people stand in their relationship with God, his law is within them. Whether or not your children have accepted Jesus Christ as their Lord and Savior, God's law is within them. His law is their conscience. His law tells them about good and bad.

You can teach your children to pay attention to their conscience. Their conscience not only warns them against doing bad things, but it also warns them that bad things are happening around them and that other people may have bad things in their hearts.

For instance, I introduced my children to their conscience (which I call "God talking to you through your guts") during Saturday morning cartoons. As they watched cartoons, I watched their faces. As they made different facial expressions, I asked them how they felt in their heart. When they laughed, of course they were feeling "good." But then certain things (violent, monstrous, etc.) came on, and the expression on their faces would become one of fear. When I asked them what they felt then, they said "bad" or "scared." I told them that when they feel that way, they have power over the situation and can change the station or turn off the TV. I empowered them to take action when they had those bad feelings.

From there, I told them that when they felt that same bad feeling, they would know that there is something bad or wrong happening and that they should think of how they can get away from or change whatever is bad or wrong. This bad feeling warns them that they need to do something. Perhaps all they need to do is come and get their dad. Or perhaps they need to get away from whatever or whoever they are around at the time.

Teach your kids that God speaks to them through their guts. When kids become sensitive to this, they can become aware of potential danger and also know what to do if they have that sense of danger.

Be aware, however, that our consciences are not the final word. We have been given a new heart, but as fallen creatures we can sometimes deceive ourselves in our judgments. Our consciences need to line up with what the Word of God says.

The Spirit Within: God Warns Kids

Throughout history, God has seen fit to provide warnings to his people. People need to listen to the warnings and take heed. Kids especially need to be trained how to listen to God's warnings because kids are so small and vulnerable. They can be taught as young as three years old to pay attention to God speaking to them in their guts.

Along with knowing that there is some danger around them, kids need to be instructed what to do:

- Come directly to Mom or Dad
- Walk away from the people they are near
- Turn off the medium that is making them feel bad
- Close the book

It's important that your tots not feel powerless when they have this bad feeling inside. If they feel powerless, they will feel paralyzed. When my kids saw bad things while watching TV, they first felt paralyzed, as though that awful stuff on TV had control over them. They needed to be equipped to stop and think about their options and to be enabled to make a decision to change their situation.

Refer to Chapter 20 and read through the comments on Matthew 2:13–14 and Genesis 7:5–10.

The Spirit Within: God Flows Through Kids

Aren't preschoolers wonderful? Unlike adults, they have no preconceived notions about anything. They look to their parents to lead them and guide them and teach them about the world. Their little minds and spirits are open. Because of this, we must both protect them from certain things and introduce them to certain things. As parents, we are the gatekeepers for our children. Along the way, we teach them to be their own gatekeepers, but in the preschool years, they need us to do this for them.

How does God flow through kids? The power of God flowed through the Lord Jesus, and the sick were healed. The power of God flows not just through adults, but through children, too. The only requirement is that the person be open to the Spirit of God flowing. This openness is created when parents create a framework for it in the minds and hearts of their children.

The gifts of healing, given by the Holy Spirit, do not need any special importation in order to flow through a person. If you, as parents, pray for people who are sick, encourage your three- to five-year-old to stand by and join you. Ask your child to hold his or her hand near the sick person and simply ask the Holy Spirit to send his power to touch the sick person. Then ask your little tike if his or her hand has become warm or tingly. Those that minister healing prayer to the sick have found that this occurs sometimes but not all of the time. This is one evidence of the gift of healing flowing, but they may not feel anything. The Holy Spirit sometimes flows in healing power without any manifestations at all.

The Holy Spirit's healing power can flow through children relatively easily. If this happens with your child, that's great. If nothing happens when your child prays, that's okay, too. Your children are learning that God called us all to pray for the sick, and people will be blessed even if they don't get healed. Again, we are creating a reasonable expectation of God's sovereign ability to flow through his children, even the littlest of children.

A few warnings for when your children pray for the sick:

- Never let them physically touch the sick person when they are praying.
- Never let other people put their hands on your child when the sick are being prayed for.
- Allow your children to tell you when they feel the Spirit of God is speaking to them about specifically praying for a particular person. You decide if it is okay for them to pray for that person, and you accompany them and oversee what is occurring.

Safety and Sanity Tips

Remember, you are the adult. It is your job to protect your child in every way, even spiritually. Your preschooler is immature and should not have the responsibility to take care of adults. Don't allow anyone to ask your child personally to pray for them. Make sure people know they must go through you. If people are healed at the hands of your child, others will pursue your child. As parents, you must ensure that your children are left to be children and are not left with adult responsibilities to meet the needs of adults.

Even children are given gifts of the Holy Spirit, and it's okay for them to be mentored into mature use of those gifts. Just because a child is able to be used by the Holy Spirit to effect the works of Christ does not mean that the child has the maturity to handle the situation. You are the adult. God has given you charge over your child. If you have an uncomfortable sense from God about your child praying for a particular person or in a particular circumstance, then disallow it. You must also trust what you hear from the Lord, and your child must learn the value of parents' protection and guidance.

The Spirit Within: God Comforts Kids

Our children will go through many aches and pains in life. It's part of the human experience. Sometimes you will be available to comfort them; sometimes you won't. They need to know how to experience the comfort of God when you are not there.

For example, when you are comforting your daughter, begin to pray out loud. Ask the Lord Jesus to come. Ask the Lord Jesus to wrap his arms around her and pour out his love to her. Ask the Holy Spirit (the Comforter) to come and cuddle her with his love. Ask the Holy Spirit to touch her heart and her mind and her soul, and bring her peace.

You can also tell your children that when they are lying in bed, if they feel lonely or sad or bad, they can ask the Lord Jesus to wrap his arms around them and hold them.

While comforting your son, for instance, you can ask the Lord Jesus to come and wrap his arms around him, look into his eyes, and tell him how much he loves him.

Or, while comforting your daughter, you can tell her that she can invite the Lord Jesus to come into the room, and she can talk to him, tell him everything on her heart, and ask him to touch her heart.

Remind your children now and then that they can pray and ask the Lord these same things whenever they feel bad. Tell them after they pray to just be still for a little while and wait for God's peace to come to them.

Word from the Wise

The Apostle Paul tells us that we need to comfort others with the comfort we have received from God (2 Corinthians 1:3–7). As parents, you will comfort your tots over and over again, but your job is to also show them the comfort that comes from God. When you aren't with them, they need to know how to receive God's comfort. When they need your warm arms around them, pray with them like this: "Lord Jesus, come to Lara now and wrap your loving arms around her. Holy Spirit, I ask that you would come and touch my little girl's heart and comfort her now, in Jesus' name." Let Lara know that she can pray this even when you aren't with her.

Chapter 14

Growing Kids with a Conscience

Parents, it's your job to teach your children to be socially and morally responsible human beings. They don't become that way on their own.

The Lord gives each person a conscience, but parents help the conscience to develop in a healthy way. Parents teach tots, through actions and words, "the right thing to do." They do this through teaching them about the necessity of controlling their bodies and then controlling their outside world and their inner world. With each of these developments, toddlers will be growing their conscience and, along with the Holy Spirit, will develop their inner sense of right and wrong.

There's nothing worse than an out-of-control child. These children become the spoiled brats of tomorrow, the classroom problems for teachers, the teenage delinquents of the future. Out-of-control children come from permissive parents and from parents who are overly controlling without affection. You can learn to avoid these parenting errors.

Self-Control

Parents need to train children in the fine art of "self-control." Self-control is the ability to control one's behavior, one's own body movements.

When do you start teaching your son or daughter about self-control? As soon as he or she can crawl or walk.

Stopping Motor Movements

This is the first stage in the development of self-control, for toddlers to stop their movements! Yes, that's right, stop their movements—control their bodies. This would include such things as not touching things they should not touch, staying in one place when told to stay where they are, stopping their actions when it appears they are about to hurt themselves or someone else.

Of course, this is learned through your toddler hearing the word "no." Each time you say "no," you train your child in the fine art of self-control. However, inappropriately saying "no" has its negative effects (see Chapter 15).

Training your toddler to not touch things is a very important developmental step. (This is where permissive parents miss the boat and create spoiled kids.) Some experts tell you to take everything important out of the reach of your toddler. While you must keep everything dangerous (like medicines and poisons) out of reach of toddlers, you should not keep all "off-limits" objects out of reach. How will they learn if they don't practice?

While you will surely place valuable things up high, you ought to leave some objects within reach of your toddler that are clearly off-limits. They need these objects to practice on. As your toddler learns to keep her hands off objects that are off-limits, you can bring out (or down) more of the valuables. When you have your children well trained and they come upon a new object, they should be looking to you to see if it's okay for them to touch it.

Don't let your children touch everything they see while out shopping, and don't let them push every button on every contraption in every store. While these things may serve a distractibility need for you, you are short-changing your children by encouraging their lack of self-control. They need to learn to control their behavior in public and at home, and they shouldn't touch things that aren't theirs unless they have permission and it is appropriate. This is a choice you are making not to control your children, and you are giving them the message that they are not required to control their behavior in public. What will they be like when they get to school?

Word from the Wise

"A person without self-control is as defenseless as a city with broken-down walls." (Proverbs 25:28)

Teaching self-control is an essential element of parenting. It is God-inspired, God-required.

Control and Concentration

Toddlers learning how to control their body is positively correlated with their ability to concentrate and not be easily distracted.

Overactive Tots

Do you think your 12- to 24-month-old is much more of a squirmer and mover than other people's kids? That may be. At this stage, there can be significant differences in the amount of activity seen in toddlers. However, the good news, is, by age three or four, these overactive kids seem to even out with their peers.

Once they pass from their fourth year, their activity level will be fairly consistent over their growing-up years. This is when you'll be able to see what your child's true nature is in terms of needs for physical activity.

Word from the Wise

"But after he had taken the census, David's conscience began to bother him. And he said to the Lord, 'I have sinned greatly and shouldn't have taken the census. Please forgive me, Lord, for doing this foolish thing.' (2 Samuel 24:10)

It's a parent's job to teach a child what is right and wrong and how to make amends to God and others for bad choices.

Hyperactive Tots

The hyperactive toddler is not simply more active than the overactive toddler. Hyperactivity is about a child …

- Not being able to respond to commands to stop a behavior.
- Exhibiting a behavior that is clearly not appropriate to the situation.
- Being able to respond at only one speed—immediate, fast, impulsive.
- Showing restless movement, rocking, swaying, fiddling, wiggling, squirming, and playing nervously.
- Exhibiting disorganized activity.
- Not actually running faster than other children.
- Displaying other physiological, behavioral, or learning problems.

Hyperactive boys are far more common than hyperactive girls. If your toddler is hyperactive, you are probably frustrated and exhausted. Even though your toddler may want to follow your commands, he or she may not be able to. Punishment does not help the hyperactive child's behavior. Your tot may have some neurological damage, may have ingested lead, or may have been deprived of oxygen at birth. Your family may need special help. Consult with your doctor, and get a referral to a specialist.

Starting, Stopping, and Slowing

Research reveals that as children pass from ages three to five, they increase in their ability to go slow. For most tots, it's all or nothing in terms of speed.

When asked to draw lines slowly on a paper, younger toddlers will just draw the line quickly. As they grow a little bit, they start slowly but then finish fast in a jerk. Slow is difficult but gets better by age 5 or 6.

Toddlers respond to commands, but not in the way you might think! If they stand on the line waiting for you to say "stop" or "go," no matter which one you say, they will lunge forward. They respond to being told to do something, and they can't quite distinguish what to do with different commands. So, it's easier for your toddler to respond to "do" rather than "don't do," and "fast" rather than "slow."

Toddler Tales

Just after we moved into our house, the neighbors across the street came to welcome us. They brought their two daughters, two and four years old. The girls ran about our house, and picked up and broke at least half of our collector toys. They wanted to run upstairs and explore our bedrooms. I blocked the stairs by sitting on them, and they tried to push past me in front of their parents, even though I told them they couldn't go upstairs. There was no acknowledgment or recognition from the parents that the girls were doing anything wrong, and the girls were not called to account in any way for all the toys they had broken. Welcome to the neighborhood!

Self-Control and Problem Solving

Given a choice, toddlers will tend to make the choice that is the easiest and fastest, although not necessarily the best. Here is where you have the opportunity to help them develop their thinking. Here's how:

- Stop them before they make their choice.
- Explain to them the consequences of various decisions.
- Start asking them to think about what their options are and what the consequences of their choices will be.

When you facilitate problem solving in your children, your help them increase their ability to control their behavior before they act. You help them see that it is better in most cases to think before they act.

Children as young as two can be taught how to think before they act—to use reflective problem solving instead of impulsivity.

As you role-play with your children, you can create scenarios in which people have to think before they act (for example, the firefighter rescuing the person in the burning building—ask your tot about the different ways the firefighter could get to the person, which way would endanger him, which way would be the safest, which way would be the fastest for the victim, and so on).

Impulsivity and Boredom

You teach children to sustain their attention through intentionally thinking before acting. Children who are left to be impulsive, without parental intervention, will

Safety and Sanity Tips

It's a lot of work to train your toddler. The investment of your time and energy now will spare you much grief in the future.

continue to make quick decisions. They will not stop and think things through, and they will not come up with the best solution. This is a skill they need parents to teach them. Children left to act impulsively get bored quickly. They cannot sustain their attention on anything in particular. This is the video addict (requires no real thinking, only a quick response) instead of the chess player (requires great thinking before acting).

Locus of Control

Locus of control starts with the realization that you can control things that directly affect you. Teach your children that they can make decisions, take action, and reap the consequences of those actions, positive or negative.

Locus of Control and Parental Responsiveness

Your valuing and affirming what is inside your child helps them develop an internal locus of control. They gain confidence to trust themselves, which means trusting themselves to make decisions. When they make good decisions, they feel good about who they are and become internally motivated. It all works together.

Respond to your children when they talk with you and ask you about things. Don't ignore them or push them away.

Of course, this doesn't mean going with your child's every whim and allowing your toddler to become a tyrant. It means hearing out your kids and valuing what they say, even if it is necessary to overrule their request. Parents still need to be parents and maintain control of their home. Remember, children feel secure when their parents are in control, but they need to be given opportunities to take control over themselves in age-appropriate ways. Over the course of their years with you, you should be constantly putting more control into their hands so that they will be capable and competent adults when they leave home. It's a process. It starts when they are about two!

Locus of Control and Self-Esteem

Locus of control and self-esteem are closely linked. Simply stated, when your toddler knows she can control something about her world and does control it, she feels good about her ability to do so. She feels good about herself. Toddlers (and others) have a sense of helplessness if they come to think that nothing they do can change anything—they give up, they stop trying, and they become passive victims of the world.

Instilling Internal Locus of Control

It is important that tots be given opportunities to make decisions about themselves and for themselves. These, of course, should be appropriate for their age. (You don't ask your toddler if he'd like to move to another town—that's your decision!) Toddlers can be asked …

- What they'd like to wear for the day.
- What sort of cereal or sandwich they would like.
- Where they would like to keep their special toys.
- How they want their stuffed animals arranged.
- Whether they want to paint or draw.
- Whether they'd like to play with their toys outside or have you fill their little pool.
- Who they would like to have over to play with.
- Who they want to invite to their birthday party.
- What storybook they'd like you to read to them.
- Whether they'd like to go shopping with you (only if someone else will be at home and there is truly the option).
- What they'd like to buy a friend for a birthday present (within a set dollar range).

Benefits of an Internal Locus of Control

When toddlers know that they have some ability to control what happens to them …

- They learn not to fear the world.
- They feel confidence in themselves.
- They do better at school.

- They allow themselves more challenges.
- They become independent.
- They can act decisively.
- They are not self-centered.
- They make decisions to help others because they want to, not because they are required to by an authority figure.
- They think for themselves and are better problem solvers.
- They are willing to take calculated risks.

When tots believe that they have the power to affect their world and determine what happens to them, and that they are responsible for their successes and failures, they develop an internal center of control, which makes them feel good about themselves. Their self-esteem is high. They also do better academically when they get to school.

Keep in mind that if your children are raised with an internal locus of control, they will be able to consider the human voice, but they will also be able to hear the voice of God. Why? Because they have been taught to tune into what is inside of them. The Spirit of God lives within. A child who has an internal locus of control is at peace within. Since the Spirit of the Lord speaks as a still, small voice, you want your children to be able to hear him when he calls.

> **Safety and Sanity Tips**
>
> You may feel that your world is more sane if you can make all the decisions for your toddler. While this may help you in the short run, it will drive you crazy over the long haul. Encouraging independence now will give you more peace of mind later.

Dangers of External Locus of Control

Parents who make every decision for their children, who believe children should be seen and not heard, and who do not encourage or support decision making in their children raise children who …

- Feel powerless.
- Feel helpless.
- Tend to be taken advantage of by others.

- Suffer from depression.
- Have no motivation.
- Never reach their potential, unaware of what that potential might be.
- Do poorly academically.
- Have no self-confidence.
- Fear the world.
- Remain dependent on others.
- Have no decision-making skills.

When tots are overly controlled by their parents, they develop an external center of control. They come to believe that they are unable to affect their world. They stop trying. They become passive. Eventually, even if they do succeed, they think it was a fluke or luck. In extreme cases, kids and adults who believe this about themselves become depressed, and they give up.

Self-esteem is integrally connected to our perception of whether we can affect our world.

Development of Morality and Altruism

As Christians, morality and altruistic behavior are highly valued and taught to us throughout the Bible. Jesus taught specifically about moral issues and about altruism. Why? Because these are things that are foreign to our selfish sinful nature. In addition to teaching children to be sociable (learning how to communicate and get along with people) and spiritual (learning how to communicate and get along with God), we need to teach them how to go the extra mile by doing the right thing (when tempted to do wrong) and by thinking of others (even though our human tendency is to think only of ourselves).

Moral Thinking

Moral thinking and moral behavior are uneven in children as they develop. As parents, you want to instill good moral thinking in your children, but don't expect them to make perfect moral decisions as they grow. Eventually, their moral thinking and mental maturity catch up with each other, but for now, it's your job to plant the seeds that support the development of a good, solid internal moral code.

How can you do this? The following parenting styles are found to enhance moral thinking:

Dr. Mom Speaks

As you talk with your toddler about godly morality and principles, provide an explanation with the lesson. For instance: "God doesn't want us to steal. When we steal, other people get hurt. Something that they need or love gets taken away from them. If people take things from us, it hurts our feelings. We shouldn't take things from others."

- Help your children understand how their actions will be experienced by another person—teach them the perspective of others.
- Help your children to understand other people's needs and expectations.
- Foster your children's empathy for others by showing empathy yourself and by showing compassion and understanding for the empathy they feel for others.
- Help your children learn how to recognize and share their emotions.
- Give your children reasonable control over their actions, and ensure that they know they are responsible for their actions.
- Give fair and consistent discipline.

Arbitrary assertion of parental power has a negative effect on moral thought and altruism.

Moral Thinking and Car Rides

Yes, indeed, one of the best places to talk about moral issues is in the car, whether your child is 2 or 12 or 16.

Driving in the car can be boring for children, but children want to hear what their parents think and how life should be lived. Conversations in the car can include …

- Responding to people in need.
- Identifying feelings.
- Expressing your empathy for people who need help.
- Understanding that children are not responsible for helping adults in need.
- Not touching people's privates.
- Relaying to children what to do if someone touches their privates.
- Comforting people who are sad.

- Showing love through actions.
- Stopping yourself from doing something you shouldn't do.
- Listening to the voice of God within.

Altruism

When they are as young as one or two years old, toddlers are aware of Mom and Dad's reactions to themselves and others. They are picking up on the value of altruism that young!

Helping, comforting, rescuing, defending, and sharing are what altruism is all about. Children learn altruism by watching their parents step in and compassionately respond to someone in need. Altruism isn't taught by words; it is taught by actions. What you tell your children about helping others must occasionally be reinforced by what they see you do.

Altruism becomes a value to children when they have an affectionate relationship with the adult who is demonstrating the altruistic behavior. Affection for the adult motivates children to pattern themselves after the adult.

Altruism and Play

Structured role-playing with children also teaches altruism. (Remember, only when children approach the age of four will they be ready to begin to practice being altruistic. Before this age they are watching and learning from you. Now, they will begin to practice altruism for themselves.) When your children have friends over, or even with your own children, you can give each child a role (a fireman, a person caught in a burning house, a doctor, a sick person, etc.) and ask them all to play the roles of helping the person who is in danger or who is hurt or sick. Playing roles as "helpers" contributes substantially to the development of altruism in children. Have the children change roles. It has been shown that children who have this sort of training are more likely than those who haven't to spontaneously offer to help a hurt classmate or friend.

Altruism and Praise

Be careful not to overpraise your children for altruistic behavior. You don't want them to do good things to please you; you want them to do good things out of the goodness of their heart. Keep your praise to the acknowledgement of the fact that they were helpful and that the person they helped is now better off because of what they did. Overly praising your tot will actually inhibit future helpful behavior. Recognition is what is necessary.

Altruism and Response to Aggression

If your tot is aggressive toward another tot, this is a perfect opportunity for you to demonstrate altruism to your toddler. First, you respond to the hurt child in a compassionate manner. Then you talk with your tot about how the other child has been hurt. Wait for a little contrition; encourage the two to make up and be friends. When your child's heart is in the right place, lead him or her into an apology and into behavior that will make up for what has been done.

Altruism and Preparing Food

Researchers have found that children's altruistic behavior is positively correlated with whether they are included in food preparation and cooking. Unfortunately, other household chores don't have this kind of effect on children.

When children know that their work makes a contribution to the family (food preparation and care of younger siblings), that the work must be done, and that the family is better off for the work being done, they will become more altruistic to others outside the home. This applies even if there is no adult present.

Altruism and Respect for Authority

Children who are required to be respectful to their parents and other adults show higher levels of altruism than children who are allowed to disrespect their parents and other adults.

Altruism and Mood

Children who are depressed will not be altruistic. Depression is all about internal conflict. When children are consumed by their own inner struggles, they don't think about the needs of others.

Positive mood contributes to positive behavior. Help your tot pump up his mood before you teach lessons on altruism.

Altruism Starts with Observation

The first step on the road to altruism is for children to observe when someone is angry, hurt, sad, fearful, or tired. Your toddler may pay attention to these signs in others naturally. If your toddler doesn't attend to these things, naturally you will need to teach him or her to pay attention to others.

Altruism and Parental Responses to Aggression

Your responses to your children when they exhibit altruistic behavior have an effect on how much altruism they exhibit. Mothers who have reported on their children's altruistic behavior when they were first the aggressor (and then responded to the victim in an altruistic fashion) found the following:

- **Explanation with moral values.** When moms and dads respond to a toddler's aggression by telling their child …

    "You have hurt this child."

    "It is wrong to do (whatever the behavior was)."

    "Don't do that again."

and then withdraw affection temporarily from their child, altruism was seen more frequently.

- **No explanation and removal.** When moms and dads respond to their toddler's aggression by …

    Saying something like "Stop that"

    Yanking or dragging the child away from the situation

    Physically restraining the child

    Physically punishing their child

altruistic behavior was infrequent (Zahn-Waxler, Radke-Yarrow, and King, "Child-rearing and children's pro-social initiations toward victims of distress." (*Child Development*, 1979, 50, 319–30)

Altruism and Empathy

Toddlers are very aware of the emotions of those around them. They feel everybody's pain and joy. Alleviating someone else's pain also alleviates their pain. If the other person feels good, they can feel good. This is natural empathy, and natural empathy motivates altruistic behavior.

Natural empathy is something found in families in which there are close relationships. Your toddler won't necessarily feel this way about a complete stranger—at least, not without a little teaching from his or her parents. Your tot may react emotionally to the stranger's pain but not necessarily do something to alleviate that pain.

At their age, this is a good thing! You don't want your toddler feeling responsible for "fixing" a stranger's emotional problems, especially "adult" problems. Training children to respond to strangers with altruistic behavior is inappropriate in the preschool years because of the danger it puts them in. Adults with ill motives try to gain the empathy of a child to lure them away from Mom and Dad. If your child is one who naturally responds to everyone out of empathy, you will have to guide him or her and say: "Your feelings for people are really good, and God is very pleased with you, but God will find other ways to take care of people you don't know. But by all means, don't stop showing your kind heart to our family and friends."

As your children get older, you can teach them about altruistic actions toward strangers. You may exhibit some in front of your children, but remind them that they should not do this on their own unless Mom or Dad is holding their hand and they have Mom or Dad's approval. But for now, their personal safety is a higher priority.

> **Toddler Tales**
>
> When she was three and a half years old, I picked up my daughter from playschool. The teacher pulled me aside. She told me my little girl always looked for ways to be kind to other kids, noticed when they were sad or frustrated, and consistently gave them hugs and showed them kindness. When she was 20, a man spilled his freshly poured coffee all over the floor of a coffee bar. My daughter jumped up quickly to the counter and bought him a replacement cup. They live what they learn.

Chapter
15

Discipline in Love

What is discipline? The word *discipline* comes from the word *disciple*, which means "to teach, guide, or instruct."

The Bible tells us, "Teach your children to choose the right path, and when they are older, they will remain upon it." (Proverbs 22:6) Proverbs 13:24 also tells us, "If you refuse to discipline your children, it proves you don't love them; if you love your children, you will be prompt to discipline them." In the Book of Deuteronomy, we read, "So you should realize that just as a parent disciplines a child, the Lord your God disciplines you to help you." (8:5)

Discipline is the actions that a parent takes, for the good of the child, to help the child to know with certainty what behaviors are acceptable and good. Discipline means having the willingness, diligence, and consistency to call the child to account for behavior.

For the most part, discipline is all about training your sons and your daughters. This book is full of ideas and options for training your toddler into acceptable behavior. When parents are responsive both in providing guidance and in responding to errant behavior in the ways already presented, most of their work disciplining their children has already occurred.

What Is Discipline and What Is Abuse?

When the word *discipline* is used, most people think of physical punishment. Discipline is about calling your children to account and drawing a firm line around what is acceptable behavior and what is not acceptable behavior. For the most part, this can and should be done without physical punishment.

Physical punishment is discipline when ...

- All other options for dealing with the particular behavior have been exhausted.
- It is for the benefit and good of the child.
- It is for the safety and security of the child.
- It is for the safety and security of another person.
- It is not about parental anger.
- It is used appropriately and sparingly.

Word from the Wise

"To learn, you must love discipline; it is stupid to hate correction." (Proverbs 12:1)

Discipline is essential to learning—and not just learning correct behavior. Poor discipline can lead to laziness, can foster poor learners in school, and eventually can affect your child's calling and use of talents in life.

Physical punishment is abuse when ...

- It serves to produce no long-term benefit for the child.
- Your anger is involved in the discipline.
- It is to "get back" at the child.
- The punishment exceeds the minimum required for behavior modification.
- The form and duration of punishment is inappropriate.

The Necessity of Parental Control

The Lord disciplines those whom he loves. (Hebrews 12:6) Why? Because in our humanity we are self-serving, self-centered, and sinful, and without discipline we cannot know love. The Lord tells us that we are to love others as we love ourselves. The person who is self-serving, self-centered, and selfish hates himself, loathes himself, and takes out his hatred on others. The person who knows self-control and gains the ability to control his inner and outer worlds has a love for his own self—and out of that love, loves others.

Secular researchers have discovered what Christians should know because of their understanding of the nature of God. Researchers who study parent-child relationships went to nursery schools and observed three- and four-year-olds. They assessed their behaviors and attitudes. They looked at children who were …

- Competent—happy, self-controlled, self-reliant.
- Withdrawn—sad, poor social involvement.
- Immature—lacking self-control, highly dependent.

They observed the children with their parents and rated the kind of parental control the parent had over the child, how much the parents demanded maturity in their children, how well the parents talked with their children, how well the parents listened to their children's opinions and feelings, and how nurturing the parents were toward their children. The researchers also made home visits.

What they found was that children who were …

- Happy
- Self-reliant
- Able to face challenges

had parents who …

- Exercised a good deal of control over their tots.
- Demanded responsible and independent behavior.
- Explained things to their tots.
- Listened to their tots.
- Provided emotional support for their tots.

Parents of withdrawn children were controlling and demanding and provided no emotional warmth for their tots. Parents of immature children exercised little control over their children and were only moderately nurturing.

Parenting Styles

Over the years, researchers have categorized three basic types of parenting styles—permissive, authoritarian, and authoritative—that produce three different types of children.

Permissive Parents

Permissive parents …

- Seldom discipline their children.
- Give in to their children's whims and demands.
- Do not insist that children have household responsibilities.
- Allow children to regulate themselves.
- Avoid control.
- Attempt to use reasoning with their children.
- Attempt to behave in a way that will not upset their children.
- Consult their children on discipline.

Result: Children are dependent, not socially responsible, highly aggressive, lacking in self-control, and immature. With boys, permissive parenting results in anger and defiance.

Proverbs 19:18 reads, "Discipline your children while there is hope. If you don't, you will ruin their lives." Permissive parents who don't exercise control over their children raise children who remain children, immature in every way.

Toddler Tales

In our multiunit living complex were six rugged concrete staircases that would rip apart anyone's skin if they fell down them. Our toddler had to learn to climb only our stairs, nobody else's. She thought it only a game when I took her away from the other stairs, said "no," and directed her to our stairs. I did this over and over. The stern words and redirection didn't work. She just laughed and did it again. It was no laughing matter. With great anxiety I realized that physical punishment was necessary. A slap on the thigh each time she tried to climb the other stairs finally taught her the limits. In a few tries, she knew to only go up our stairs. It broke my heart, but I knew I did what had to be done.

Authoritarian Parents

Authoritarian parents ...

- Have an absolute set of standards (rules, requirements, restrictions).
- Shape, control, and evaluate their kids based on those standards.
- Value obedience for its own sake.
- Value hard work and preservation of order at all costs.
- Discourage or disallow verbal give and take with their children.
- Sometimes reject their children.
- Are controlling.
- Are demanding.
- Mete out severe punishment for defiance.
- Exercise authority arbitrarily without explanation to the children.
- Do not allow children to be involved in any decision making.
- Believe they have an absolute right to exclusively control their children.
- Lack empathy toward their children.
- Have low self-esteem.

Result: Children are dependent, lack empathy for others, have low self-esteem, have no internal controls, are obedient, lack affection, are frequently sad and withdrawn, are timid, have difficulty establishing relationships with other children, are unassertive, are joyless, see only mediocre development of social responsibility, and aren't very self-reliant. Boys often become angry and defiant, aren't good problem solvers, are aggressive, are impulsive, are coercive, and eventually become juvenile delinquents.

Colossians 3:21 says, "Fathers, don't aggravate your children. If you do, they will become discouraged and quit trying." Ephesians 6:4 says, "And now a word to you fathers. Don't make your children angry by the way you treat them. Rather, bring them up with the discipline and instruction approved by the Lord." Restrictive and hostile parents raise troubled children.

Authoritative Parents

Authoritative parents …

- Expect children to conform to parental requirements while at the same time expecting independence and self-direction.
- Direct children in a rational manner.
- Encourage parent-child verbal give-and-take interactions.
- Provide reasons behind demands, rules, and discipline.
- Use power when necessary.
- Set standards and narrow limits on children's activities, and enforce them consistently.
- Do not see themselves as infallible.
- Recognize the rights of parents and children.
- Don't yield to children's attempts at coercion.

Result: Children are independent, are socially responsible, have a happy and positive mood, are obedient, are self-reliant, are achievement oriented and domineering toward age mates (in girls), are friendly and cooperative (in boys), are able to control aggressive impulses, are not coercive toward parents, show adequate self-control, have high self-esteem, can approach new situations with confidence, show low aggression (in boys), and are altruistic.

In Paul's first letter to Timothy, he describes the attributes of a man eligible to become an elder of the church (3:1–5). The list includes the requirements that he must have a life that people don't speak negatively about, show self-control, live wisely, have a good reputation, be able to teach, not be a heavy drinker, not be violent, be gentle and peace-loving, manage his family well, and have children who respect and obey him. This list resembles the qualities and characteristics of an authoritative parent. Restrictive but warm and accepting parents raise healthy children who honor their parents and God.

Not a Democracy

Studies have been done with families who attempted to operate as a democracy, allowing children to self-determine and have an equal part in decision and policy making. Highly democratic parents produced children who were above average in …

- Their ability to plan.
- Fearlessness.
- Leadership.
- Aggressiveness.
- Coerciveness.
- Cruelty.
- Bossiness.
- Physical vigor and activity.
- Social involvement.
- Egoism (self-centeredness).

Children raised in democratic families use both verbal persuasion and physical force to get their way in spite of harm to others. They are seldom the ones victimized by others' aggression, but they also are less likely to offer help to others.

A family is not a democracy.

Warmth and Affection Must Undergird Discipline

Discipline is necessary to raise a healthy son or daughter. But discipline without love and affection is harmful to a child's development.

Those who know the Lord understand this completely. The Father first offers us his love. When we choose to be his children, he disciplines us as is good and right and necessary to help us become all that he desires for us to be. In the same way, love and nurturance make the discipline of children wise, not cruel.

Safety and Sanity Tips

Limiting spanking to a bare hand on bare buttocks protects you from going too far, and protects your toddler from physical and emotional damage.

Dr. Mom Speaks

Authoritarian parents are at risk of physically abusing their children. They have a high need to control their children, have little tolerance for children, are unable to express themselves effectively, and are usually cold and emotionally unavailable. They resort to physical punishment to try to get their children to "obey" them. They emphasize "the rod" without "love, comfort, and nurturance." Their gospel is incomplete.

How to Use Physical Discipline Effectively

Rarely, but almost certainly, there will come a time when physical discipline is necessary. Here are some guidelines.

Physical Pain

No loving parent wants their little child to feel physical pain. Quite the contrary, it's our job to protect our child from physical pain. Instructions in this book attempt to give parents enough resources that any resort to the use of physical punishment is an option only after all others have been attempted—and then, only the most minimal amount is employed to deal with the problem behavior. On rare occasions, administering a small, brief amount of physical pain becomes necessary.

Your preverbal toddler will most often respond to your direction not to touch a forbidden object or do a forbidden behavior. When redirection and words alone are ineffective, a small flick on the hand associated with the word *no* will quickly teach the toddler that touching the object will bring about his own pain. To avoid pain, he must avoid touching the object. Take your child through the routine of behavior that is expected and explain the behavior and your expectation. Then, if he doesn't do as told, give a little flick on the hand and expect him to do it again and again until he gets it right. And when we say "pain," it's more the sting of rebuke than actual physical pain.

There are toddlers who will ask "why" about everything, including why you are setting the limits you are setting. While a good clear explanation is preferable, remember that you don't need to get into an argument with your child about these limits. This is where it is a mistake to try to reason with a toddler.

Training at home should eliminate the need for training in public.

The Boundaries and Limits of Physical Discipline

When your toddler does something that is …

- Clearly off-limits for touching
- Clearly dangerous
- Clearly hurtful to another

you must deal with it quickly and assuredly.

If you are doing a good job in training your child, the need for physical discipline should be small. If you have had to spank your toddler more than three or four times throughout their preschool years, you need to ask yourself what else is going on with your child that is causing problems. If the child's behavior is troublesome after this, you should be delving deeper for answers. Continued physical discipline is not the answer. Talk with your pastor, a Christian counselor, or, in more ordinary cases, your friends who have raised toddlers. Find out how either you or your toddler can adjust behavior to avoid too much physical discipline. Let them observe your toddler's behavior, and be open about your own faults and shortcomings. Sometimes all you need are some handy practical tips.

Once your child is fully verbal and has sufficient emotional and intellectual development, physical punishment is no longer an effective tool in shaping the development of your child. Physical discipline beyond the preschool years is inappropriate, unnecessary, and unproductive for your child.

Setting the Sights and Sounds of Discipline

You should have a specific look on your face and tone in your voice when you deal with your toddler in a disciplinarian way. Your little one needs to know you mean business.

Yelling, shouting, screaming, and the like don't encourage your child's respect; they encourage your child's disdain and rebellion. Good and effective discipline is done with a calm, strong voice. Even if your child yells, you should not yell. Keep track of your tone and volume. If you yell, your child will yell louder and it will be a power competition between you. When you speak quietly and intently to your child, they will stop yelling because otherwise your child won't hear what you're saying. Don't be as childish as your toddler; rise above and be the adult. You should also be beginning to teach your child not to scream at you. Respect for authority is important, and appropriate discipline such as "timeouts" or restriction of privileges can be enforced if screaming persists.

If you do this consistently at home, you will need nothing more than a quiet, gentle, strong tone when out in public. Your child should mind you in public by your very look and sound.

Less Is More

Do not get yourself into this type of scenario with your children: "Please don't do that. You're hurting Mommy's feelings. You know that is a bad thing to do. Mommy doesn't like it when you do that—why don't you stop? I'm going to be mad at you if you don't stop that. You're such a bad little boy. God doesn't like you when you do that. You don't want God to be mad at you, do you?"

Parents don't need to give a defense for the behavioral expectations of their children to a three-year-old. Be clear, direct, and to the point, and then move on. "No" means "no," period.

Word from the Wise

"The more words you speak, the less they mean. So why overdo it?" (Ecclesiastes 6:11) When discipline is necessary keep your words to a minimum. Sometimes saying less is much more powerful than saying more.

Biting

A small spoonful of baking soda usually cures biting. She needs to know in no uncertain terms that this will not be tolerated. With baby biting, you can't afford to give your toddler another chance or a second warning. Your baby's safety is at risk. Your toddler must know "now" that she is never to do that again.

Preverbal vs. Verbal Toddler

Physical discipline can be a slap on the hands, a flick with the fingers, a little pinch, or a hand spanking.

Discipline for the preverbal tot can involve a slap, a flick, or a pinch accompanied by "no" and the tone and the face. Be consistent, firm, and unyielding. Make sure you get eye contact with your little rascal. Your kids have to know that you are dead serious.

Discipline for your preverbal or verbal tot can include spanking. As Proverbs 23:13–14 says, don't fail to correct your children. They won't die if you spank them. Physical discipline may well save them from death.

Nevers

Never engage in any of the following:

1. Never slap children anywhere on the body other than their hands, their buttocks, or the backs of their thighs.
2. Never slap children with anything other than your hand. You need to know at all times how much pressure and pain you are administering. If you can feel it, they can feel it.

Some advocate switches, sticks, belts, and other objects. Use of objects to discipline your children is not necessary or advisable. Some parents use these sorts of objects with restraint, but there is the risk that you will go too far because you lose the ability to know how much pain your child is feeling. It is unnecessary and no more productive than the use of your hand. Parents who go overboard will tend to do it with objects.

Some advocate 5 to 10 swats. This goes beyond what is necessary for effective discipline. You job is to end the dangerous behavior—not break the spirit or the will of the child.

3. Never spank your tot more than three hand slaps.
4. Never spank your tot unless you are calm and controlled.
5. Never give chances ("If you do that one more time …"). This is a license to your toddler to do it one more time. Giving chances trains your child not to obey until you get really angry.
6. Sometimes parents discipline in anger because they have waited too long to deal with the problematic behavior and have allowed themselves to build up

too much anger. Never wait until you can't take it anymore to discipline your toddler. This is selfish on your part and destructive for the toddler personally and for your relationship with your toddler. If you truly can't handle dealing with your toddler, seek professional help. Waiting until you reach the end of your rope and then exploding with anger toward your toddler is very harmful.

7. Never guilt-trip, shame, curse, or name-call your toddler in order to bring about obedience.

Natural Consequences

Always ask yourself, "Does this behavior have a natural consequence?" In other words, do I need to intervene or will the natural consequences be enough for my tot's behavior modification?

For example:

- Your four-year-old needs a playmate and tries to engage your two-year-old. He offends your two-year-old, who refuses to play with him anymore. Now he is alone. This may be enough for him to want to treat his younger sibling better.

- Your toddler seems disinterested in her food and plays with it. Remove the plate. She has no dinner. She can't have the plate back unless she eats.

- Your toddler gets mad and rips pages out of his book. No more book.

- Your toddler runs the child's shopping cart into you, and it wasn't an accident. No more shopping cart to push.

- Your toddler won't come in the house when called (or won't stay in the yard). She must stay inside for a number of days while watching her friends play outside. Next time she must come in when called or will have to stay in longer.

- Your toddler throws his wooden blocks around. Take the blocks away for a week. Bring them back with a warning.

No discipline or reprimand is necessary. Removing or preventing the activity often brings results on its own.

Timeouts for Extroverts and Introverts

One effective method of behavior change for extroverts is isolation. Set them apart from interactions, acknowledgement, or reinforcements from others, and they soon extinguish the behaviors that reaped them those consequences.

- Send them to their room.
- Set the egg timer for three to five minutes.
- Tell them not to come out of their room until the timer goes off.

This strategy won't work for introverts, who love being in their room with all their toys and books. The solitude does them a world of good in terms of personal pleasure and contentment. They'll get lost playing and thinking and will have no thought of why they ended up there. In fact, it may have the reverse effect of reinforcing their behavior!

A timeout for an introvert is better spent sitting on a chair or standing in the proverbial corner while the egg timer counts down. Keep this child from solitary activities!

Food and Bed

Remember, sometimes behavior problems exist only because little ones are hungry or tired or you've stretched them beyond their capacity. Pay attention to your children so that you know whether they are really exhibiting behavior problems or whether they just need to be fed or put to bed!

Most often, a miserable toddler is a tired toddler. Discipline is for intentional misbehavior, not human nature.

In the Car

If you are in your vehicle with the kids and they are not responding to your verbal reprimands, you must stop the car to deal with them. Sometimes kids think they can get away with more because your hands are tied up with the steering wheel.

Assess the situation. Are they just hungry or tired? If so, you may have to just let them cry and whine (ignoring them) until you get home and put them to bed (unless they fall asleep on the way). If you know they are well fed and rested and there is a serious behavior problem, pull over, get their attention, and reprimand them.

Your children need to learn young that they cannot act up in a vehicle because it puts everyone in danger. Spank them, if necessary, but don't swat at them while you're driving. This is totally unsafe for everyone and is not an effective way to get their attention.

Parental Provocation

Don't provoke your children to anger (Ephesians 6:4) and then use their response as justification to discipline them. Don't have fun at your kids' expense; don't humiliate your children in front of others or tease them until they break, or they will do this same thing to those smaller and younger than themselves.

Don't bully your boys. Let's not create bullies. Your son will store up his anger and take it out on someone else, somewhere, someday.

Fear of Discipline

If you say that you love your children too much to discipline them, you are operating in error.

If you fear that disciplining your toddler will cause your child to reject you, you're wrong. This fear is all about your personal insecurities, not what is good for the child. The truth is, not disciplining your child will result in a rejection of you.

> ### Word from the Wise
>
> "A youngster's heart is filled with foolishness, but discipline will drive it away." (Proverbs 22:15) Healthy discipline helps guide your children from infancy to maturity. You can't expect innate wisdom in your children, and the selfish sinful nature is present at birth.

Are you afraid to discipline your toddler for fear of becoming abusive, like your father or mother? This is one good reason that anger should not be associated with discipline, but it's not a good reason to not discipline your developing son or daughter.

Your children need you to discipline them—to not do so is to let them down and to teach them to be selfish tyrants. Children don't become "wonderful people" without curbing their selfish and self-centered tendencies.

If you love them, you won't allow them to grow up to disrespect you or God. God loves us as adults and yet must discipline us. Are you more knowledgeable or loving than God himself? You accept God's love and his discipline. Your children are entitled to receive both from you so that they don't go astray and so that they experience consequences for their actions.

Sometimes one parent won't discipline and leaves all of the discipline to the other parent. Are you making your spouse discipline for two? Parents need to equally participate in disciplining their children; to not do so leaves the child to disrespect the parent who won't discipline.

Threats

A threat is a dare. If your child is into a serious power struggle with you, he will take you up on your dare, not to reap the consequences of the threat but to let you know that no matter what you say, he will do what he wants to do anyway. This is a bad place to get to with your children. You don't need to say "If you … then …." Just state the rule "You must not …." Leave it at that. If the child violates the rule, he must be disciplined. But now it is not a threat; it is just a reality of life. Break the rule, reap the consequences. The issue of power and control is removed.

Never threaten to abandon your child, especially not at the store! This is always inappropriate. It threatens children's basic sense of security, and they learn they can't trust you. This is not beneficial to the parent-child relationship.

Parents Prone to Spoiling

Parents who are prone to spoiling their children usually …

* Had trouble having children.
* Adopted children after futile attempts to have their own children.
* Try to make up for all they didn't have in life by indulging their own offspring.
* Are mental health professionals trying to prove they are great and perfect parents.
* Have little tolerance for their own frustration and give in to their children to avoid their own feelings and reactions to their children's demands.

Toddler Tales

On Easter Sunday in a Catholic Church, a little four-year-old girl left her parents' side and went to the font of holy water. She proceeded to splash and play and be silly. Her parents sat there. By failing to act, her parents were training her to be a brat!

Dealing with the Vicious Child

In Chapter 23, you will find guidance on dealing with aggression between siblings and playmates, and how to teach conflict resolution to the very young.

Most of the time, with most children, following all of the guidelines set forth in this book with your toddler will be enough to deal with toddlers fighting. However, some rare children are sometimes downright vicious. My good friend was telling me about her granddaughter, who, when small, was so vicious that she would lunge at her cousins with her clawed hands and gouge chunks of skin out of their faces. They have lasting scars. They used to call her the "devil child." Yes, there are kids this vicious.

If your child's aggressive and violent behavior is out of the range of "normal," you will need prayer and professional help. There are many reasons why your child may be vicious.

Some parents wonder if there is something demonic about what they see in their child. If you suspect that there could be a truly evil element to your child's behavior, be cautious. Please refer to Appendix H for guidance in how to address this concern.

Assessment for Child Sexual Abuse

A toddler who is vicious should be assessed for the possibility of sexual abuse. Deep-seated anger may be causing your little one to act out in a vicious way.

Medical Evaluation

A seriously violent toddler should be seen by a pediatrician and have a thorough medical evaluation. Has your little one suffered any head trauma? Damage to certain areas of the brain can cause violent behaviors.

Corporal Punishment

No matter what the underlying cause of the vicious aggression by your child is, your toddler must stop hurting others. You must protect the innocent, and you must restrain your child. Very few situations require you to spank your child, but this is one of them. Keep in mind that this is not for ordinary sibling rivalry or tussles between playmates—this is the program for the seriously physically hurtful toddler.

- **Isolate your child.** While you must punish your child for the behavior, you should also not add humiliation to the problem. Deal with your child alone, in private. Don't make the punishment also something that other children could ridicule your tot over. This will only provoke more aggressive behavior toward the other children.

- **Calm yourself down.** Even if your toddler is violent, it is no reason for you to become violent. Violence is a risk if you deal with your tot while you are furious. Spank only when you have complete control of yourself.

- **Explain.** Make sure your toddler knows exactly what he or she did wrong and why it was wrong. Use the conflict-resolution strategies from Chapter 23. If your child is not curbing the aggression by using those strategies, continue on this list.

- **Spank.** If your tot is not responding to the conflict-resolution strategies, you may need to spank. Don't spank through a diaper; this is useless. If your tot is in a diaper, spank the tops of the back of the thighs. Otherwise, pull the pants down and slap a bare bottom (not more than three times).

- **Love.** Let your tot have the tears, and say that you love her but that she can't hurt other people any more. Let her feel remorse and a bit of alienation/rejection. Don't wipe away her tears too soon or rescue her from the pain of her emotions. Let her feel it. She needs to feel it. She should not get your positive affection until she demonstrates a contrite heart. Then love her and cuddle her and lead her into apologies, forgiveness, and reconciliation with the person she hurt.

Proverbs 20:30 states, "Physical punishment cleanses away evil; such discipline purifies the heart." The devil tempts everyone to do the wrong thing, adults and tots alike. For some, fear of the punishment of the Lord for sin stops them from giving in to the temptation. Teaching toddlers to stop and think about whether their behavior will draw physical punishment will have the positive effect of helping them resist the temptation to do the wrong thing.

> **Safety and Sanity Tips**
>
> Much spanking can be avoided by using the 5-second count. Tell your tot exactly what is expected or what is forbidden. Let your child know that if the behavior is not corrected by the time you count to 5, you will indeed administer a spanking. Begin the count, slowly. Seldom will you get to 5 before Junior is running off to do as he was told.

The Outcome of Love and Healthy Discipline

The Bible also tells us that if we discipline our children, they will bring us "happiness and peace of mind." (Proverbs 19:17)

The love and fellowship with your child will eventually cause them not to want to misbehave. Discipline alone will never produce a peaceful, well-behaved child. When your children have enjoyed your fellowship, they come to not want to do anything that would cause you to disdain them or be disappointed in them. They will want to live up to the godly expectations you have of them. The desire to please you in a healthy way is a good thing. Law and grace: The law is the commandments of God. Grace is God's divine assistance to obey them.

Eventually, this is the type of motivation that will transfer from you to God for your children. They will not want to sin because they will not want to lose God's favor. This is a biblical and godly principle of living. Through parents, children come to develop their knowledge and concept of God.

Chapter 16

Dealing with Nighttime Disturbances

Most often, sleep terrors and nightmares mean nothing more than that there has been a bad dream or their sleep has been disturbed for some innocuous reason. Occasionally, sleep disturbances can take on a spiritual dimension.

First, let's consider nightmares.

Nightmares

Sometimes we can find an explanation for nightmares and sometimes we can't. Three possible contributing factors to nightmares are stress, food, and objects.

Stress

I once had a nightmare that a black panther was crushing my head in its jaw. At the time, I was studying four hours a day for three and a half months to take my psychology licensing exam, working part-time to feed my children, and being a mom with preschoolers. My nightmare represented the intense pressure I was under. The result? One cracked molar from clenching my teeth at night—and a frightening nightmare! Sometimes the stressors of the day cause nightmares.

In the daytime, talk with your tot about what they saw in their nightmare. Can you make any sense out of it? They could be upset about something at home, issues with friends, issues from playschool, or someone who may have hurt them without your knowing about it. Cuddle, listen, and give them a chance to unload their stress.

Food

Have you ever heard of a "pizza dream"? Lots of people correlate their nightmares with having eaten a ton of spicy food before bed—or eaten too much before bed, period. Also, it has been said of old not to eat "Welsh rabbit" before bed because it will give you nightmares. This dish is made from cheese, and certain cheeses have been clinically found to cause people bad dreams at night. What is your babe eating before bed?

Objects Can Cause Nightmares

Sometimes people can't sleep at night or have nightmares because certain objects in their room are emotionally or spiritually disturbing.

One time a young woman I was counseling reported that she could never sleep at night (not for years). She had been sexually assaulted by a family friend, and this friend had bought many stuffed animals for her. They were all in her room. On the surface of it, they looked innocuous. I suggested putting them all in the garage for a week to see if it would make any difference. It did. She slept like a baby. But to test further, she brought them back in. Again she had trouble sleeping. She removed them again. Again she was sleeping. She realized that she needed to get rid of them permanently.

Deuteronomy 23:14 tells us that as the Lord moves around your camp at night to protect you and defeat your enemies, he must not see "any shameful thing" or "he might turn away from you." The stuffed animals were shameful to the Lord. They represented an abusive man, a man who had harmed one of his innocent children. His protection was returned to the young woman when she had removed the "shameful thing" from her home.

Look around your child's room. What do you see? Do you suspect that anything in the room could be disturbing? Ask the Holy Spirit to give you "eyes to see" as you stand there surveying her room. Any object that stands out to you should be removed for testing. Remove one object at a time. See what the result is. You need to test any objects that are suspicious.

Objects may not be a problem in your child's room, but if they are, you can permanently remove them. If the object causing the problem is one of your child's favorite things, it must go away silently and mysteriously. You can't expect a toddler to understand that the object may be causing nightmares. It must be "lost" until the child is old enough to understand. And be very, very sure about the object before you destroy it. You don't want your child to have her heart broken for nothing! Use common sense and don't go on a frenzy. Keep testing until you are absolutely certain.

Most nightmares, while frightening, do not have a truly evil connection. Most are just bad dreams.

Comforting Your Child

Don't get into a discussion with your child in the middle of the night about the content of their nightmares. Listen to the basic details of the nightmare and save the rest for the daytime. You don't want to encourage them to remain up at night for any longer than is absolutely necessary.

No matter what the reason for the nightmare (if there is one), put your little one back in bed (if they have come to you), gently comfort her with a gentle stroking on the head or back, assure her everything will be alright, pray and ask God to send his Holy Spirit to comfort her and kiss her goodnight.

Sleep Terrors

Sleep terrors are when a child wakes up screaming and terrified for no reason. There is no bad dream. The only thing they recall may be vague, fragmentary images.

If your child wakes up with sleep terrors, go to them (or return them to their bed), speak soothing words, and rub their back until they fall asleep. Since there were no bad dreams, they will usually go back to sleep quite quickly.

Things That Go Bump in the Night

Sometimes, a child is not just having nightmares or sleep terrors. Sometimes children see things that scare them. It is your children's fears that need to be dealt with.

Your child may see things when they are wide awake or when their eyes are closed (but they are not asleep). What might they be seeing?

As Christians, we know there is a seen and an unseen world. We know that God is spirit, that the Holy Spirit has no physical body, that there are angels of light and angels of darkness. We also know that Jesus was seen by many after his death in the form of a physical body. We also know that after Jesus' death on the cross, the bodies of dead people appeared to many in Jerusalem (Matthew 27:50–53).

The Bible describes a number of creatures and spiritual entities never seen in the physical world. Ezekiel writes about the "living being" he sees in a vision the Lord gives him, which he cannot identify as anything alive on this Earth. It is some type of spiritual creature. The Book of Revelation (4:6) also refers to "four living beings." These "living beings" are described as distinct from the angels. There are other entities that humans can't see in the physical world but that the Lord allows us to see.

At times, God the Father has allowed people to see angels (of light and of darkness), spirits of dead people, and other spiritual creatures that he has created. Some adults and children today report seeing these things. It seems that some people are more able than others to see things in the unseen world.

As a parent, your priority is to get your little ones sleeping soundly, peacefully, through the night.

Help for Your Little Ones

Having counseled with parents who have children who could see all sorts of spiritual entities and having had two of my children see such things, I came to learn that the Lord has provided us tremendous resources to help people get a good night's sleep. I have never had to counsel with a child or their parents after they began to pray the kinds of prayers I learned to pray over my own children.

Helping your children to get a good night's sleep is one more way you can share your faith, demonstrate to them that you serve a mighty and awesome God, and make them fearless of evil because "the Spirit who lives in you is greater than the spirit who lives in the world"! (1 John 4:4)

I pray that these prayers will be a complete solution to your child's troubled nights, but if they aren't, please consult your pastor or a professional counselor for additional help.

First Things First

Your concern begins when your children see things in the unseen world; those things usually cause them fear. You don't want your children to be afraid or tormented by the things they see (even if you can't see them).

When children see spiritual things, you don't need to talk them out of their reality, you need to pray so that their reality changes. As Christian parents you can, and should, acknowledge what your child is experiencing and then tell them that Mommy and Daddy will pray and ask the Lord for his help.

Caution

If your child's problems are spiritual in nature, you want to make sure that you don't scare them. What follows is not material that you should use to initiate a discussion with your child if they are not reporting any nighttime problems. The guidance offered below is for use when your child comes to you. You must decide, based on your particular child's personality and sensitivities, whether it is in your child's best interests to discuss any of the following information. For some children it will be better for the parents alone to pray what they can pray without bringing it to the attention of their child. The most minimal intervention is always the best. Remember the goal: Help your child get a good night's rest. The goal is not to give your wee ones a complete education about the spirit world. Remember, the scripture tells us to be innocent of evil. (1 Corinthians 14:20)

What Parents Can Do

It's best that parents deal with their children's spiritual nighttime problems without involving their children. Sometimes this is not possible. But before you discuss strategies that your child can use (see "Defensive Strategies," later in this chapter), start by doing all you can do in prayer.

Anointing with Oil

Remember how Moses told the children of Israel to mark their doorposts with blood to protect them from the spirit of death? The blood on the doorposts was a sign to the spirit of death. The sign identified which houses the spirit of death was not allowed into! The spirit of death had to pass over those homes and not harm their firstborn sons. (Exodus 12:12–13) This is a biblical example of how God protected children from a spirit.

Later he used both blood and oil to anoint the doorposts of the temple to keep it spiritually clean. In Deuteronomy 11:18–21, Moses instructed the Israelites to write the Ten Commandments on the doorposts of their houses and on their gates so that they and their children would flourish. Moses took anointing oil and blood and sprinkled them on Aaron's clothes to make them holy. (Leviticus 8:30) In early spring each year, the priests were to put blood on the doorposts of the temple and the four corners of the upper ledge on the altar to make atonement for the temple. (Ezekiel 45:18–20)

Marking doorposts can protect children from some spiritual harm. Writing the Word of God on the doorposts of houses will help you and your children to flourish. Anointing with oil can bring holiness to a person.

What does all this mean for your children? Simply put, if you anoint your children's door and window with oil and, as you do this, pray for the protection of the blood of Jesus over the door and window, some of the spiritual things that were bothering your children won't bother them anymore. Please refer to Appendix H for basic instructions on anointing a room with oil.

Toddler Tales

When she was three, my daughter occasionally woke up screaming, "Witches, Mommy, witches!" She said she saw witches in her bedroom. After anointing her bedroom and praying, there were no more witches. She slept soundly.

Until we moved to a new house! Then my son said in the night he saw snakes on the ground and about eight witches in our home. We hadn't anointed it yet. After anointing, the kids reported no snakes and no witches.

This is not something parents need to talk with their children about. If your child sees spirits in their room at night, go ahead and anoint your child's bedroom door and window, and see if your child complains again about seeing them.

Bedtime Prayers for Little Folk (and Big Folk, Too)

How much Jesus loves children! Jesus is ready, willing, and able to come to our children at night and stand guard over them. We only have to ask.

Being on the offensive—preventing these things from bothering your child in the first place—is always preferable to being on the defensive.

Angels Standing Guard

When Daniel called out to God, the Lord told him that he had heard Daniel's prayer but that he was blocked from responding for 21 days because of a territorial demonic spirit. The Lord told Daniel that it was his Archangel Michael that came to help him deal with that spirit. (Daniel 10:12–14) The Lord tells Daniel that "there is no one to help me against these spirit princes except Michael." (v. 21)

Michael is known as a warrior angel. Daniel 12:1 says that Michael stands guard over Israel. Revelation 12:7 says that there was a war in heaven and that Michael and the angels under his command fought the dragon and his bad angels. Michael and the angels under him are powerful, and their job is to fight battles against bad spirits. We should tell our children that God has some powerful angels that work with him and help him against those bad spirits. You can ask the Lord to send some of those angels to stand guard over your children as they sleep!

So what exactly do you ask? "Father God, I ask, please, that you would send warrior angels to come and stand guard at the four corners of Ashley's bed to protect her as she sleeps tonight."

Lord over Your Night

Deuteronomy 23:14 tells us that "the Lord your God moves around in your camp to protect you and to defeat your enemies." In Genesis 28:15, the Lord tells Jacob that he will be with him and protect him wherever he goes. We are told in 1 Samuel 2:9 that the Lord protects his godly ones. In Ezra 8:21, the children of Israel were ashamed to ask the king for protection from their enemies and instead prayed that God would protect them and their children as they traveled. God heard their prayer. In Psalms 5:11–12, David asks God for protection so that all those who love the Lord can be filled with joy. David asked the Lord to surround his people with his shield of love.

When your little rascals go to bed, hopefully they aren't going anywhere else. They are staying put. You want the Lord to stand guard over them as they sleep and put his shield of love around them, so you pray: "Lord Jesus, please come now and be Lord over Ashley's night tonight and surround her with your shield of love."

Defensive Strategies

If you have anointed your child's room with oil and are praying the two prayers above every night and your child is still having spiritual disturbances, try the following.

Dr. Mom Speaks

There is no need for parents to get into huge spiritual discussions about demons and creatures and such with their toddlers. Doing the anointing and nighttime prayers is enough for nearly every sleep problem. Only if these aren't enough should you provide specific instructions directly to your toddler. Don't ask for a creature for protection unless your child sees creatures. Don't make issues out of nonissues!

Angels of Light

If your child says he sees angels in his bedroom at night, we want to be sure that any angels visiting him are from the Lord and not from the enemy. Since the enemy can disguise his angels to look like angels of light, the angel should be "tested" to make sure it's one of the good ones. 1 John 4:2 guides us on this: You can tell your tot that next time he sees the angel he should ask the angel, "Did Jesus Christ become a human being?" Angels from the kingdom of darkness can't answer "yes" to that question. If he says, 'yes,' ask him what he came to tell him. Most angels from the Lord's kingdom are messengers. When they appear to people, like to Joseph, they have a message. If God is sending your child an angel to deliver a message, you want to know what it is.

Angels of Darkness

What if the angel of light says "no" to the previous question? Then the angel your child sees may be evil. You don't want these angels in your house, let alone in your child's room. I have provided some suggested prayers to pray for the spiritual protection of your house and property (see Appendix H). Pray them every day for a couple of weeks and see if your child still sees dark angels in his room.

These prayers may suffice. If not, you should instruct your toddler to deal with the dark angel. Tell your tot that if the dark angel comes again they may pray: "Lord Jesus, please come right now and take this bad spirit out of my bedroom." As a last resort, you can instruct your child to say to the dark angel: "In Jesus' name, get out of my bedroom right now!" Ah, the power of Jesus' name!

Safety and Sanity Tips

For you to keep sane in the years preceding your children all getting into school, you must have your rest. For you to get your rest, your little ones need their rest. Don't resign yourself to getting up with them every night because of their spiritual reports. Take action—pray!

As parents, you won't be in the bedroom with your tots when they see the spirits. First, you want your children to know how to pray. But if they wake up screaming and terrified, in you go! Now it's up to you to say in a spoken voice: "In the name of the Lord Jesus Christ, I command all spirits that aren't from Almighty God to get out of Ashley's bedroom right now!" Then ask the Holy Spirit to come and comfort your daughter and bring her peace. Pray the nighttime prayers discussed in the section "Nighttime Prayers for Little Folk (and Big Folk, Too)."

Dr. Mom Speaks

One couple came to me because their little girl told them that when she's sleeping at night, people take her away and make her watch other people get hurt. It's not important to find out any more details. The priority? Help the little girl sleep. I told her parents how to anoint her room and pray nighttime prayers. Her terrorized nights ended. No psychotherapy was necessary.

Creatures

Your child may initially be afraid of all spiritual creatures because they all look scary. But, the Lord has good creatures in his kingdom that do work for him. Perhaps your child is seeing one of the good creatures. As mentioned earlier, it's okay for you to tell your child about the Lord's creatures.

What do children need if they are being frightened by creatures they see at night? First, they need to know if it's a friend or foe. If it's a friend, it can stay. If it's a foe, it must go.

If your child tells you he sees a creature in his room, pray and ask the Lord Jesus to remove any creatures that are there that aren't from him. Ask your child if the creature is still there. If it is, it's from the Lord. Tell him it's a good creature. If the creature leaves after this prayer it was a bad one, but your child has learned how easy it is to get rid of the bad ones.

Tell your child that anytime there is a bad creature, they can pray like you did and ask Lord Jesus to take it away.

Another option is to ask God the Father to send a bigger, more powerful creature to protect your child from the one bothering him!

Keep a smile on your face and don't act too serious. You have to be playful about this stuff. You have to let your children know that you aren't afraid of the creature and that they don't have to be afraid of the creature, either. God's going to give them a much bigger creature to watch over them.

Toddler Tales

My son was at a sleepover. At night he saw a creature, like a dragon, coming from above, trying to bite him. He was afraid. We prayed and asked the Lord to provide one of his creatures to protect him from the creature. This dragon-creature came after him again. My son saw a slithering creature under the bed come up and defend him against the dragon. Later my son saw this slithery thing in his room at home. He could see it moving around his room. He wasn't afraid of it because he had already seen it defend him. He knew the slithery one was a "good one" from the Lord. He was no longer afraid of anything he saw at night.

As parents, you can pray and ask Father God if he would please send one of his creatures to watch over your child at night.

That should do it!

Part 5

Protection for Your Child

Part of your responsibility as a parent is to keep your children safe. In this part, you will learn about protecting your children from emotionally disturbing events and disasters in life. You will learn about protecting your children from your negative feelings about an ex-spouse, your marital conflicts, and toxic family members. Additionally, you will learn how to hire safe babysitters for your toddler and how to equip your child in case of abuse or abduction.

In the final chapter of this part, we deal with child abuse and abduction. Because of the high incidence of abuse against children, this tragedy may strike your family. If your little one is abused, you can learn how to lead him or her into healing in the Lord Jesus to free the soul and mind of the trauma they have sustained. We also consider when and how to seek professional help.

Chapter 17

Hiring a Babysitter

Parents of preschoolers need regular breaks to maintain their sanity and their marriages. One of the most anxious moments for parents is leaving their children with a babysitter. In this chapter, we focus on finding a "safe" babysitter. Parents today are concerned about child abuse and protecting their children from this tragedy. This chapter identifies risk factors when selecting a sitter. You will learn how to find the safest possible babysitter.

We'll focus on hiring a teenage babysitter, but people hire adults as well, and sometimes relatives watch kids. For the most part, the same principles apply.

It is important that your sitter know how to deal with your children in an emergency, how to deal with them when they act up, and how to deal with any special medical needs.

It is also important that you learn how to talk with your children after the babysitter goes home to make sure that the experience has been a good one; if it hasn't, you need to know about it. Parents can't presume that "no news is good news." Parents need to dig for information with their children without being police interrogators.

Keep in mind that when you find a great babysitter, she is not just your employee; she becomes a small part of your family. You develop a relationship with her as she develops a relationship with you and your children. The relationship may extend for years while she's babysitting, and it may shift to friendship when she moves into her 20s. If you've been good to her and maintain the relationship, she may be willing to come back when your kids are teenagers so that you and your spouse can get away for that second honeymoon!

Guidelines for Finding a Safe Babysitter

Parents should follow many guidelines when trying to find a safe, competent babysitter. Most of these are provided in checklist form in Appendix C, along with other resources like a sample medical consent form (Appendix A) and a list of information you should leave with your sitter (Appendix B).

Aside from the basic requirement such as babysitter and first-aid courses, there are some important issues to consider in finding a "safe" babysitter.

Personal referrals are always worth a lot, but don't forget that you still need to make your own assessment. Ask other parents, nursery caregivers, your local Christian high school, or the youth group leader at your church for referrals. Relatives may seem like the first option, but you ought to still consider the following criteria. Pay attention to your children's responses to the relative, and still do the follow-up debriefing.

Interview and References

Interview a teenager as you would interview anyone else looking for a job. You should never just call someone and ask if that person would babysit your children.

You want to conduct the interview at your house when all of your kids are at home. It's best if Mom and Dad can do this together so that you both meet all of the candidates and they meet both of you. Make sure that your children are around as the interview takes place. Invite the potential sitter to come and spend an hour or two with you and the kids. You might invite the candidate to dinner one night. Observe what happens: Does the potential babysitter attempt to interact with your children? Do your children seem to take to the person or shy away? Does the teen seem to like children? Is she a "warm" person?

Ask for references, and call them. Are the references solely character references? The babysitter doesn't have to be a Christian, but does she share the same values as you do? If the teen has never done any babysitting, a character reference may be the only kind she has. Are the references people who have hired the teen to babysit their own children? Is the reference someone who has observed the teen take care of children at a church nursery, preschool program, or day care? Ask the reference not only what kind of person the teen is, but also specifically what he or she has observed about how the teen has cared for the children directly. Ask if the reference has ever seen the teen deal with an obstinate child, a crying child, or a child with pants full of poop!

What are the ages of children that the teen has babysat before? Does she have previous experience with children the age of yours? Has she ever changed diapers or put toddlers to bed?

Ask the teen what kind of occupations she is considering for the future. Do any of their responses indicate a love for children? Does she want to be an elementary school or kindergarten teacher? Teach kids swimming lessons? Work at a day care? You want a teen who has a love for children and enjoys them. Of course, even a teen with no interest in an occupation involving direct contact with children could be an excellent choice. If they have a love for kids you'll see it when they interact with your children.

Ask the teen if she ever felt she made a mistake when babysitting. What did she do to learn from that mistake? How would she do things differently if the same situation arose again?

Toddler Tales

> When I was 15, I was hired to babysit a three-year-old. I knew nothing about three-year-olds. I had no idea that I couldn't let the child play alone in the backyard while I watched TV. Next thing I knew, the child was missing. The toddler had left the backyard and was walking down the sidewalk alone. You can be sure those parents never asked me to babysit again. I wasn't a bad teen—I just had no clue what three-year-olds were capable of and how closely they needed to be watched.
>
> The moral of the story: Find out how much experience the potential babysitter has with kids the ages of your kids.

The interview should never take place on the same day you need a sitter. Plan to find a sitter at least two to three weeks ahead so you aren't rushed. Also, you may want to hire the teen for an hour or two at first while you're at home so that you can get some extra housework done, mow the grass, or clean out a closet. You may want to hire someone just so you can go to the store to get a few groceries. Hiring a sitter for a short time the first few occasions will give you a better sense of whether you want to leave that person with your children for a whole evening.

If you are considering another mom to babysit your kids, observe the relationship she has with her own children. What have you observed about her parenting?

Well Trained

Most advisors will tell you to hire someone who has taken a babysitter or first-aid course. Yes, it's preferable if the teenager has had a course. But this in and of itself should not be the deciding factor.

Has the teen ever changed poopy diapers? Is she willing to change your child's diapers? Is she willing to help your child wipe his bottom if he needs help?

Safety and Sanity Tips

What do you do if your child starts to avoid the babysitter? Does this mean you have to find a new sitter? Not necessarily. In asking the debriefing questions, you may find out that Junior doesn't like your sitter anymore because he doesn't want the sitter to wipe his poopy bottom. He won't wipe it himself. What do you do? Tell the babysitter to leave his poopy bottom alone even if you have to put him in the tub when you get home and wash it yourself! There are issues not worth losing a good sitter over.

Has the sitter ever fed children before? Has she ever put kids to bed before?

Has a child ever had an accident when she was babysitting and needed some kind of first aid? What did she do?

How does she like to put kids to bed?

Has she ever had to deal with a child who was having a temper tantrum? What did she do about it?

Has she ever felt that she needed to discipline a child? How did she do it?

Has the teen ever called anyone else for advice while babysitting? One thing you want to know is that you have a resourceful teen. You want to know that if she doesn't know what to do, she will call and ask either you, her own parents, or someone else.

Does your prospective teen go to church? Will she read Bible stories to your kids at bedtime and pray with them before they go to sleep? Will she pray with them before meals? Your babysitter is standing in your shoes while you're gone. If these things are important to you, discuss them at the interview.

The best-trained teen is one who has little brothers and sisters (that is, as long as they are the kind and loving type, not the hostile and dominant type). Most, but not all, oldest children of these big families have already learned how to do all the things you want a babysitter to do. (One thing to note, though, is how the younger children in the family respond to their care-taking older sibling. Pay attention to any alarm bells.) These kids don't need a babysitter course!

Social Group and Peers

One of your interview questions needs to be about the teen's social life. What does she do with friends and peers? If she has no social life, don't hire her. Socially isolated teenagers are too risky. They may be sweet and nice, but they are in the high risk category of caretakers. This doesn't mean that every social introvert is a danger to your kids. We're talking here about weighing the odds. You are learning about what the red flags are. Lack of a social life is a serious red flag when it comes to teen babysitters.

If a sitter is hard to get hold of or is very busy with friends, it's usually a good sign. Try to nail her down to be at your house now and then.

Male vs. Female

Both male and female babysitters can be safe for your child, and both can be dangerous. It's not exclusively about gender. But let's look at the issues.

Females are generally safer than males. Why? Both male and female teens are dealing with issues of sex drive. But males are usually struggling more. Teenage boys who are experiencing high sex drives are more likely than females to experiment with children, possibly yours.

Boys who were sexually abused as preschoolers often start to push their abuse away from themselves and onto others when they are teens. You don't want your children to be the ones they push their abuse onto. Do you know whether the boy has been sexually abused? Although you may not want to ask this question in an interview with the teen, you should keep your ears open in case you come across a piece of information like this. Of course, just because a boy has been sexually abused doesn't mean he will pass his pain onto your children, but we're talking "odds" and risk factors here. This is a high risk factor.

Who are the safe teenage boys? They do exist. The safe teenage boys are the ones who have not been sexually abused themselves, who have good social relationships with peers, and, most important, who have a good solid male relationship with their fathers.

Dr. Mom Speaks

A good friend called one day to ask me about choosing a babysitter. She had in mind a young man, an only child, who was living with his single mother, with no father in the picture. He was a social outcast. As a psychologist and family therapist who specialized in treating sexual abuse, both victims and offenders, I told her "No way! Don't hire him to babysit your children." I went over my guidelines with her. She decided I didn't know this kid well enough and hired him anyway. Six months later, she called to say that he had not only sexually molested her baby girl, but that he had done it in front of her two preschool sons. She ended up with three traumatized children. My heart sank. The situation had been preventable.

Females can be a danger to your kids, too. Again, if they are socially isolated, find someone else. Whenever there has been child abuse by a female sitter, we discover that she has no friends and is a social outcast—and always available to babysit! Also, lots of teenage girls are not child-oriented at all. You will pick up on this in an interview. You want someone who likes to be around children, not someone who just wants to earn a few bucks.

Word from the Wise

"… God sent the angel Gabriel to Nazareth … to a virgin named Mary. … Gabriel appeared to her and said, 'Greetings, favored woman! The Lord is with you!' Confused and disturbed, Mary tried to think what the angel could mean. 'Don't be frightened, Mary,' the angel told her, 'for God has decided to bless you! You will become pregnant and have a son, and you are to name him Jesus.'" (Luke 1:26–33)

God did not pick just anyone to bear his son. Can you imagine the requirements he must have had of the young teenage woman he chose to entrust his baby son to? Mary was given an awesome responsibility.

In the same way, it behooves us to make sure the people we choose to entrust our children to meet our requirements because they have an awesome responsibility!

Guidelines for the Babysitter

It's your responsibility to inform and instruct your babysitter on all sorts of things—from emergencies to disciplinary issues, to diet, to medications, to what's off-limits, to food, to bedtimes, to activities. You can't presume that a teenager is a mother or a doctor or a trained emergency response person. Even though you can't teach the teen everything, you can teach her some basic things. Make sure she knows to call for help when she doesn't know what to do.

Emergencies

You must instruct the babysitter in what to do in case of an emergency. Leave a list of emergency contacts for the babysitter (see Appendix B).

Your babysitter must be able to contact you or another adult in an emergency to ask what to do if she doesn't know. She should have your number when you are gone. If she can't get hold of you, it's best if she can fall back on her parents.

In the United States, you must leave a medical consent for treatment form with your babysitter dated for that day. Both the babysitter and an adult over the age of 18 should be listed. Consider your babysitter's parents or a neighbor. Make sure your neighbor knows and will be at home that night. If you do print up a form on your computer, you can print off a new form each time you go out and put a new date on it.

Your medical consent should have your medical insurance information on it, as well as any allergies your children have to medications. Adding your names and contact information will give the emergency room personnel everything they need, and they will be able to contact you, if necessary. Check Appendix A for a sample letter.

In Canada, this isn't necessary because parental consent isn't required for an emergency. Two doctors at the hospital can give consent for your child to be treated.

Does your babysitter know what to do if one of the children gets a burn? A heat burn? An electrical burn? A chemical burn? A sunburn? A friction burn?

What about a bleeding nose? Scrapped knees? Does the sitter know where the bandages are? Antibacterial creams? The first-aid kit? Can the babysitter give your child pain medication for a headache? Where is the pain reliever kept? In an emergency, the sitter shouldn't have to search your house to find these sorts of things, and you should provide explicit instructions for her so that she knows what to do.

The worst position you can leave your babysitter in is to have a lack of knowledge in an emergency. The information in Appendix B is very helpful. You might not stop to think that the sitter needs to know the exact street address of the home or the nearest two cross streets in case she has to call for emergency services. You need to provide all of this information.

Contact Info

Leave all possible contact information with the babysitter. Make sure the sitter feels free to call you. If it is impossible to contact you for whatever reason, make sure you provide additional adult resources for the teen if her parents aren't available.

Disciplinary Policies

You need to be explicit with the sitter about what to do if a child has a temper tantrum, hurts one of the other children, won't cooperate, won't go to bed, and so on. When things go wrong, you want to know that your sitter knows the right thing to do by you and by your children.

You want to be sure to debrief the sitter when you come home to find out whether there have been any behavior problems and how she handled it. You know your children best and can guide your sitter in how to handle them.

Medical Issues

If your children have any special medical needs, give proper instruction to the sitter. You should have the potential sitter over while you're there and let her do the things needed for your child while you are there to offer guidance. If your child needs an inhaler or a respirator, or uses a catheter or whatever, the sitter needs practice under supervision before being left alone with your child. After you bring the sitter over and explain the medical issues and provide some training, let her go home and think about whether she still wants the babysitting job. You don't want a hesitant teen. Either she can deal with it or she can't. If the sitter gets nervous in an emergency, your child will suffer.

Friends and Phone Calls

What is your policy on your babysitter having friends over while on the job? You need to explicitly say what is not acceptable. What about making and receiving phone calls from friends?

Remember, you are an employer! You are hiring a person for a job. When you go to work, does your boss let you have your friends come to work for the day? Does your boss let you make personal phone calls?

Even though phone calls may seem like a small issue, if the teen is absorbed on the phone, that means she isn't checking regularly on your kids (even if your kids are in bed). It also means that if you're trying to call, you won't be able to get through. If the teen has a cell phone, ask her to restrict calls or turn off the cell phone while babysitting. If her parents need to reach her, they can call your house number. Make sure your sitter knows that you're paying her to attend to your children, not her friends, but do so as a kindly suggestion.

Friends and boyfriends are a no-no. Your sitter ought to know that right up front.

Debriefing with Junior After the Babysitter Goes Home

Parents need to get into the habit of debriefing with their children. It starts with babysitting, playschool, and preschool. You must stay in touch with what is happening and what has happened with your children.

You need to know how things went with the babysitter from your kids' perspective, not just the babysitter's.

When trying to get information out of children, you need to ask open-ended questions; "yes," "no," "fine," and "okay" are not the answers you need. Here are the types of questions to ask your little ones:

- What did you do that made you happy?
- What did you do that made you sad?
- Tell me one fun thing you did.
- Tell me one thing you did that you didn't like.
- Tell me the best thing about (name of babysitter).
- Tell me the worst thing about (name of babysitter).
- Who came over when we were gone?

These basic questions should give you an idea of whether your children were safe with the sitter, whether the sitter was engaged with the children, or issues you may need to talk about with the sitter.

Be sure to watch your children's faces when they respond to you. If they have been told not to tell you something by the sitter, they will pause before answering and then avoid the question until they come up with an answer. In other words, if someone has told them not to tell you something and you ask a question about "the worst thing that happened," the thought of the bad thing will come to their mind first. They will have to try to search for a lie or a way to distract you or avoid the question.

Just because there are no bruises on your child doesn't mean everything went well.

Some parents install spy cameras to check up on the babysitter.

You want to know that the kids had fun, that they felt safe, and that they really liked the babysitter. You'll get a genuine feeling for that when you ask those simple questions.

You may find out about a gap in the babysitter's knowledge that you can then fill her in on later. You may find that the kids loved her and she was great. That will make you feel great, too.

Merely asking your kids these sorts of questions also helps them develop their ability to talk about when things go well and when things don't go well. Teaching your children that you are interested in them, in what happens with them, in what makes them happy, and in what makes them sad sets them up to know that they can confide in you.

Other Babysitter Issues and Options of Note

You can glean a lot of good information from moms and dads who already employ babysitters. Get all the tips and advice you can. Ask about local sitters and names you've been given, and find out what other families have experienced with them. When sitters have not done a good job and have been fired, those families' names won't be on the list of references.

Never Too Desperate

Never be too desperate to go out for the evening. Some teens today will take advantage of that. They may call just before they come over to say that a friend was going to sleep over that night. Then they have the audacity to ask you at the last minute if you mind if the friend comes along to babysit your kids! It may happen that your babysitter just shows up at your house with the friend and gives you a story that implies that you'd be cruel not to let the friend help babysit for the night. Be ready to tell the sitter to "forget it."

Never be so desperate to go out or keep your plans that you buy into this sort of thing, even if you have to waste your $100 tickets to the symphony! It's not worth it to allow a teenage babysitter to think she can pull these kinds of stunts.

You are hiring a babysitter to set aside everything else in her life for a couple of hours, for good money, to focus her attention exclusively on *your* children. If a friend is there, your children are not the primary focus or concern. And what do you know about this friend?

Driving the Sitter Home

If it's late at night and the sitter lives down the block, she should be walked home. If she has to be driven home, I recommend that the mom drive them home, for a couple of reasons. Moms are the ones who are most likely the primary caregivers for their preschoolers and are better positioned to debrief with the sitter. The debriefing can happen on the drive home.

Another issue involves the teen girl being alone in the car at night with the dad. If the marriage is strong at the time, it's probably not an issue. If the marriage is weak, I don't advise it. You just don't want to provide any sort of temptation in any way if a marriage is shaky. If you've chosen a really nice young woman to watch your kids, a connection can start with a vulnerable man in a car late at night. Don't even think of putting your husband or her in that position. Even if you and your husband both know he's a totally safe man to be around, your teenage sitter may still be uncomfortable having the dad drive her home. If you want to keep her, put her at ease.

Paying the Sitter—the Double Blessing

Don't leave your sitter feeling uncomfortable about money. At the interview, ask her what hourly fee she feels is fair for the number of children you have. Tell her what you think is fair. This is a contract in which both parties need to feel valued and respected. Three children are more work than one! You need to pay more. Remember, these teens can go out and get a job for $6.50 an hour and may have much less work than looking after your children!

Agree on the fee. Then when you arrive home, have your money in hand and just give her the money. Don't give her a check. Why make her have to go to the bank? Be prepared. If you don't have the exact amount, pay her more. Remember, you want her to want to come back again. If she's a great sitter and your kids love her, bless her with a financial reward so that if she ever has two families wanting her the same night, she'll choose yours!

If you're short on cash and can't give her a cash bonus, remember to give her a little something on her birthday and at Christmas. Leave little special things for her when you can—cards, trinkets, stuffed animals, special chocolates, etc. (Of course, you're already leaving her snacks for her evening. I'm referring here to doing a little extra now and then.) Perhaps you have tickets to an event that you can't use. Or buy an extra ticket and take her with your family. Make sure she knows how much you appreciate her!

Word from the Wise

"Since I was so sure of your understanding and trust, I wanted to give you a double blessing." (2 Corinthians 1:15)

The Apostle Paul knew in his heart what he needed to do for those people whom he could trust and showed understanding to him. Give them a double blessing. If you find someone you know you can totally trust your kids with and who is totally understanding and loving toward your children, you should praise them and be generous with compensation.

Chapter 18

Emotional Protection for Your Child

One of the jobs you have as a parent is to protect your children physically, spiritually, and emotionally. Protection involves keeping harm from coming to your children. You lock your doors to keep out robbers, you pray for spiritual protection, and you make conscious decisions for emotional protection.

Protection from Divorced Parents Who Don't Get Along

Parental pain causes child pain. The more pain you are in, the more pain your child is in. Divorce brings pain for an entire family system.

The Toddler World

Toddlers suffer the most from parental pain. Remember, their world is very small. You and your household are their world. When there is pain in their home, their whole world feels like it's collapsing around them, on them.

Because of their age and maturity level, divorce hits toddlers harder than any other age group. This is because of their immature emotional development and their lack of verbal skills. They need stability, predictability, and consistency. Divorce throws their world into a tailspin.

What Your Toddler Can Understand

Toddlers have no comprehension of what divorce means. The only thing they know is that Mommy and Daddy aren't living with each other anymore and that Mommy and Daddy are angry at each other.

Trying to go into any detailed talks with your toddler about your marital situation is not necessary, helpful, or healthy. Your children need to know these things:

- Mommy and Daddy both love them.
- Mommy and Daddy will both spend time with them (presuming that the other parent actually will be involved in your children's lives).
- Mommy and Daddy aren't going to be living in the same house.
- Your kids are good, and they did nothing that made Mommy and Daddy not want to live together anymore.

> **Word from the Wise**
>
> "The Lord is my rock, my fortress, and my savior; my God is my rock, in whom I find protection. He is my shield, the strength of my salvation, and my stronghold, my high tower, my savior, the one who saves me from violence." (2 Samuel 22:2–3)
>
> As God the Father cared for Samuel, you also must care for and protect your children.

Regression

Divorce and its aftermath, including the continued level of stress between Mom and Dad, will cause toddlers to regress in their developmental achievements. Indications of regression were previously mentioned at the end of Chapter 8.

Minimizing the Disturbance

While divorce may be a reality, all of the pain that comes with divorce does not have to fall upon your toddler's shoulders. You can do specific things to keep your toddler's world as stable and pain-free as possible under the circumstances:

- Keep your toddler in a steady routine at home (no matter how you feel).
- Talk with your ex-spouse about keeping the same kind of bedtime routine at both homes.
- Keep taking your toddler to regularly scheduled activities (no matter how you feel).
- Do what is necessary to enable your toddler to see the other parent (no matter how you feel).
- Never stop visits with the other parent because of failure to pay child support (this is not your child's issue, and children are never to be held for ransom by one parent against the other).
- Find a confidant for yourself.
- Deal with your pain outside of your house as much as possible.
- Deal with your pain when your child is out of the house as much as possible.
- Ensure that your son or daughter is sound asleep before you allow yourself to grieve your own pain.
- Don't cry about your marital situation in front of your child—your tot can't handle your emotions.
- Do not argue with your ex-spouse within earshot of your toddler (just because they are in another room doesn't mean your tot can't hear you).
- Do not get into arguments with your ex-spouse on the phone while your toddler is in the house.
- Do not talk negatively about your ex-spouse when other adults visit your home.
- Never threaten your child that bad behavior will mean not seeing the other parent.
- Don't allow other people to talk negatively about your ex-spouse when your children are in the house (or at other people's houses, if your children are there).
- Maintain at least a businesslike relationship with your ex-spouse as it pertains to facilitating his or her relationship with your son or daughter.

Remember:

- No matter what sort of adult relationship you had with your spouse, it is not indicative of the kind of relationship your ex-spouse can or will have with your son or daughter.

- The fact that your ex-spouse didn't spend much time with your children while married is irrelevant to how much time or involvement he or she may want with them after a separation.

Your issues with your ex are not issues for your children. Your children do not need to know the details of any of your marital problems. If there was open fighting, the children already know that Mom and Dad didn't get along. That's all they need to be told: "Mom and Dad didn't get along. Mommy and Daddy won't be living together anymore. You will see Mommy at her house and Daddy at his house." Anything more than that is not in your toddler's best interests and can't be justified.

Recovery from the Disturbance

While toddlers will regress because of the disturbance of the separation or divorce, they will eventually catch up to where they were and where they should be.

It takes about two years for a child to become acclimated after the separation of parents.

How can you help?

- Be nurturing.
- Help your child express feelings.
- Consider that bad or regressed behavior could be because of stress—listen to your child.
- Allow the regression, but slowly set the expectation that your toddler must do what he or she is able to do.
- Continue to set clear limits for behavior, be understanding of acting out, be gracious, and be kind, but don't remove consequences. (Kids still need to apologize if they hurt someone, they still need to help wipe up the food they threw on the floor, and they still need to brush their teeth, for instance.)

- Be as consistent as possible.
- Get the help you need to deal with your feelings about the end of your marriage.
- Speak of your ex-spouse in a positive way in front of your tot.
- Remind your tot how much the other parent loves him or her.
- Tell your tot good stories of things that happened with the other parent.

Self-Control as a Parental Discipline That Blesses a Child

The end of a relationship and your pain from it cannot be used as any reason to lose control of yourself. Under duress, you must rise to the occasion and do right by your children. They cannot control their environment, but you can. You must get the help you need while, at the same time, being the parent your toddler needs you to be. Protecting your toddler from your personal pain and from the pain that comes to children because of parental conflict is one way that you bless your children and give them the best you can give. It's a choice. It's something you do for your kids, whether you feel like it or not!

Remember, the person you might have to protect your child from might be yourself—your anger, your animosity, your pain, and your words. If you are having trouble controlling your emotions or words around your children, recognize your need for healing from your own pain and find a good Christian counselor to help you heal.

Options for Communicating with Your Ex-Spouse

If the relationship between you and your ex-spouse is bitter and communication is next to impossible, try these options:

- Get call display. Talk with your ex-spouse only when you feel you can handle the call.
- If you see your former spouse's number on the call display, pray. Ask God the Father to send his angels to protect this conversation. Ask the Holy Spirit to come and bring you comfort and peace so that you can speak with your ex. Ask the Lord Jesus to give you the words to speak and help you to hold your tongue.

- Leave phone messages back and forth to make arrangements for visitation.

- If you're putting a court order visitation in place, ask your lawyers to write in a specific visitation schedule, and follow it. If you can't stop being nasty to each other, pay your lawyer to do all of your communicating with your ex-spouse's lawyer. Yes, this is expensive, but the emotional cost to a child who hears his parents in conflict is more expensive.
- Use a mediator.
- Write notes or letters, and send them back and forth.

Godly Childrearing

If you have custody of your children, you have the responsibility before the Lord to raise them in a loving and peaceful environment.

Prayers for Your Little One

Don't forget that during trying times, you need to be upheld in prayer by those who love you, and you need to uphold your children in prayer. Ask your pastor, Christian friends, and Christian relatives to intercede for you and your children.

Remember to pray for your toddler daily. Ask for God's protection, love, and comfort to come to your child.

Ask the Lord to strengthen you daily and give you wisdom as you seek to raise your tot to come to know the love and grace of your Lord and Savior, Jesus Christ.

Protection from Other Disasters

Your kids don't need to know everything. From September 11 to the murder across town, your preschoolers should not be bombarded by news, information, graphic details, and parental discussions about disasters and tragedies. They should not be watching the blow-by-blow news coverage of life's horrors.

It's your job to protect the minds of your little people. In the same way we take precautions to keep out burglars by locking our door, we sometimes need to turn off our TV or radio.

What can you do?

- Tape the news and watch it after your toddler has gone to bed.
- Set your toddler up to play in another room while the news is on, and keep the volume low.
- Plug in the earphones and listen to the news.
- Discuss disasters …

    … after your toddler is sound asleep.

    … while your toddler is at playschool.

    … while your toddler is out in the yard playing.

- Don't try to explain in detail any disaster to your tot. (If your child asks what's going on, tell him or her only the most basic information without details.)

> **Safety and Sanity Tips**
>
> Buy your toddler a cassette or CD player with headphones. When you have to talk about stuff a little one shouldn't hear, put in a favorite kids tape and let your child dance around to it. Your tot will be oblivious to what you're saying.

Dealing with Reality

The only reality toddlers know is what is happening in his own home. Remember, their world is their home. They have no interest in what is happening on the next block, let alone across town or across the world.

Let them be kids—don't allow the cares of the world to drop down on their shoulders.

If your kids ask "What's happening, Dad?" simply tell them …

- Some people have been hurt, but they are getting help.
- Some people are fighting, but they'll work it out.

> **Dr. Mom Speaks**
>
> As one of my colleagues once said, your home is a greenhouse. You don't take the plant out of the greenhouse into the world until it is strong enough. You must protect your children from life's adversities until they are strong enough to handle them.

If you are upset or crying over a disaster and they ask "What's wrong, Dad?" simply tell them …

- Daddy is mad about something that happened, but after Daddy thinks about it for a while and prays about it, Daddy will feel better.
- Daddy is sad about something that happened. After Daddy thinks about it for a while and prays about it, Daddy will feel better.

If your toddler tries to comfort you and tells you he or she will take care of you, the appropriate response is: "Thank you for wanting to take care of Daddy. But sweetheart, it's not your job to take care of Daddy. It's Mommy's job and the Lord's job and Daddy's job to take care of Daddy when Daddy is feeling bad. You go and play—everything is going to be okay."

Protection from Toxic or Destructive Family Members

Just because they are your relatives doesn't mean they are good for you or your kids.

Depending on how toxic your family members are, you will need to consider …

- Keeping your children away from them completely.
- Making visits with them short and sweet.
- Making sure there are no sleepovers at their house.
- Making sure you or your spouse is always present in case things get out of hand.
- Making sure you don't visit unless the family members are sober or not under the influence of drugs.
- Having visits only at your house, where you have greater control over the environment.
- Staying at a hotel when you visit.
- Excusing yourselves, going for a walk, or going somewhere else if things start to get out of hand.

Keep an eye on your children to see how they are reacting to family members you are concerned about.

Don't ...

- Make your children kiss or hug any family member they don't respond naturally to.
- Let your son or daughter sit on the lap of any family member you feel uncomfortable about.
- Let your child be alone, go for a walk, or play in another room with any family member you or your child is uncomfortable around.

Remember, your responsibility to protect your child includes protecting him or her from those you are related to, if necessary.

Protection from Your Marital Conflicts

Most parents think that when they fight behind closed doors, their children don't hear them. Nearly all adults who come to therapy over childhood issues will tell you of all the fights they heard between their parents when they were in bed, presumably asleep and out of earshot. Just because it looks like Junior is sleeping doesn't mean he is. And just because Junior was asleep when you started fighting doesn't mean he'll stay asleep during your fight.

When children hear their parents fight, it is very disturbing for them.

I remember one day I heard my parents fighting. They were fighting over the stove. Mom wanted a new gas stove and wanted Dad to convert it from oil. Mom became so mad that she threatened Dad that if he didn't deal with that stove, she would pack up us kids and move to the city. Wow! That was the only time I'd

Toddler Tales

My daughter's preschool teacher loved her because she showed caring for others who were having a bad day by hugging them or patting them on the back.

One day my husband and I took a drive up to the mountains. Our three-year-old was in the car. An argument ensued. We were both angry and raised our voices to each other. Our daughter started crying.

The next day at preschool she bit a child.

ever heard my parents fight—and to hear that our family might split up? I just started bawling and bawling. I was demolished inside. When my parents heard me crying they came to me and told me that everything was going to be okay. Dad said he'd change the stove over, and that was it. Sheesh! Why put me through that agony? I'm sure the result would have been the same if they had gone out to the garage and sat in the car and had that fight!

Your toddler is emotionally immature. You need to be mindful that even if they are quietly present, they are hearing and are aware of everything going on. Just because you don't hear them doesn't mean they aren't listening to every word you say and picking up on every emotion you feel. As the Lord is a strong shield around us, so should we be a strong shield around our toddlers and protect them from the adult world. Let them enjoy just being a kid.

Chapter 19

Child Abuse or Abduction: A Parent's Worst Nightmare

Our worst fear as parents is that our children could be abused or abducted. We look at our children and see how vulnerable they are, and it can be scary. What can we do to protect them? In this chapter, you will learn some valuable information about how children are targeted by sex offenders—information that will better enable you to protect your child.

Children need to know how to hear the Holy Spirit telling them when there is danger. You will learn how to teach them this.

You will also learn how to empower your tikes through real-life stories of how God's people were helped out of abuse, abduction, and captivity. Through these biblical stories, you can teach your children the kinds of prayers they can pray if anything bad happens to them. And, God forbid, if your child is ever abducted, you will learn the kinds of prayers to pray that will have the most chance of effecting freedom and escape for your precious little one.

What Every Parent Needs to Know About How Abusers Select Their Victims

As professionals have worked with sex offenders over the years, they have come to learn what these people are looking for when they search for a victim and what steers them away from particular children. Parents are now able to equip themselves with information they can use to help reduce the odds that their child will be targeted by an abuser.

The General Traits of an Adult Male Sex Offender

Sex offenders don't have any particular "look," are not identifiable by any particular profession, and can range in age from 15 to 80.

Some teens sexually touch those younger than them but do not go on to become molesters as adults. These are teens who were not sexually abused themselves (generally), and their touching of youngsters is more about sexual exploration in puberty than the beginnings of a life-long problem as a sex offender. Both male and female teens sometimes abuse children. The high-risk checklist is in Chapter 17.

Life-long sex offenders who are male begin in their youth, driven by inner conflicts and trauma from their own sexual victimization. These men are driven to sexually touch children and generally have more than 100 victims by the age of 65. Sadly, they don't retire. Some 80-year-old men are abusing their great-grandchildren. They have just moved from one generation to another.

The typical child molester is a timid man, is unassertive with adults, and is quiet, with a lot of fear. He may be outgoing, but he still lives in fear. I have worked with sex offenders who were very colorful and strong-looking. They used their suave, debonair style to seduce children.

Child abusers are child-oriented and are most often known to the children. They want to gain children's trust. They are friendly with the children and their parents. Abusers don't want to alarm children or make them afraid because they will lose their relationship with them. Abusers find it titillating and exciting to go a little further sexually with a child each time. They are working to disarm the family so that alarm bells won't ring. Generally, those who abuse children are nice, friendly people.

A child molester is not just meeting a sexual need or drive when seeking out children for sexual contact. To him, children "feel safer, less threatening, less demanding, less problematic than a relationship with an adult." (*Handbook of Clinical Intervention in Child Sexual Abuse,* Suzanne M. Sgroi, M.D. Massachusetts: D. C. Health & Company, 1984, pg. 27)

According to the American Association of Pediatrics, one of five adult women report having been sexually assaulted as children and one of ten adult men report having been sexually assaulted in childhood. In eight out of ten cases, the victim personally knows their offender, who is an authority figure the child knows and trusts (www.medem.com/MedLB). The U.S. Department of Justice cites that six out of ten rape or sexual assault incidents were perpetrated against them by a friend, relative, or neighbor in their own home (www.usdoj.gov).

Prefers Company of Children Rather Than Adults

At family get-togethers, sex offenders prefer to hang out with children instead of adults. They drift toward wherever the children are. They like to play with the kids, rough-house at times, and have kids sit on their laps. During these rough-housing times, they make their first contact with a child's privates. They pass it off as an accident. When they have kids on their laps, they put their hand on a chest or breast. They begin what looks like inadvertent touches to a child's crotch. They sometimes have an erection while a child is on their lap. Play becomes the means to desensitize a child to touch.

Familiarity and Accessibility

Abusers don't look far for their victims. They choose kids they have regular contact with. Abusers will work on children for up to two years to desensitize them toward advancing sexual touch. If your child is ever sexually abused, the likelihood will be that it will be by someone you know. Someone you know well.

Abusers will offer to babysit a child or take a child on trips or on outings. Ask yourself why an adult man would want to spend so much time with your child. One family I knew had a friend who offered to take the 10-year-old daughter on drives he made to another city. The parents didn't know that he was fondling her the whole way there and the whole way home. No matter how badly you need a break from your kids, be wary of men who want to spend time alone with them and offer to take them off your hands. If you aren't the one initiating the request for child care, see it as a red flag.

Violent vs. Nonviolent

The majority of sex offenders don't use violence to gain power over their victims. They like to gain power through more implicit means. If they can befriend the children, the kids may feel an allegiance (not telling on a friend). If they can give the children something like candy or toys, the kids may keep quiet to keep getting the treats and may feel that if they tell, they won't get their treats. Kids may also feel that they are betraying the person who was good to them. If the abuser is doing otherwise good things for the family and the parents really like him, a child may keep quiet because he or she doesn't want to see the parents' friendship upset by telling. If the abuser is a person who just shows the child attention and affection, the child won't tell to avoid losing this, even though he or she feels in the spirit that something is wrong. Sometimes nonviolent abusers threaten a child not to tell, but this is mostly unnecessary.

While some sex offenders are violent, they are by far in the minority. Violent offenders don't consider the personality of the child when choosing one to abuse. They are looking for accessibility alone. These offenders are the ones who might grab a child at a mall or playground and not know the child at all. They go to a place where children are, just to get whatever kid they can get their hands on. Again, this type of abuse is very rare.

Nonviolent offenders need opportunity and accessibility, but they are looking for a particular type of child in a particular type of situation.

Naive, Compliant, Trusting

Nonviolent abusers are looking for children who are sexually naïve. They want to teach the child something, show the child something. They will exploit the child's sexual ignorance.

Abusers look for compliant children. They need victims who won't put up a fight or resistance. They look for shyness and timidity.

Abusers look for a child who will trust easily and quickly. Many children are so naïve that they trust anyone and go to anyone. Parents can see this as a loving nature, but an abuser will see this as an opportunity. An affectionate child is a more vulnerable child.

The Strong Child

For the most part, child molesters are cowards. Who but a coward would go after a child? Child molesters are afraid of confrontation, even by the child. When a child shows signs of being assertive and verbally capable, offenders shy away.

Most often, if a child looks at the offender and says "Stop it," "Leave me alone," or "I'm telling my Mommy/Daddy on you," the offender will stop. Offenders know they will go to jail for what they are doing. They feel threatened by children who have the guts to tell on them.

Assertive children aren't chosen by most sex offenders (although they may be by a violent offender who just grabs them and runs). Children who appear competent and talkative are avoided.

Incest offenders actually breathe a sigh of relief when a child finally tells on them. Some incest offenders live in a silent hell with their addiction; when the child tells, it is often the first step of their getting help and being accountable.

The Father

Offenders are afraid of strong men. Remember, internally they are cowards. Children without a strong relationship with their father are more vulnerable than children who have a strong relationship with their father.

One of the things an offender does when scoping out the next victim is to assess the threat of the child's father. If the father-child interactions show that the child is close to the father, the molester will avoid the child. If the father talks with the child, shows interest and affection, and does things with the child, the offender most likely will leave that child alone.

Emotionally distant fathers are no protection for their children. They can be big and strong, but if they have no relationship with their children, they are no protection for their kids. Whether absent emotionally or physically, an absent father leaves his children vulnerable.

What Can You Do?

Parents should be the ones to teach their children about their bodies. They need age-appropriate information about sexual issues. Refer to Chapter 6 for more information.

Do you have a shy, timid, compliant child? Focus on teaching your child to develop verbal skills. Help your tike learn how to speak up. Pay attention to whether your kids are comfortable around particular people who may be of concern. Ask open-ended questions about how your child's tummy feels around anyone you may be concerned about. Watch your child's nonverbal language.

If you have such a child, especially if there is a weak relationship with the father, never let this child out of your sight! Leave him or her only with people you know to be safe. Shy, timid children need more protection because they are at greater risk.

Hearing the Voice of God When Mom and Dad Aren't Around

From the time children begin to talk, you can begin to help them discern the Holy Spirit. Here is what you need to teach your little ones:

> The Holy Spirit lives in your tummy. If there is danger, the Holy Spirit gives you a rotten feeling in your tummy. When you feel a rotten feeling in your tummy, the Holy Spirit is telling you to run away from whoever you are near and run to Mommy or Daddy.

You can also tell your child this:

> No matter how nice a person talks or how nice that person looks, even if Mommy and Daddy know them, if the Holy Spirit ever gives you that yucky feeling in your tummy, you need to listen to the Holy Spirit. Come directly to Mom and Dad if your tummy starts feeling bad.

Check out Chapter 13 on how to train your child to listen to the Holy Spirit.

You need to affirm to your children that they can trust their gut because the Holy Spirit speaks to them that way. You ought not to talk your children out of the reactions they have to adults. Kids are very sensitive to people who have ill agendas. Let your children have their reactions to adults. Their reactions should tell you something as much as they are telling your children something.

No matter how nice some people look, how nice they talk, or how sweet they smell, if there is evil lurking in their hearts, kids will pick up on it. You have to make sure your children know this and then equip them with the proper instructions for when they are sensing a reaction to certain people. At the same time, we don't want to frighten our children. Keep your instructions and comments brief and to the point. Parents who have themselves been sexually abused tend to say too much to their children out of their own fears. Less is more.

Toddler Tales

One day my three-year-old son came up to me at church and told me that there was a man in the church basement who gave him a really bad feeling in his tummy. He told me that it was the Holy Spirit talking to him. I told him he was right. Interestingly, my five-year-old daughter had made the same comment on the same man another time. In fact, the man gave me the creeps, too! I told my children that no matter where they might be in the church, if they saw that man, they needed to walk or run the other way.

My kids were taught that the Holy Spirit speaks to them in their gut. Was that man a sex offender? I don't know. I do know that there are sex offenders in our churches every Sunday, and I want my kids to stay away from anyone who gives them the creeps. Better safe than sorry!

Teaching your children sensitivity to their gut does not instill fear in them. It empowers your children to know what to do in difficult circumstances. They are learning to listen to the voice of God rather than the voice of man.

Dr. Mom Speaks

Most fear comes from lack of knowledge and feeling powerless. Not knowing what to do contributes to fear. The more you know, the less you fear. Equipping your children with knowledge of what they can do if they end up in a bad situation will not instill fear in them—it will give them confidence in themselves and in their God!

The Kinds of Prayers God Answers for Children

When kids are being abused, or if they have been abducted, they usually pray the wrong kinds of prayers. They pray and ask God to make the person stop hurting them.

Kids need to know that when they pray, they can't ask God to make someone else stop doing what they are doing because God gives everybody free will, even when they are bad people. God lets people choose to do right or do wrong, to do good or to do bad. When they choose to do wrong, he doesn't stop them.

Children have often felt let down by God because the abuser didn't stop abusing them after they prayed. Many children have had their faith destroyed over this type of thing.

This does not leave children without power. But they need to be taught the kinds of prayers that they can pray that do not contradict the free will God gave everybody.

If you go directly to the Bible, you can find the kinds of prayers that men of God prayed when they were imprisoned, held captive, or chased by someone trying to harm them. God makes provision for his people when they are in trouble.

Word from the Wise

"… your Father knows exactly what you need even before you ask him! Pray like this "…." (Matthew 6:8–9)

Your children need to know that when they are in a dangerous situation they should ask God specifically for what they need. Do they need food? Ask for food. Do they need help getting away from someone bad? Then they need to ask for help to get away from someone bad.

Your children must be taught that they can ask God for very specific things if they ever get lost, if they get into a bad situation, or if a bad person ever tries to hurt them. You can empower your little people with the power of almighty God. They need to feel like they have some strength and power even though they are small. They *do* have strength and power because they have a powerful God.

At the same time that you will learn what your child can do, of course, you realize that your child may be abducted and killed. It happens way too often. But as parents, if this horrible thing were to happen to our children, we want them to feel as brave as they can, as confident as they can, and as fearless as they can. It is double harm for children to be abducted and to suffer fear. You may do everything in your power to protect your children, and they may still be abducted. As a parent, the only thing I may have control over is to instill in my babies something of the Lord that they can draw on if this horror should befall them. Children may be too small to fight physically, but they can put up as big of a spiritual fight as David did against Goliath! You want your children to be able to talk to God in such a way that they can believe that they can defeat their big foe, just like David did. How do you do this?

You give your children spiritual knowledge and spiritual tools. You teach them how people in the Bible escaped danger and death. You teach them the kind of prayers God has been known to answer for his people when they were captives.

Equipping Your Child to Face Danger: Little Bible Studies for Little People

The following Bible studies will teach your children biblical principles so they will learn how to ask for God's help if they are ever abducted or someone is trying to hurt them.

John 14:6–14

Jesus sat down with his disciples one day and taught them that they can only come to his Heavenly Father through him. He went on to say that if they need to ask his Heavenly Father for anything, they must ask in his name.

Comforting words for your child: "Jesus told us that we can ask anything in his name and he will do it for us. If we ever are in trouble, we need to start asking God for some things. Whenever we ask God for things, we ask him 'in Jesus' name.'"

Acts 16:18

A man named Paul was close to God. He healed many sick people and made evil spirits leave people. He did this "in Jesus' name." One day a girl was bothering him a lot. He knew that an evil spirit was inside her. He spoke to the spirit in her and said, "I command you in the name of Jesus Christ to come out of her!" And the spirit left the girl right away.

Comforting words for your child: "If people are trying to hurt us or do bad things to us, it is because there is a bad spirit in them. Just like Paul, we can order that spirit to leave that person 'in Jesus' name.' We just need to look right at the person and say, 'In the name of Jesus Christ, I order you evil spirit to get out of her (or him).' Children have just as much power as adults do to tell an evil spirit to leave a person. This is because we are Christians, and our heavenly Father is the powerful one and helps his children when they call out to him."

Safety and Sanity Tips

Tell your preschooler. "If anyone tries to hurt you or take you away from Mom or Dad, you just look that person straight in the eye and say loudly, 'In the name of Jesus Christ, I order you to let me go right now!' or 'In the name of Jesus Christ, I order you to stop hurting me right now!'" Ask your child to practice saying these things with you until he or she can do them very assertively and in a commanding way.

Genesis 19:16–17

A man named Lot was in a city that became very dangerous. God's angels grabbed hold of his hand and rushed him and his wife out of the city to safety. The angels talked to this man and said "Run for your lives!"

Comforting words for your child: When people are in danger God can send his angels to show them the way to safety. If children ever get in danger they can ask God to send angels to show them the way out, too.

Matthew 2:13–14

When Jesus was a baby, an angel came and talked to his father. The angel told Joseph that Jesus was in danger and that he should run away to a place where Jesus would be safe. Jesus' parents took him away to a safe place. After the danger was over, an angel told Joseph he could go back home again.

Comforting words for your child: "God knows when people are going to be in trouble, and sometimes he tells us how we can run away from trouble before it happens."

Numbers 10:9–10

Once God told his people that when they are in trouble, they should make a loud noise. He told them that when they make the loud noise, he will remember them and come and rescue them from their enemies. The Lord told the people to blow a trumpet. A trumpet makes lots of noise.

Comforting words for your child: "Sometimes when people are in trouble, they need to make a loud noise. Not only will God hear them, but other people might hear them, too, and help them."

1 Samuel 17:45–47

David was just a boy when he was chosen to fight the giant Goliath. He was small. He didn't have big weapons. He knew that all he had was his mighty God and that God could help him fight his enemy. And God did.

Comforting words for your child: "If we are ever in a place where there are big people all around us with guns or other weapons, even if we have no weapons, we have God. God doesn't need weapons to rescue his children. Remember, God can shake the ground! We can ask him to fight against the bad people for us."

To learn other ways that God provided a way of escape for his people, see Genesis 7:5–10; Genesis 19:16–17; Isaiah 51:9–11; Psalm 141:8–10; 1 Samuel 27:1; Psalm 3:1–8; Psalm 17:13; Psalm 139:1–12; Genesis 32:9–12; Exodus 3:7–10; 14:13–14; Judges 3:8–10, 15; 2 Kings 13:4–5; Acts 27:42–44; Judges 6:14–16; and 2 Kings 6:8–23.

What to Pray If Your Child Goes Missing

If one of your children is abducted or goes missing, the prayers you can pray as parents are, in essence, the same kinds of prayers that you teach your children to pray.

Parents need first to pray for prevention. You need to pray for spiritual protection over your children every day.

Second, parents need to pray prayers for foreknowledge and wisdom. Pray that if anybody has any evil intent toward your children, both you and your child will witness it in your spirit and the Holy Spirit will divert you away from the danger. Practically speaking, if you are driving to a particular park that day for an outing and you get the sense inside that you shouldn't go or that you should change your plans, you should change your plans. You have to trust that after you have asked for God's divine wisdom on something, you should trust it, just like you teach your children.

God the Father knows what is in everybody's heart, including those with ill intent. He can communicate that information to you or your children. If your children tell you that they really feel bad about going somewhere and doing something, pay attention to them—they may be feeling the heart of God about that situation. This is not to say that you should let your children determine where you go and what you do all the time. However, you need to learn to listen to the hearts of your children so that if God is trying to speak to them or to you through them, you will be able to discern that.

Third, if your children go missing, you need to take both human action and supernatural action. You need to do all the right things to contact neighbors and the authorities, and then you need to pray. Just praying for a safe return is not enough. You need to ask specifically for what you want and for those kinds of things that God can answer for you. Remember, God gave everybody a free will, and he allows people to choose evil.

Ask God to give your child the guts to be bold and speak out the things you've taught. Ask God to show your child a way to escape. Ask God to lead another person who can rescue your child. Ask the Father to be a mighty shield around your child. Ask the Lord Jesus to go and stand over your child with his mighty sword drawn against anyone who would attempt to harm your child. Ask the Holy Spirit to go into your child and speak to his or her heart and give thoughts and ideas of anything your child can do to escape. Ask the Father to remind your child to make a big noise so that someone might hear him or her!

Spiritually speaking, you can also ask God the Father to send out his angels to do a few tasks. You can ask the Father to send his angels to lead your child on an escape path. You can ask the Father to send his mighty angels to go to each person involved in taking your child and to have those angels bind up every evil thing operating in or through those people and shut down those evil forces.

Ask the Lord Jesus to put his comforting arms around your child and stay with him or her throughout this ordeal.

Chapter 20

If Your Child Has Been Traumatized

What is trauma? Children have been traumatized if they have experienced, witnessed, or been told about an extreme stressor that involved the threat of death or serious injury to themselves or someone they are close to.

Trauma arises when a child's response involves intense fear, helplessness, or horror. Trauma arises not only from being victimized by child sexual abuse, physical abuse, verbal abuse, or spiritual abuse, but also from witnessing someone else get abused or hurt. Trauma can result from witnessing or enduring a natural disaster, being in a car accident where people are badly hurt, or being told about horrific things that have happened to people or animals. Sometimes children are traumatized by hearing their parents fight or hurt each other. Children can also be traumatized when animals are hurt.

Potential Signs and Symptoms of Trauma in Children

Has your child changed?

- Was he once a contented little guy who now shows signs of aggression that you don't understand?

- Has he reverted to being afraid when you leave him? Has he become more clingy than he was?

- Is he having trouble falling asleep or staying asleep?

- Has he started talking in his sleep, or has he started having nightmares regularly?

- Does he seem more hyperactive than usual, or is he having increased outbursts of aggression?

- Does he seem more irritable and angry? Does he exhibit disorganized or agitated behavior?

- Has he started wetting the bed again or reverted to "baby talk"?

- Has he started to shut out the world? Have you found him in the fetal position sucking his thumb? Does he seem to be "glazed over" at times? Lethargic?

- Has he developed fears of specific places or people?

- Has his drawing and artwork regressed? Is his artwork illustrating anger? Is he using yellow or green to color his people?

- Has he started to tell those he loves that he hates them?

- Does he seem unable to remember things like he once did? Is he having trouble learning?

Safety and Sanity Tips

Even when toddlers misbehave and do things you don't understand, they must find safety in you.

If you have seen a shift in your child's usual behavior that has continued for at least a month, it's within the realm of possibility that he has been traumatized.

The Brunt of It All

A traumatized child is vulnerable to parental anger, discipline, punishment, and aggression. The traumatized child is not functioning as he or she should, and when this is misdiagnosed or misinterpreted by parents and other care-givers, the goal of the care-givers may be to "whip the child into shape" through increased discipline.

This is a serious mistake for the traumatized toddler. Now he or she will not only have confusion over the trauma sustained, but he or she won't be able to understand why you are angry.

What Has Happened to My Child's World?

If your son or daughter has been traumatized, his or her inner world has collapsed.

The Issues of Safety and Trust on Learning and Memory

You will recall from Chapters 1 and 5 that these years with your toddler are critical for the establishment of trust in a child's environment. Children are busy learning about their world. A feeling of safety will help them to grow in a healthy way. Safety is freedom, freedom to grow.

When the sense of safety is threatened, the mind seeks to protect itself. In the process of protecting itself, it stops letting in a lot of information. Learning and memory are severely curtailed by significant stressors.

Powerlessness

Toddlers are learning what control they have over themselves and their environments. One of their significant developmental accomplishments is to achieve a sense of autonomy, giving them a sense of personal confidence and achievement. Trauma strips that away.

Toddlers are little. They have no power when it comes to older children, teens, or adults. They have no ability to control an environment when people bigger than them are doing bad things to them or to others. Toddlers can't stop adults from talking about things that scare them.

You are providing a "safe" world for your toddler. But with trauma comes the collapse of what had once appeared "safe." Your toddler loses part of himself or herself.

Providing the Setting for Children to Tell You When They've Been Hurt

Parents need to provide an environment that is conducive to toddlers' ongoing communication with them. You set the stage for conversation when you ...

- Talk with them directly.
- Listen to them intently.
- Teach them a language to express themselves.
- Create opportunities for them to "share" with you.
- Initiate conversations that would set the stage for them to "share" trauma if they have been traumatized.
- Assure them that they are safe and secure with you and that, no matter what they tell you, you will react with calm reserve (on the outside, even if you're screaming within).

Fear of Anger

Nobody likes anger. Nobody likes to be around someone who is angry. Children are no different. Children's fear of adult anger can be the very thing that stops them from telling their parents about the hurt they have sustained. Even if you try to convince your children that you won't be angry at *them*, it won't necessarily matter. Anger is anger, and they will avoid it.

As a psychologist working with traumatized children, I worked hard to set an open arena where my children could freely come to me if they were hurt. When my daughter was four, a man grabbed at her chest. She didn't tell me until she was five. Why? Fear of anger. Even with assurance that I wasn't angry at *her*, she knew only that I would be angry. She didn't want to experience my anger, whether it was directed at her or not.

After this incident with my daughter, I came to understand that I had to find some way to talk with my children about these sorts of things so that fear of anger wouldn't stop them from telling me if something bad happened to them.

Toddler Tales

When the little girl told her grandmother that her dad (grandma's son) was touching her privates, Grandma said, "Don't tell your grandfather—he'll kill him!" The little girl never told another soul, and the sexual abuse continued until her late teenage years.

You must listen to children when they try to tell you that they have been or are being hurt. You must think ahead and plan how you will respond to your tots.

Getting Around the Fear of Anger

If you want your children to be able to tell you if someone has hurt them, these are the kinds of messages you need to give them:

- Big kids, teens, or adults who hurt little children are people whose hearts are aching.

- Sometimes people with hurting hearts can't call out for help.

- When people hurt little children, it's their way of calling out for help.

- It's our job to help people or to try to get them the help that they need.

- If someone hurts them, they need to tell Mom and Dad about it so that they can get help.

- When they come to Mom and Dad and tell them they have been hurt, Mom and Dad will do whatever they can to see that the hurtful person gets the help needed.

Things that you could say to toddlers that will inhibit them from telling you when they have been hurt:

- "If anyone hurts you, we'll have them sent to jail." Most of the time, kids are hurt by people close to them or the family. They don't want people they know taken away by the police, so they won't tell.

- "If anyone hurts you, they will be in so much trouble." Kids don't want to get people in trouble because they know they don't like to be in trouble. This won't help them to tell you anything.

> **Dr. Mom Speaks**
>
> The new message to my children paid off! My third child came to me one day to tell me that one of her friends needed help—could I help him? She knew he needed help because he reached over and touched her between her legs. I calmly called his mom to have a talk. It worked!

Leading Your Child Through Inner Healing with Jesus

Loving parents who have a good relationship with their children are perfectly situated to be their toddler's counselor! There is no reason why you can't learn how to lead your child through some healing exercises and learn some things that will help him or her heal from whatever has hurt him or her so deeply. In some pieces of recovery your child will need a professional's help, but Mom or Dad can do a lot with a toddler.

When I first started as a young therapist, I saw lots of children, including two- to four-year-olds. After a few years, I figured out that if I could engage the parents in the healing process, the children could get much better much faster.

After all, if your child already trusts you and you can handle hearing what has happened, you can probably do enough without the aid of a professional counselor at this age (with a little guidance from a professional, of course). However, if you are freaked out by the details of your child's story, you should entrust this job to the professionals immediately. Also, what you do now doesn't eliminate the possibility that your child may need a professional's help later, but it reduces the likelihood that your tot will need *a lot* of therapy later!

The Truth and the Light

The truth is the truth. Telling the truth can elicit a lot of pain. As they say, "Sometimes the truth hurts." But it hurts only for a short time if it is "told." Only when the truth is kept secret does it hurt for a long time. In fact, it keeps hurting until it is told!

Jesus' words are true in all circumstances. The truth will set you free in every way.

Bringing forth the truth allows the light of the righteousness of the Lord Jesus Christ to shine into and obliterate all darkness. Tots need the light of Jesus to shine in them. They need to be free from their pain. Helping them work through their truth, with the light of the Lord Jesus Christ, will release their pain.

> **Word from the Wise**
>
> "And you will know the truth, and the truth will set you free." (John 8:32)
>
> The truth: The single most important ingredient in becoming free from the negative effects of trauma.

Four Parts of Healing from Trauma

Simply put, once victimized, every person has four main tasks to heal from their abuse:

1. Face what actually happened (facts of the event, what left them vulnerable to the victimization, how they feel about what they saw or experienced, what they feel about each person involved, and so on).

2. Face how they've adapted their everyday lifestyle in reaction or response to the victimization.

3. Face the abuse's effects on their intimate relationship (for example, with their spouse, including sexual effects).

4. Disconnect from all connections with the kingdom of darkness that have arisen because of the trauma (or sin against the child).

> ### Safety and Sanity Tips
>
> Only a finite number of tears are attached to any specific incident of pain in life. Once those tears are shed along with the facts of what created the tears, the tears will reach their end.

What Abused Toddlers Need to Do to Heal

While your child is just a toddler, he or she, with your help, can deal only with no. 1 in the previous list. You and your spouse can deal with no. 4 without your toddler present. Toddlers, by virtue of their age and life history, are not yet old enough to deal with the other two points here.

Interestingly, when small folk have the opportunity when they are little to go through step 1 (and you go through 4 on their behalf), the chances that they will ever have to go through steps 2 and 3 are remote. This is where the world lives in a perpetual lie. There is no such thing as "scarred for life" when we have faith in Jesus Christ and when we have the resources of the kingdom of light at our fingertips.

> ### Word from the Wise
>
> "Instead, we will hold to the truth in love, becoming more and more in every way like Christ, who is the head of his body, the church." (Ephesians 4:15)
>
> Truth and love need to be found together. When you respond to your children, you need to respond like Christ, in love. Only then will the truth come out and will your children be on the path to freedom and healing.

> ### Word from the Wise
>
> "One day some parents brought their little children to Jesus so he could touch them and bless them, but the disciples told them not to bother him. Then Jesus called for the children and said to the disciples, 'Let the children come to me. Don't stop them! For the Kingdom of God belongs to such as these.'" (Luke 18:15–17)
>
> Your tots need to know that the Lord Jesus welcomes them unto himself. Let's bring our children to the Lord, in good times and in bad.

Inner Healing for Your Toddler

Please see Appendix H for suggested prayers to lead your toddler through inner healing.

Children's goals for inner healing should be …

- To express as many details of what happened as possible.
- To identify who hurt them or what they saw happen to someone else, or to articulate how they felt about what they were told about what happened to someone they care about.
- To identify their anger, confusion, or helplessness, and allow their feelings to come out with their verbalizations.
- To talk about where Mom and Dad were when this happened, and how they felt about Mom and Dad not being there.
- To talk about their fears of the trauma happening again.

Additionally, your goal should be …

- To assure your children of your love and that you won't let the situation that left them vulnerable arise again. (For example, say "Christy will never baby-sit at our house again!" or "We won't talk about the people in the war around you again.")

Trouble Verbalizing

If your tot has trouble putting his words together, get out the crayons and the paper and let them draw. If he has been traumatized, he will eventually express it in his art.

When you see something unusual in his art, ask him to let his picture speak. Ask him to tell you what the picture is trying to say.

Spiritual Disconnection and Victimization

If your child has been traumatized, it's possible that the kingdom of darkness has gained some ability to harass him or her at a very deep level. Because Mom and Dad have complete spiritual authority over their toddler, they are able to break any bonds with evil that may have arisen from their child's trauma. If you suspect your toddler may need this sort of help, please refer to Appendix H for suggested prayers.

If You Have Hurt Your Child

Apologize for any intentionally or unintentionally inflicted pain you have caused your child. Do not ask your child for forgiveness; say only you are sorry. Forgiveness is to be motivated by the child when ready, not the parent.

Don't ask your child to pray for you to help you stop whatever you've done. It's not a child's responsibility to do this for a parent. If the child prays and you do it again, the child not only will be disappointed in you, but now he or she may think that God can't even help. God is then seen as someone not strong enough to help. Spiritually, for your child, this is a dangerous place to tread.

If you inflict pain on your child and feel a compulsion toward hurting him or her, seek help. Go to Chapter 22 for additional help.

Videotaping Your Sessions

You may want to consider videotaping your inner-healing session to assist the police. If possible, when you do this, roll the video tape without your child's knowledge or awareness. Make sure that you ask open-ended questions and don't put words or people's names in your child's mouth. You don't want to spoil any evidence that you may uncover of a crime. You don't want to spoil the opportunity to have someone incarcerated if they are hurting children.

Videotaping your inner-healing session may spare your child having to repeat the story to many people (police, prosecutors, and others). This is a protection for your toddler in the long run. It's much easier to take a "clean" videotape to make a police report than for an officer of the law who doesn't know your child to try to elicit a statement.

Rebuilding Safety and Security

You have an opportunity every day to help your toddler resume normal, healthy development. But you have to take a few steps back before your child can start to move forward again. Your tot won't really lose much time when Mom and Dad are working with him or her to this end.

If your child has been traumatized, he or she will regress. Allow this and rest in it. Don't discipline your tot for this. Junior needs to get back to knowing that he has a safe and secure world with Mom and Dad (and other care-givers).

Although you will want to be more tolerant of odd behavior, the limits must still be firm regarding aggression to people, property, or animals. If you are working with your child on the inner-healing exercises and the aggression is increasing instead of decreasing, see a professional who specializes in trauma recovery.

Finding a Therapist for Your Child

Refer to Appendix D for guidance in finding a therapist.

Dealing with Courts and Lawyers

Being involved in a court case, no matter what your role, responsibility, culpability, or expertise, is stressful. Court actions drag on for years. They take their toll on everyone. Having said that, going to court is often the only way to stop an abusive person from finding more victims, and it may be the only way that your child can get the medical or psychological resources needed to fully recover from the trauma.

Criminal Actions

In most locales, there is no statute of limitations on the criminal prosecution of sex crimes. This means there is no immediate need to press criminal charges or proceed with criminal charges. The prosecutor will influence when charges will be leveled and investigated, and when the trial will be. However, you are not completely powerless in these decisions.

Won't your child make a better witness at age seven instead of age four? Or three? Or two?

You decide when you will make a police report. Check your state laws to see if you have to report all child abuse or only abuse in which the child is at risk to be abused again. In some jurisdictions, the law states that you must report child abuse if the child is in need of protection. Find out what your options are.

Even if you must file a police report right away, you may be able to discuss the timing of the prosecution with the prosecutor.

Civil Actions

There is a statute of limitations on a civil action against anyone. In most locales, you must file an action within two years of the incident or within two years of the discovery of the incident. In some locales, you must file within 10 years or the action can't be brought to court. If your tot has been abused and you are considering a civil action for damages against the abuser, you should contact a local attorney as soon as possible to discuss the situation and keep your options open. Make sure you ask the lawyer, even if you don't file an action on behalf of your child in infancy, whether the child will be able to file his or her own action upon reaching adulthood.

Court Considerations

As parents, it's your job to protect your child. If your child is victimized, you must assess what is in the best interests of your child.

You are weighing a number of factors:

- You are angry as parents and want to see the offender brought to justice.
- You are concerned for other children in the community and feel a sense of obligation to expose the offender to prosecution so that others will be spared your grief.
- Your child is in pain, and you don't want him or her to go through further pain through involvement in a court action.
- Your child has been hurt and deserves to be compensated for injury and treatment.

Consult with people you know and trust. Some decisions are made for you, and some you have control over. Make the best decisions you can for your toddler.

Part 6

Temper and Tantrums: Dealing Humanely with Our Humanity

Whether it's your toddler or yourself who is having a bad day, you will learn how to deal with the tough times that everybody experiences at some time.

Children fighting with friends or siblings is yet another challenge for parents. Teaching your children how to resolve their conflicts gives them skills for life.

Moms and dads need to be able to identify when and if their mental state is negatively affecting their parenting. Learn the signs and symptoms of depression, anxiety, and post-trauma stress disorder, and learn what to do when you need pastoral or professional counseling or medical help.

Chapter 21

Tantrums, Whining, and Other Annoying Stuff

Is there a child alive who has never had a tantrum? *Tantrum* is a word used to describe a state where a child is totally out of control or appears so. What to do? What to do? And whining, what everyone loathes hearing! How do you extinguish that behavior quickly? Then there is keeping kids from annoying you in the car and dealing with those nasty words you don't want to hear coming out of their mouths. Read on.

All About Tantrums: Taming the Ugly Side of Humanity

Real tantrums are typically seen in young toddlers, not older children. By the time your child reaches four, the tantrums should be over. Children older than four may throw a tantrum, but it will be different in motivation and intent from that of a younger child.

Let's start with the younger tots (sometimes the older preschoolers, too).

Totally Tired

Do you get cranky and miserable when you are exhausted? So does your toddler/preschooler. Just put your child to bed. Don't argue or try to reason with an exhausted tot. It's a waste of time and energy and will only serve to create a bigger scene. Put the kid to bed. (Maybe you need a nap, too!)

Overstimulated

While it takes an inordinate amount of stimulation to get the best of an extrovert, your little introvert may reach his limit far sooner. You need to know if you have an introverted child and be careful not to overstimulate him or her. Your child needs to be removed from situations before reaching that limit. Get to know your child, and try to figure out how much is too much. The parents of an introvert have to adjust to shorter outings. You need to pay attention to how many people are in the house and how much commotion there is, and make sure your introvert can have some time alone or just with you to settle down. Calm little introverts can totally shock parents and "not be themselves." Actually, they are being themselves; their limit has been reached.

No Control over Anything

Children can reach the tantrum stage out of complete frustration that they don't have control over anything. Let your child make some decisions that are within his or her control. For instance, if your toddler is having a tantrum getting into the car, allow him or her to pick out a favorite hand toy or stuffed animal to take along. When your child gets into the car seat without a fuss, offer a little praise for the good behavior.

Pay attention to when your child has a tantrum. Step back and assess the situation. If it is a situation that repeats in your routines (like at bath time), think of one little decision your tot can make around that time to provide a little sense of control. With bathing, your toddler may have a favorite bath toy or fancy face cloth to hold on to while getting into the tub or after successfully getting into the tub without fussing.

Too Much New Stuff, Can't Handle It

Little ones can get totally overwhelmed with too many changes in their environment or routine. If your child gets overwhelmed easily, stay with a predictable routine and prepare him or her for changes ahead of time (if possible). When introducing your toddler to a new situation or new people, describe the situation ahead of time in a calm and positive way. Let your child know what to expect when you get there (who will be there, what you will be doing).

Your judging child (see Chapter 2) will need a routine and more structure (lack of structure can cause him an overload of frustration). Your perceiving child will move with the changes more easily, but when things are too structured, that can overload his or her frustration. Again, you have to get to know your child in order to regulate his or her life so that the two of you can live in peace and so that when your tot "loses it," you'll have an idea how to change things next time.

"I Don't Know What Else to Do with Myself"

When children experience a lot of stress or tragedy, they can end up so overwhelmed with their emotions and stress that they don't know what to do. So they have a mental meltdown. This is more typical of children who don't have the language or expertise to say what they are thinking or speaking—such is the importance of helping them to express their feelings from a young age.

When children have tantrums from mental meltdown, they need love and assurance, not discipline. They need a parent who will just pick them up and hold them, no matter how much they are kicking and screaming. They need to know that even though they may feel like their world is falling apart, it really isn't. They need to feel their world securely around them. For a toddler, that means feeling Mom or Dad's arms firmly around them. You need to just hold them until they settle.

The Medical Side

Certain medications can affect your child's mood and behavior. Some antihistamines are harder on your child than others in terms of mood. If your child is on medications and you are concerned about tantrums, ask your doctor if the medications have emotional side effects and if moods will be affected.

Food affects your child. Sugar in any form (candy, pop, or desserts) winds up children for a while and then lets them crash. That's a huge impact on mood! Greasy, deep-fried foods also carb up children. They may not get a sugar high, but they may still get a carb crash after the stomach tries to deal with all that fat!

Or a child's thyroid can be off. Food allergies could be causing behavior problems. Serious concerns require a check with your family doctor or pediatrician.

Parental Response to Tantrums

The most important thing to remember when your child has a tantrum is this: "The child is having the tantrum! Not you!" (Hopefully not you.) Your child's behavior or emotions don't dictate your behavior or emotions. If you are calm and your child is having a fit, read on. If you and your child have both lost it, consult Chapter 22.

> **Word from the Wise**
>
> "Those who control their anger have great understanding; those with a hasty temper will make mistakes." (Proverbs 14:29)
>
> It behooves us as Christian parents to model anger control for our children. We must control our responses to our children and act wisely under pressure rather than reacting without thought.

Mom, Dad, keep a grip on yourself. You have to make a decision when your child has a tantrum. You have to try to quickly ascertain what has produced the tantrum. Your response will be dictated by the cause. Yelling at the child, scolding the child, or punishing the child won't end the tantrum—in fact, if little Susie knows she can make you lose it by losing it herself, oh, what power she wields over you! Your daughter needs to know that even if she loses control, you will *not!* Now is the time to invoke your thinking function.

1. Talk to your daughter calmly.
2. Tell her exactly what is going to happen.
3. Do it.

Your options for telling her what is going to happen are as follows:

- "You are tired. I'm putting you to bed." Then put her to bed.
- "You're hungry/thirsty. I'm getting you some food/drink." Get her what she needs.
- "Mommy needs to help you calm down. We are leaving the mall right now." Leave the mall.
- "Daddy is going to hold you now and squeeze you and love you." Pick her up, hold her firmly, speak softly, tell her you love her, and wait for her to get a grip on herself. Don't move until your child is peaceful.
- "We've had a long day. We all are going to go home and rest." Go home and rest.

Younger preschoolers' tantrums aren't always a behavior problem. They are usually a cry for help!

Now for the older preschoolers (sometimes the younger tots, too):

Sometimes tantrums aren't about a child's inner world collapsing, but rather about the child trying to control Mom, Dad, siblings, or friends (or other people's parents). When a child acts up to get you interested in their every movement, you cannot reward that child with a loving hug or kind understanding. If a tantrum is thrown for some secondary gain and the child doesn't get the secondary gain, there is no reason to repeat the behavior.

Without lecturing or yelling (which feeds into an attempted parental manipulation), try the following:

- Leave the room. Lend no ear to the emotional display. Avoid eye contact and arguing. Tantrums need an audience. Remove the audience; the tantrum has no purpose to continue.

- Tell the child directly and firmly that you will not respond to this type of behavior and that it is unacceptable. Then stop interacting with the child and carry on with your business. Avoid eye contact and arguing.

- Don't even think of trying to reason, barter, or otherwise negotiate with a child who is having a hissy fit.

- Sometimes just providing a distraction will be enough to end the tantrum. Make a funny face at the child (not mean, funny). Ask if the child would like you to tell a joke. Have a joke ready.

- Walk over to the CD player and let the child know that he or she can listen to a CD. Invite the child to come and choose one. If the tantrum continues, leave the room.

- Get down on the floor with the blocks, and ask the child if he or she wants to play with you. Or, pull out a book, sit down, and start to read it out loud. This is not rewarding the tantrum. It is ignoring the bad behavior and showing how to switch to doing something much more worthwhile.

- Notice something novel in your surroundings, and point it out to your child.

Some children just test their environment to make sure it is as stable as they hope it is. They may make some sputterings, but when you don't engage them with a big reaction, they just carry on with other things.

Don't dwell on tantrums—move on quickly.

Long after the tantrum is over, hours and hours later, ask your child if he or she remembers earlier that day being upset, and ask if he or she can think of any reason for becoming so frustrated. Debriefing afterward can yield some valuable information for the parent and may result in preventing future tantrums.

If your preschooler becomes violent toward you or others, you must restrain him or her in a safe way that doesn't hurt. Your child cannot be let loose to terrorize others. The line must be drawn.

When my extroverted daughter was a preschooler, she got so frustrated at times that she got verbally and physically out of control. There was, of course, no reasoning with her. My choice of action was to sit on her. Well, not in a way that would hurt her—only to restrain her. I took her to her bedroom, laid her on her bed (fighting and flailing the whole way), and straddled her with my feet locking down her legs and my hands loosely holding down her arms. The weight of my body wasn't on her as I was on my knees. From this position, I could stop her from moving while at the same time telling her that I loved her and that everything would be okay. It didn't take her long to settle down.

This type of incident happened again a couple of years later. That time I sat with her on the floor and held on to her and spoke the soothing words "I love you, everything is going to be okay." When she was 12 years old she asked me if I remembered these two incidents. Of course I did. Her comment: "You really loved me then, didn't you, Mom?" "Yes," I said, "and I still do." My little extrovert learned that even when she spins out of control, she can do something to get a grip on herself.

With the modeling she had from her mom, she began to teach herself how to soothe herself. Even as a little girl, when she felt overwhelmed, she would go into the bottom of her closet and rock herself and call on the Lord Jesus to come and help her. She would stay there until she gained a sense of peace. She's 20 years old and finds her way to the Lord's peace in the same way. She has learned to get a grip on herself from the way her mom helped her get a grip on herself as a preschooler. What children learn now gives them skills for living throughout their lives.

Dealing with Screeching, Screaming, and Whining

Children who screech, scream, squeal, and whine should be ignored. Their goal is to get you busy with them one way or another. Small children learn that whining is functional; it gets you to do something for them. By whining, they can control the world! Well, at least they can control you! This is unacceptable behavior, and they need to know it right from the get-go.

At the same time, they need to know what the correct behavior is. If they come to your side in that whining voice, state calmly, "Mommy doesn't hear whining; Mommy only hears nice talking." The moment they change their voice, turn to them and ask them what they want. Normal, appropriate attempts of children to communicate with their parents should not be ignored.

The screeching and squealing is your children's attempt to get you stirred up. It can be their way to try to get you to dote on them. It could be their way to get you off the phone with your friend and onto them. They figure that if they annoy you enough, you'll give in to them one way or another. You must resist and hold firm. Giving in to these childish behaviors trains your children to be rude, and while this may get them something at home with you, it certainly won't get them far at school and in the real world. Nobody is going to put up with that!

Ignoring children to punish them is wrong. Ignoring them to extinguish bad behavior is correction. Ignoring them must end when the appropriate, acceptable behavior is demonstrated.

If your child whines only after they have tried to talk with you over and over and you have ignored them, you are the problem. Make sure that you acknowledge your children and their needs when they are speaking to you appropriately. They shouldn't have to misbehave to get you to listen to them. If you can't meet their need right away, tell them you can't help them now but that you can help them very soon. Hand them a little egg timer and tell them that when the sand runs out, you'll be able to do what they need you to do. Be sure to praise children for successfully waiting for you.

Is your child whining because he or she can't get you to interact in any other way? Parents of whining children need to ask themselves if they are making reasonable attempts to meet the needs of their children. Parenting preschoolers is a real challenge, and sometimes parents can become resentful of their tots and resist doing the things for them that they should be doing as parents. Remember, your preschoolers are completely dependent on you. It takes nearly two decades of parenting for them to become competent enough to meet their own needs on a daily basis without some assistance from you.

Toddler Tales

One mother didn't want her children to bother her while she was cooking dinner, so she put ear plugs in and ignored her son. She wouldn't even listen to the most normal thing he might say. The more he tried to interact with her, the more she acted like he was invisible. This child was getting a message from his mother—"What you have to say isn't important to me." The young boy grew into a young man who resorted to yelling and screaming at his mom in attempts to be heard.

All human beings need to be heard, especially by those who love them!

Car Travel with Toddlers and Preschoolers

Today's parents are blessed with advances in technology and food packaging that weren't available to their parents.

The best way to prevent problems in the car is to prepare ahead of time. You can avert nearly all traveling ordeals by good planning. Of course, your child may still kick up a fuss now and then, humanity being what it is. We'll address that in a bit. First, here's what you need to have in your car (or minivan) at all times:

- **Things to keep their hands busy:** Small toys, crayons, coloring books or coloring sheets (Crayola ColorWonder Markers and paper), washable markers, file cards to draw on, stickers, sticky tabs, stamps, slinky, silly putty (as long as your child doesn't eat everything within reach), and small stuffed animals or beanie toys. Visit a "dollar store" and get a bag of junk toys. Pull out a new one each trip.

- **Things to keep their minds busy:** Picture books, stories on cassettes, your own voice reading them their favorite book (they can hold the book and turn the pages when you say "beep" on the tape), and music or stories on cassette or DVD on a children's player with headphones. Say to your child, "Tell me when you see a dog," "Tell me when you see a postal box", and so on. If you have one of those video players for the vehicle, put in a tape of your children goofing off.

- **Things to keep their voices busy:** Sing-a-long cassette tapes. You can sing with your kids, ask them to sing a song, ask them to tell you everything they see out of the window, and teach them praise songs, camp songs, and the ABCs.

- **Things to keep their tummies satisfied:** Individually packaged cheese sticks, granola bars, fruit bars, crackers, miniature juice boxes, raisins, dried fruit, small bottles of water, Cheerios (or other cereals like Shreddies or Chex), lunchable snack packages, and carrot sticks.

- **Things to soothe the soul:** A special polar fleece blanket that is kept only in the car for car rides (a small piece of fabric that just covers the body, not a big blanket), children's Bible stories on cassette, classical music, and peaceful worship music.

Every family vehicle needs a permanent plastic container with a lid that keeps kids' car supplies and snacks always available. You never know when you will have to pick up the kids on a moment's notice and drive. Waiting until you leave the door to grab a few things for the car will only produce ongoing stress for you and for your children. Make sure you have wet wipes, paper towels, a face cloth that can be wetted with water (with a zipper-lock bag to put it in after use), spare diapers or pull-ups, and an extra set of clothes.

You can't expect children sitting beside each other in a vehicle not to fidget and begin to irritate each other. Before long, the fight is on. Always keep your children beyond arm's reach of each other. You can't allow your children to terrorize each other in the car. Don't ignore their fighting because there is always an underdog (unless you have twins or triplets who are the same size and developmental stage). If the car is small and there are no other options than for the kids to sit right beside each other, put a pillow or a piece of cardboard or something else between them so that they cannot easily focus on each other.

If you are younger parents and have a long trip to take, consider driving at night while the kids are sleeping. Daytime trips will require regular stops to let your little ones burn off some steam, have a snack, and go to the bathroom. Those nonstop trips of "life before children" are over!

> **Safety and Sanity Tips**
>
> Boredom is part of life. Sometimes moments in life are just boring. Children can't be getting stimulated all the time you're driving in a vehicle. If you've tried everything possible and your child is still fussing, let her fuss and ignore her. She is just going to have to learn that sometimes there is nothing to do but sit there, be quiet, and be bored.

As with other annoying behavior, you don't want your kids to think that their misbehavior can control you. If they are fighting, don't threaten to take them home unless they stop. They may indeed want to go home! You also don't tell them that you will pull over and stop the car until they behave, unless you are going somewhere that they really want to get to quickly (like a friend's birthday party). If the kids get to the point that one or all become totally out of control, you may need to stop to discipline each of them. See Chapter 15 for more direction here.

Potty Mouth

Children learn their words from those around them. If your child has "potty mouth," he or she learned the words from somewhere. Children imitate words before they know what they mean.

The first time your child utters an unacceptable word, if you ignore it, there is a good chance that it won't be repeated. If your child does repeat it, keep calm and don't show your inner reaction. Say that it is a word that your family doesn't use and that your child shouldn't use it again. Carry on with other things, and don't focus on the utterance of this word.

Most often, this is enough. If the child doesn't find any use for the word, he or she won't repeat it.

If your son sees at playschool or at home that kids using these words get attention from adults, he may repeat them as an attention-getting strategy. Another possibility is that if a few kids at preschool are using these words regularly, your child may think that this is the ordinary thing to do. So first, ignore; second, point out that the words used are unacceptable to members of your family; and, third, if the words continue to come out of his mouth, more is needed on your part to deal with it.

If your daughter is learning these words from you or your family, it is a contradiction for you to use them and not allow her to use them. Curbing bad language starts with Mom and Dad.

Words that we find unacceptable are usually words that people use to express negative emotions. When negative emotions are expressed, they are usually expressed with some intensity. If your child is repeating a bad word, he or she is probably first saying it in anger, grabbing at a word to express that anger. If you've told your daughter that the word is not acceptable in your home and she uses it again when she's angry, go to her and ask her what has made her upset. Help her find other words to express her anger. Tell her that when she's angry, she needs to use "these" words to tell us how she feels and not "those" words. She must have enough acceptable words in her vocabulary to express herself sufficiently. Kids need a "feeling" vocabulary, and you need to teach it to them.

You can also make up silly words to replace ones that are unacceptable, that only you and your child know the meaning of.

Like everybody else, children hate to be ignored. Ignoring behavior to extinguish bad behavior is a corrective measure, not punishment. Your child should know that they will not be attended to for bad language. Mommy doesn't hear anything but nice talking!

Word from the Wise

"May the words of my mouth and the thoughts of my heart be pleasing to you, O Lord, my rock and my redeemer." (Psalms 19:14)

You can now teach your children what it means to come before God, confess your sin, repent, and ask for forgiveness. Lead your child in the words he needs to say to tell the Lord he's sorry for using potty talk and ask for the Lord to forgive him.

When You're About to Blow Your Stack

Praise be to God that we have a loving heavenly Father! God is so good, always and all ways. The Father knows all about parenting. While he has enjoyed the intimacy of relationships with his children when they are obedient, he has also felt the frustrations and anger that every parent feels when children misbehave. One thing we experience that God the Father has never experienced is the depletion of our human energy. We have a God who needs no sleep or rejuvenation or sustenance. He never tires, but we do!

The toddler years are the part of the family life cycle that features the greatest extremes:

- The greatest amount of laughter and fun
- The greatest amount of exhaustion and fatigue

To date, I have not met any parents of preschoolers who have not, at one time or another, reached their wit's end. It may occur only once or twice throughout years with toddlers—or it may occur many, many times.

My Scariest Story

While I was attending Fuller Theological Seminary, studying for my Master's degree, my eldest daughter was three and my son was a year old. Those were very stressful days, attending school full-time and caring for my little ones.

One day I came home about 9 P.M. My husband, who was also studying full-time, handed me my son, who was screaming and crying incessantly, and left for the library.

I tried to settle him down, but he wouldn't stop screaming. I was so stressed out that I didn't have anything left in me to give him. I started to shake. All I could think was that I had to *"shut him up."* His screaming was driving me crazy. I soon realized that no matter what I did to try to comfort him, because I was so stressed he wasn't going to get calmed down. I knew I was no help to him.

I took him to his bedroom (my daughter was already in bed) and set him in his crib. I left him screaming in his crib as I closed his door and told him I loved him. I walked down the hallway, closed another door and sat on the sofa. I was shaking uncontrollably. The thought that kept racing through my mind was to pick up my son and throw him against the wall to shut him up. I couldn't even believe I had such an evil thought.

I cried out to God for his help. I begged the Holy Spirit to come to me. I asked the Lord Jesus to come and stand guard over my home and protect me from all evil. One thing I knew for sure—I had to keep my hands off my son! I needed to stay away from him. He was doing nothing wrong; he was just a tired little guy. He fell asleep in his crib. As I called out for God's help, I praised him and thanked him that I had enough self-control not to hurt my son.

That was one of the darkest moments for me as a mother. I know I did the right thing, but it was hard. It took all I had in me to do what I did. I'm so thankful I never hurt my precious son. This was the first time I realized that sometimes parents need to protect their children from themselves.

I encourage you, no matter how rotten you feel, to protect your children from yourself when necessary.

Protect Thy Child from Thyself!

Do you know that God the Father himself recognized that he needed to protect his children from his fury?

Word from the Wise

"Whenever the Tabernacle is moved, the Levites will take it down and set it up again. Anyone else who goes too near the Tabernacle will be executed. … But the Levites will camp around the Tabernacle of the Covenant to offer the people of Israel protection from the Lord's fierce anger." (Numbers 1:51, 53)

God doesn't tempt us to sin and make him angry. He provides safe boundaries to keep us from paying the consequences of violating his laws.

God the Father made a rule: "No one but the Levites is to touch the Tabernacle." The consequences for breaking the rule were that those who touched the Tabernacle would be killed. God the Father did not leave his children vulnerable to accidentally touching the Tabernacle. He provided a barrier between the Tabernacle and his children. The barrier was the Levites. They were to camp around the Tabernacle to protect the people from doing what the Lord found offensive. What were the people being protected from? The Lord's fierce anger.

This is an important principle of parenting: Protect your children from your anger. Don't just set rules for your children, but provide a barrier between them and the chance that they will break those rules and arouse your anger. This is "protecting our children from ourselves."

If you know that your children might do something with objects around the house that would make you furious, protect them from it. For example …

- You have a family heirloom. If your children flushed it down the toilet, you'd be furious. Lock it up.
- You have a sentimental breakable object. If your children broke it, you'd be furious. Keep it out of reach.

Toddler Tales

One day I came home to find that my nephew had somehow gotten our electric drill and had drilled in and out of the foam stuffing on our arm chair several times. Where was my sister when this was happening?

- You have a favorite pair of high heels. If your children put them on and broke the heel, you'd be furious. Put them on the upper shelf in your closet.
- You have electric tools. If your children damaged something while playing with them, you'd be furious. Keep your tools locked up.
- You have crystal bowls or stemware. If your children cracked them, you'd be furious. Set them up out of reach, or box them for storage until your children are older.

Protecting Your Child When You Feel You May Hurt Them

When you are so angry that dealing with your children could turn ugly, abusive, or regretful, you must put them in a safe place and keep your hands off them. Here are some ideas:

- Let your spouse take over. Back off. If your spouse is at work, can he or she come home?
- If you're home alone, put your toddler in the crib or a bedroom, leave the room, close the door, and let him or her cry or scream. If your child tries to leave the room:

  Hold the door shut, and hold the knob so it can't be twisted.

  Sit outside the bedroom door holding the door.

  Say that you love your child but that you are too upset to deal with him or her or help right now.

  Hold the door shut either until your child falls asleep or leaves it alone.

  Say that your child can't come out until Mommy or Daddy comes in.

  Keep a barrier between you and your child until you cool down.

  Go and sit and pray.

  > Father God, I ask that you would come to me now, and protect me and my household from the evil one. Please send your mighty warrior angels to surround my home and battle every evil thing that is attacking my household and me this day.

Holy Spirit, please come to me now and comfort me. Please flow through my body and settle my spirit and my soul.

Lord Jesus, please come now and hold me in your arms. May I rest in your care and love right now.

Take out your Bible and read Psalms 25, 28, or 31 out loud.

Wait for the Lord's peace before you return to your children.

- If your toddlers are three or four years old, you may be able to look at them and tell them that you are too upset to deal with them right now. Tell them to go to their bedrooms, or family room, or wherever until you calm down and that then you will come to them.

- Call a friend or family member and briefly tell what kind of state you're in. Ask if that person can come over to watch the kids so that you can get a grip on yourself. When that friend comes over:

> **Toddler Tales**
>
> One day, when Dad came home, the three-year-old son went to him and said, "Mom says to stay out of the kitchen until dinner. Mom says she's frazzled, but she'll be okay after she eats."

If someone is at your church and the door is open, go there and pray. Any other churches closer to home that are open? Go in and pray.

Go to the mall and walk it off.

Go to a park and walk.

Go to a park with your Bible and sit on a bench, read the Word, and pray.

Sit in your car with your Bible and start praying.

Walk around the block over and over until you calm down.

- Call a friend or family member, tell briefly what kind of state you're in, and ask if you can drop off your kids there for a couple of hours.

- Call your pastor and ask if he can find someone to help you.

- If you have no other resources, strap your kids in their car seats (out of arm's reach from you) and drive until they fall asleep. Put on some soft praise music to help them and you calm down. If money is short, strap the kids in, make sure they aren't too cold or hot, and sit beside the car with your Bible and follow the directions for prayer above.

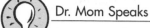

Dr. Mom Speaks

It is a sign of personal strength, not weakness, for us to acknowledge when we need help and ask for it.

- Check your community resources. In Edmonton, Alberta, Canada, there is a place called Kids Cottage. It's a place where parents at their wit's end can drop off their kids for up to 24 hours to get a grip on themselves. What is available in your community?

- Call the Distress Line (Suicide Hotline, Stress Line, Crisis Center) or any other emergency number you can to talk to another human being until you calm down.

Protecting Your Child When There's a Chronic Problem

What I mean by "chronic problem" is that you are under ongoing stress that will not change anytime soon. Typical frustrations, stresses, and fatigue can overwhelm the healthiest of parents, but some parents have more on their plate than most. This is a chronic situation.

Consider the following:

- Counseling with your pastor for underlying troubles or for support, encouragement, and intercession

Word from the Wise

"Bear one another's burdens, and thereby fulfill the law of Christ." (Galatians 6:2)

We are fulfilling biblical directives when we share our problems and struggles with other believers.

- Counseling with a professional Christian counselor to deal with underlying issues

- Joining an accountability group with other Christian moms, or at least one good friend

- Learning the method of meditating on God's comforting promises from his Word that he will sustain you by his grace

- Asking for help and intervention from a mature woman (for Mom) or man (for Dad) in the church for mentoring, encouragement, and intercession

- Seeing your medical doctor to determine whether you have any physiological imbalances (hormones, thyroid, depression, generalized anxiety disorder, mononucleosis, etc.)
- Getting involved with a Mother's Morning Out program
- Getting involved with a mother's co-op for sharing babysitting
- Putting your toddler in part-time or full-time day care or home care for a few months

Consider the Seriousness of Your Condition

You and your spouse may need to consider whether either of you are suffering such a serious emotional or mental problem that your children's safety or lives can't be guaranteed. You must seek help immediately. If your spouse becomes a threat to your children or yourself, you must talk with your doctor, a mental health professional, or the police for help and advice.

Ensuring Your Own Safety

You need to recognize if you are a threat to yourself. If you are vulnerable to hurting yourself, you must protect yourself and your children. When you have toddlers at home and you hurt yourself in their presence, you are putting untold pain in their hearts and minds.

Word from the Wise

"He led me to a place of safety; he rescued me because he delights in me. ... The Lord rewarded me for doing right because of the innocence of my hands in his sight." (Psalm 18:19, 24)

Ask the Lord to lead you to a place of safety where you can pray and seek counsel. You will be rewarded for making the right decision.

If you become suicidal or homicidal, get away from the house and call your pastor, your spouse, your family, your friends, child protective services, or the police

Safety and Sanity Tips

If necessary, drive out to the country, get out of your car, and scream your head off!

and ask them to go and care for your children. Make them safe, and then get out of the house and make the calls you need to make.

Tell others that you are a threat to yourself, and have someone go to your home to remove all medications and sharp objects. Then get yourself to a hospital emergency room immediately.

In Psalms 91:15, the Lord says, "When they call on me, I will answer; I will be with them in trouble. I will rescue them and honor them." Call on the Lord in your time of need, and remember that he directs us to bear our burdens with others. Between the Lord and loving Christian people, you can find whatever help you need.

Blowing Your Stack Safely

Yes, there is a safe way to blow your stack. Sometimes people just need to release their pent-up anxieties and frustrations.

Of course, make sure your children are safe and far away from you.

Inside the house you can …

- Pound your pillow.
- Get a punching bag.

Safety and Sanity Tips

God created crying for a purpose. When you cry, it stimulates the release of endorphins into your body. Endorphins are hormones that calm you down. That's why people feel relief and peace after they cry. (Although sometimes you end up with a headache!)

- Punch a Bobo doll.
- Squish a squishy ball.
- Get a tether ball for your backyard and hit it repeatedly.
- Set your kids up with earphones to a tape or video, go to your bedroom, close the door, press your pillow gently against your face, and scream your head off!
- Get an exercise bicycle and peddle until you are exhausted.
- Get a treadmill and walk it off.
- Take a hot shower, put on loud music in the bedroom, and "sound off."

- Sit down at your computer and type out your thoughts and feelings.
- Keep the kids out of earshot, and then call a friend and "sound off."
- Buy a tarp or canvas, paint on it every rotten feeling you have, write out your frustrations, and then cut it up and burn it in the fireplace or put it in the trash.

Outside of the house …

- Take a sledge hammer to a rock—a big rock!
- Run.
- Buy a bunch of old china, dishes, or glassware from a thrift shop and then take it out to the garage and smash it all.
- Chop wood.
- Find a big rock, paint or write on it the things you're angry about, and throw it off a bridge into a river.
- Cry.
- Blow off your steam with the Lord. Tell him everything that's bugging you and making you feel angry. He can take it!

Word from the Wise

"When Jesus saw her weeping and saw the other people wailing with her, he was moved with indignation and was deeply troubled. 'Where have you put him?' he asked them. They told him, 'Lord, come and see.' Then Jesus wept." (John 11:33–35)

Jesus was very frustrated by the people's lack of faith. He allowed himself to cry. Both moms and dads may need to cry to defuse their intense feelings.

The most effective way to rid yourself of intense negative feelings is to do two things simultaneously:

- Cry
- Talk through what is bothering you

Doing these two things together releases your soul from its bondage of pain. Crying alone won't do it. Talking alone won't do it. Some people must cry and talk with another person for relief, but some can do this on their own.

Taking Care of Yourself and Your Marriage

Recognize that as parents of toddlers, you *must* have a break from your children now and then. Don't wait until you're ready to blow your stack. Preventative maintenance is necessary for yourself personally and for your marriage.

- Go on a personal retreat. Get away for a few days.
- Go on a marriage retreat for a weekend.

Dr. Mom Speaks

The Lord Jesus himself knows how you feel with toddlers having no end of needs and demands. Do you know that the Lord often went off to the mountains alone to pray? He did this even though the crowds still wanted more from him. In his humanity, he knew when he needed a break, when he needed rest, and when he needed solitude, and he made sure he met that need. He is your example.

Chapter 23

When Kids Fight

Years ago when children fought, you'd hear parents say, "Leave them alone. They'll work it out on their own." When we leave them to work it out on their own, the law of the jungle prevails: Might makes right, the strong dominate the weak, and the ends justifies the means. This is barbaric and certainly not the way the Lord would want our children to think or behave.

It is your job as parents to socialize your children to grow into the men and women of God that you want them to become. They don't get that way without parental involvement. It's your job to train your children in the way they should go. You need to train your children how to work through their conflicts with each other.

Sibling Rivalry and Family Dynamics

Teaching your children how to work out their conflicts starts at home (presuming that there are siblings). The parents of an only child need to work with other parents and their children to teach them these skills with their friends.

If your children ages one to five seem to be fighting all the time or showing serious signs of aggression toward each other, consider the following kinds of dynamics that parents can unwittingly create that actually induce their kids to fight.

> ### Word from the Wise
>
> "The next day, as Moses was out visiting his people again, he saw two Hebrew men fighting. 'What are you doing, hitting your neighbor like that?' Moses said to the one in the wrong." (Exodus 2:13)
>
> Moses intervened when he saw two grown men fighting. How important it is for people to learn to resolve conflict in a civilized manner.

Not a Level Playing Field

Siblings in a family, especially in the preschool years, are unequal in terms of size, strength, and abilities. Might makes right in the preschool years, which means that the older and bigger dominate the younger and smaller. Doesn't the Lord teach us to watch out for our weaker brother? Are we to take advantage of the weak? No. We cannot leave or put our children in this position.

The younger children are very vulnerable in the preschool years. It'll be many years before they can be considered equals (when they are all adults!). Meanwhile, each of their ages, sizes, and abilities must be taken into consideration when there is conflict. The smaller, younger ones will always be at a disadvantage if they are left to work it out on their own.

Oldest Never "In Charge"

Because there is no level playing field among your children, one of the first rules of parenting multiple preschoolers is that the older one is never "in charge of" the younger one. No five-year-old should be left with power and responsibility over a three-year-old or a two-year-old or a baby.

You are the parent. This means that your five-year-old is not the boss of your younger children and is not responsible for feeding, diapering, or disciplining them. This doesn't mean that Mom or Dad shouldn't ask a four- or five-year-old to help them with tasks of caring for the baby, but the child is only a helper. Mom or Dad is there supervising.

Putting older children in charge of younger children sets up your children to be antagonistic toward each other. The younger one resents the older one for his illegitimate place of power; the older one is in a no-win situation because, on one hand, that child is trying to do as Mother said and, on the other hand, is straddled with a responsibility he resents because it is not legitimately his. The older child will take out his resentment against the younger one or against the parent. The younger one can end up resenting both sibling and parent.

The Danger of Favoritism

When one child sees that Mom or Dad prefers or favors the other child, the one who feels disadvantaged may attack the other out of revenge. This type of issue won't change by scolding the child who is showing the aggression. You must identify the interactions that are occurring between the victim-sibling and one or both of the parents.

Daddy's special princess may become the victim of brother's jealous revenge!

Don't Dare to Compare

You can be sure that comparing your children with one another will incite a riot. When you tell one child that he has done something wrong, bad, or not good enough while at the same time reminding that child of how well a brother or sister does it, you cause anger, hatred, and resentment between your children.

Both favoritism and comparisons can cause life-long rifts. This is not the legacy you want to leave your children.

Reasonable Expectations

The oldest child can come to resent the younger children if she feels that she is held to higher expectations than the others. While your older child is more capable and is being held responsible for her actions, she also needs to see the younger siblings held to account for their actions.

Parents can become more tolerant of a little one's misbehavior than of an older one's misbehavior. The toddler is "cute." Older children need to see you holding the younger ones to account. They need to see that the younger ones are disciplined and made to toe the line, too, according to their ability and developmental stage.

Tolerance for your younger children's misdeeds will bring retribution from your older children. They will make sure the little ones pay the price! It's better to administer the discipline than to have your older children doing so behind your back. Balance the discipline, and make sure every child is held to account—and that they all know it!

Sparks and Friction Cause Fire

If your family is overloaded with stress, your children will feel it and act out in one way or another. One of the ways they may act out is by fighting with each other. How much stress is your family under? How are you all coping? Individuals and families can handle only so much stress before it rears its ugly head as conflict in the family.

Remember, if Junior hears Mom and Dad fighting, his stress may lead him to kick his little sister.

Lead by Example, Not Preaching

Your children learn what they live. If they are exposed to their parents' fighting, they will learn to fight. They will also be full of stress and anxiety, which will contribute to their acting out with each other.

Preaching, lecturing, and guilt-tripping are not effective means of changing a toddler's behavior.

Fixing Family Dynamics

If you have one child attacking the other regularly, assess what kind of relationships exist between that child and each of you, the parents. Try to balance any imbalances. Spending more time with an aggressive child and paying more attention to that child will be a more effective way to end the aggression toward the other sibling than punishment or discipline. Consider the issues raised previously, and see if you need to make some adjustments.

Don't let sibling fighting get out of hand. If a family dynamic is causing the aggression between your children, a family therapist may be able to see what you can't see. If you need help with this, consult a professional.

Sibling Rivalry and Conflict

Children are going to fight. Sooner or later, there will be a conflict. It's not because the kids are immature or bad; it's because they are people. Even as adults, we don't like or don't get along with certain people. As adults, we choose who we want to spend time with, including siblings. Your children don't have a choice—they have to live together.

Temperament Conflicts Between Siblings

Your children may all be very different when it comes to their temperament. The greatest conflict will occur when one is an extrovert and the other is an introvert. For example, the extroverted daughter might be always getting into the space of the introverted son, who resents it and gets angry. The daughter gets upset that her brother won't interact with her the way she wants, and she can tend to be dominating and controlling with her extroversion. The introvert may push her away not because he is trying to have a bout of physical aggression, but simply because he wants to get her out of his space and will use whatever force he can muster to do it.

You have to be careful as parents not to discipline too quickly because it can look like the introvert is the one in the wrong. The introvert may have slugged the extrovert, but the extrovert may have been taunting, despite all requests by the introvert to stop. Who is in the wrong? Who needs a behavior modification? As parents, you need to get to the bottom of the story before you decide what action to take with each of your children.

In this example situation, the parents would need to work with the extrovert to help her know when to pull back, and would have to assist the introvert to help his "no" mean "no" with his sister. She has to know that her parents will back him up and that it is her responsibility to back off. What can you do for this child besides punish?

Options to Deal with the Extrovert-Introvert Conflict

With the previous example of the daughter and son, you can try these ideas:

- Find out what kinds of solitary activities she likes best, and provide her the resources to pursue those activities. Help her to discover that doing something alone can be as rewarding as doing something with someone else.

  Is she creative? Make sure she has access to play dough, a drawing pad, and paints.

  Does she like to make puzzles? Make sure she has puzzles, and direct her to them when you know she's starting to get on her brother's nerves.

  Does she like to play in the sand? With dolls? Facilitate these interests.

  Does she like to run through the sprinkler?

- Find her some extroverted friends to play with. Arrange to have them over to your house, and tell them to play with each other and leave your son to himself.

  Put her in an activity class.

  Enroll her in lessons.

- When you see that your daughter is antsy …

  Invite her to come and sit with you, and read to her.

  Invite her to come and help you prepare some food in the kitchen.

  Get down on the floor and play with her yourself.

- If it's a rainy day and you're pooped …

  Have your daughter and son each play in their own bedrooms alone.

  Have your daughter and son play in two different rooms of the house. (Make sure your daughter doesn't go to the room where her brother is.)

  Put them both to bed—they may both need a nap.

  Put them in the car and go for a long, boring drive.

When you know that there are temperament conflicts with your children, pay attention to the more outgoing, extroverted, or aggressive one, and redirect that child before he or she attacks the sibling. If the attack has already occurred, ask yourself if there is a family dynamic perpetuating the pattern.

In any event, once the attack has occurred, you will need to model …

- How people need to take responsibility for their actions.
- How people need to learn to listen to the heartache or pain they have caused another person.
- How people need to show sorrow for how they have hurt someone else and need to apologize.
- How people need to make up for the wrong they have done.

See "Teaching Conflict Resolution to Tots," later in this chapter, for more suggestions.

Stopping Things Before They Get Out of Hand

Years ago, in taking a leadership training class held to teach playground staff how to deal with children, the teacher told us that the best time to cut off an activity was at the height of fun. What? Why stop kids when they are having fun?

The logic goes like this:

- When kids are having a lot of fun, they tend to start going overboard, push too hard, try too hard, etc.
- When you are at the top, the only direction to go is down.
- A very fun activity can turn totally sour when kids get played out and then get miserable.
- When they get miserable, they start to whine, cry, or fight.
- The lasting memory is then negative for the kids and the care-givers.
- The same event or circumstances may be avoided by kids or their care-givers because it left such a bad taste for everyone.

Cutting off the activity at its peak …

- Ends the activity when everyone is still having fun.
- Prevents kids from getting too wound up and avoids eventual misery.
- Leaves everyone with a good memory of the event.
- Leaves everyone with the desire to do it again another day.

How do you cut off an activity at its peak?

- Be willing to put up with the kids whining about your stopping the activity!
- Redirect!

    Call them over and read them a story.

    Call them to the kitchen to play with play dough.

    Tell them it's time to go to the park or play in the yard.

    Tell them it's time for their nap, lunch, shopping, or whatever!

It's Not Always About Them

One day an older brother punched his three-year-old sister in the stomach. It wasn't about her. Before he left kindergarten that day, he had been kicked in the privates by an aggressive child. He was mad. He came home and took it out on his innocent sister.

When children are hurt, they don't know what to do with themselves. Aggressing toward others is one of their options to get rid of the intense feelings inside. You need to listen to your children to find out what was bothering them so much that they took it out on their sibling. The aggressive child may need your love and support before you talk with them about their response to their pain (that is, passing it on to someone else).

Everyday Stuff

Your children will get into little power plays and power struggles all the time. Here are some tips:

- When having to divide the spoils, have one child make equal amounts while the other child chooses first.

- Flip a coin.

- One plays with the item for 10 minutes, and then the other one gets it for 10 minutes—set the oven timer.

- If you have a vehicle with three rows of seating, divide and conquer—put one in the middle, one in the back, and one up front with you.

Verbal Capacity

Your toddler may be lashing out at your older child because he or she doesn't yet have the communication skills to deal with his frustrations any other way. Toddlers who don't have the words have the jerk! That is, they react almost spontaneously with a physical thrust when another child is in their space or has offended them. As toddlers' verbal capacity increases, their need to act out physically toward other children should decrease—especially since their parents should be busy teaching them how to express their feelings and how to solve conflicts along the way.

> **Safety and Sanity Tips**
>
> When you're at your wit's end and your kids are fighting, divide and conquer. Have them each go to their own rooms (or different parts of the house, if they share a room) and wait there until you come to deal with them. Then make yourself a cup of tea and relax! Open your Bible and say a little prayer. Sometimes they are just going to have to wait for you!

He Says, She Says

If your children come running to you to tattle on each other, make them face each other. Tell them to keep talking until they come up with just one story—the whole truth. Tell them Mom or Dad wants to hear only one story and then will decide who needs to be disciplined or what action needs to be taken.

What usually happens if they are both coming to tattle is that they have both done something to each other and want to be the first to tell so that you'll discipline the other one. They don't want you to hear the whole story—only their story. Many times, the one who came first will back off and want to "forget it," or will become cooperative or apologetic when seeing that Mom or Dad is going to hear what "they" did!

If you make the kids talk until they agree on one story, they won't be coming to you to do this very often. As you teach them the conflict-resolution skills they need, it will be a rare occasion that they come to tattle on each other.

No Tattling

Whoever came up with the rule of never tattling? It has always seemed to me that this was something parents told children so that they didn't have to deal with the kids themselves.

In yesteryear, hopefully no longer today, kids were given these sorts of messages:

- Don't tattle.
- Forgive and forget.
- Don't wear your feelings on your sleeve.
- Quit crying.
- Don't be a big baby.
- You get what you deserve.

As an adult, if somebody bashes you in the head or steals your money, you are entitled to go to the police for justice. Children need justice, too. In your family, you are the police, the counselor, the judge, and the parole officer.

Telling your children not to tattle can have the disastrous result of your children suffering abuse right under your nose: "Mommy and Daddy told me not to tell on anybody."

A Just God

You are trying to teach your children that God is just. Children come to know of the character and attributes of God through their parents. When you demonstrate justice in your family, you help your children to understand God. God's Word teaches the principles of getting along with each other and settling disputes.

Word from the Wise

"If another believer sins against you, go privately and point out the fault. If the other person listens and confesses it, you have won that person back. But if you are unsuccessful, take one or two others with you and go back again so that everything you say may be confirmed by two or three witnesses." (Matthew 18:15–16)

Jesus endorses dealing with offenses, not being silent about them and not ignoring them.

Conflicts with Other Kids

You teach your children how to behave socially. When your children have conflicts with other kids it's your job to show them how to solve their problems and then let them try it out themselves.

Violence

One of the first effective strategies for helping to mold your child away from aggressive violence and toward cooperative play is to work with them on role-playing with dolls. Violent behavior in many toddlers has been shown to be significantly curbed in this way. You want to role-play situations in which a person needs help. Role-play talking people through a conflict that they have with each other. In this way, you can show your children more effective ways to interact with others.

Talk about the virtues of having a friend. Does your tot want a friend? How will your child get a friend? Nobody wants to be friends with someone who hurts them. Ask your child, "If you want friends, what do you need to do and not do to have other children want to play with you?" The emphasis needs to be on what your tot needs to change.

Teach your children the social skills they don't have. If you are unable to do this, see if a preschool therapy group is available, or consider enrolling in a preschool class. Apprise the teacher of the problems, and be available when your child is there to monitor behavior and correct it every time it needs correcting. Show compassion to those your toddler offends. Ask your child to perform this behavior himself.

Positive Response Goes to the One Who Was Hurt

You don't want to give a lot of attention to the aggressive child. If these children think they can get mileage out of that, it encourages, not extinguishes, the aggression.

As a parent, show contrition, compassion, and empathy for the child who was hurt.

> **Safety and Sanity Tips**
>
> Don't forget the fine arts of diversion, distraction, and side-stepping. Sometimes simply directing your tots to other activities will end their negative focus on each other. Suggest solitary activities or ones that encourage cooperation.

Timeouts

Standing in the corner, sitting on a chair, waiting outside a room. If your toddler has been aggressive, pull him or her away from the situation and stop the play activity.

To be effective, timeouts need to be short. Remember, your toddler has a short attention span. You want your child to go from being aggressive to seeing you comfort the other child, to enduring isolation, to engaging in a talk about behavior and the hurt inflicted, to apologizing, to resuming play. If the timeout is too long, it becomes meaningless. Anything more than two to three minutes is too long. You'll remember from Chapter 2 that introverts like time alone, so if you have an introvert, their moment of isolation is more effective if they are sitting on a chair aside from others but still in the vicinity.

Apologies

You need to teach your children to apologize even when they are too little to truly understand what's going on. It's a social requirement of life. It's a value Christians have.

Having said this, while your toddler is still angry and vengeful, making him or her spit out the words "I'm sorry" in a resentful voice is not effective.

Take your son aside and talk to him. Keep your cool. Tell him that he hurt someone and that he wouldn't want to be hurt like that. Give him a moment. When his heart appears contrite, that is the time to ask him to apologize.

When he apologizes, you can encourage him to hug his friend or kiss the "boo-boo." He needs to show some tenderness to the one he was aggressive toward. Remember how you started this, by showing your child by your own behavior the kind of tenderness that needs to be shown to the victim of the aggression.

Hurt Begets Hurt

Sometimes toddlers are aggressive because they are struggling with their own emotional pain. Has your child been abused? What is your toddler bottling up inside that is boiling over onto playmates?

Listen to your little ones. If they are resistant to talking with you, consult with a professional counselor.

Toddler Tales

One night we overheard our neighbors and their children all yelling and screaming at each other. The next day we told them we cared about them and asked if we could watch their kids for a while so they could spend some time alone together. Sometimes caring for our children's friends means caring for their parents!

Hair-Pulling, Biting, Pinching, and Hitting

When kids are all bottled up inside and unable to express their feelings verbally, they often resort to a physical expression of their frustration. Hair-pulling, biting, pinching, and hitting become options for them to let another child know they are mad about something.

It is important that you teach your children how to verbally express their frustrations to you and others. The more language they have, the less physical they will be with other children.

If your children are using these techniques to express themselves, you'll need to spend some time asking them questions, listening to them, and helping them find the words to describe what they are thinking and feeling. Then you need to help them with the words to use when they …

> **Dr. Mom Speaks**
>
> Slapping or physically punishing a child in response to biting, pinching, or hitting another child teaches your child that acting out physically toward someone when you're mad is an appropriate response. After all, it's what Mom and Dad did. Kids learn by what you do!

- Want their toy back from another child.
- Want to play with particular children.
- Feel left out of the group.
- Want to use something another child is using.
- Want to play with another child's toy.

After you get your little one to tell you what was bothering him or her (before attacking the other child), comfort and cuddle your child over the issue that sparked their anger. After this is the time to help your child understand that the other child was hurt and that your child needs to apologize and make amends. Keep your cool.

Showing love to your children when they are naughty shows them that when they feel naughty, they have to think of loving the other person in spite of how they feel. The goal is that they learn the skills to deal with other children. Discipline and punishment will not stop these behaviors in toddlers (they may just be more sneaky about them so they don't get caught).

Teaching Conflict Resolution to Tots

You need to teach kids about a few basic things for resolving their conflicts. Walk them through this process:

- Each person has a story and is entitled to tell that side. (The parent needs to ask each child to tell the "facts" of what happened.)

- Each person has the responsibility to listen to the other person's story. (The parent has to make sure that as one is talking, the other child is not allowed to interrupt and get attention. The child must be quiet and hear the other one out.)

- Each person has feelings and is entitled to express them. (After the children tell their stories, the parent needs to encourage each child to tell the other how his or her feelings were affected by the conflict that just took place.)

- Each person has the responsibility to listen to how the other person's feelings have been impacted. (The parent needs to ask the listener, "Do you understand how you made Becky feel?")

- A solution needs to be found, either by the children or by the parent-mediator. (The parent needs to ask the kids if they have any ideas how they can solve their conflict. The parent hears out each child's ideas. Use this as a brainstorming session. You are teaching the children to think and find solutions. As one child offers suggestions, ask the other one what he or she thinks of that suggestion. Parents can offer ideas, too, but should encourage the children to come up with an idea that they both find equitable. If the children absolutely can't find a solution to their conflict, the parent must make a wise decision and impose it on the children.)

Yes, toddlers can learn how to resolve their conflicts. Parental involvement is necessary to teach and demonstrate. Then you need to encourage your children to use the conflict-resolution skills when they have a problem.

After teaching them these skills, if the children come and complain to you about each other, ask them to try to talk it out like Mom and Dad taught them. If they still have trouble, they can come back to you. If they haven't resolved it, guide them through the process again. Let them try to think of their own solutions and compromises. Only if they have "no clue" should you offer a few options for them to consider together. Always give at least three options so it doesn't look like you're giving the solution yourself. You want their minds to have to think in a solution-focused way.

Toddler Tales

> One day Mom was out of sight and overheard her five-year-old and three-year-old. They had just had a conflict while playing. One had yelled and one had cried. Then they stopped. One said, "I'm mad at you. I wanted to play with that car." The other said, "I thought you already played with it." The first one, "No, I didn't." The second one said, "Why don't we take turns?" The first one said, "Okay, you can go first." Mother smiled.

Teaching Sharing—Three and Older

Sharing is about reciprocity, not about one child always letting others use whatever they want. Sharing is about fairness. Sharing is not about one person always having to give something up and the other always taking.

Make sure when you are teaching sharing that both your child and the playmate give up things at times. This is sharing.

The Dominant Child

Some toddlers prey on weaker children. Your child may be the weaker child or the more dominant child. The dominant child may be the younger child!

Never let the dominant child remain in control of any object taken from another child!

Do not let the dominant child gain attention from adults. Isolation through a time-out is often necessary.

You may want to consider telling your dominant child to choose one toy for the friend to play with to "make up" for what he or she did to the other child.

If your child is the dominant one, invite over some older children to play at your house. They may be a very effective socializing force for your child as they may be able in a short time to put your child in their place!

Know How Your Children Are Behaving When You Aren't Around

It's amazing how sneaky some kids are. They can look like total angels to their parents and be little rascals behind their backs. Sometimes they are mean rascals who bully other children.

The only way for you to truly know whether your child is well behaved is to ask for feedback from other moms and dads after your child has been at their house. Or, ask the preschool/playschool or Sunday School teacher to be upfront with you about your child's behavior.

Make a specific request for this information. Don't expect other parents to tell you how much of a brat your child was that day. They are unlikely to volunteer the information (although, as a result of your child's behavior, your tot may not be asked to come back again).

If parents had previously invited your child over and don't anymore, inquire "How well behaved was my child the last time she was at your house?"

Chapter 24

Mental and Emotional Well-Being for Parents

Parents' mental and emotional well-being has a direct effect on children. It's important for Mom and Dad to be aware of how they are each doing.

Even when parents aren't aware of their mental state, their kids are. Did you know that there are little invisible antennae on top of your toddler's head? Yes, indeed, your little toddler hones in on all the emotional waves in the household and reacts to them (for better or worse—usually, worse).

Depression and Generalized Anxiety Disorder

Young parents who have work stressors, who have to move to another house or another town, who have to change jobs, who lose a job, who experience the loss of loved ones, or who have unresolved marital difficulties or unhealed emotional pain are at risk for depression and anxiety disorders.

Your mental health is extremely important to you personally, to your marriage, and to your children.

Depression

One in 10 Americans suffers from depression. Chances are, most of those suffering from depression have children. Many have toddlers. Depression is something that can creep up on you slowly. Your spouse or family members may notice before you do that you don't quite seem like yourself.

Moms are at risk for postpartum depression after the birth of their babies, but either parent may exhibit signs of depression any time. Depression can set in after there has been ongoing stress. Significant life changes can bring on stress, but when your emotional and biological systems collapse, depression can result.

Safety and Sanity Tips

Like they say, "If da momma ain't happy, ain't nobody happy." If you aren't happy, find the cause and have the courage to do whatever it takes to get your life in order.

If you have lost pleasure in most daily activities, are feeling sad or blue, or feel like you don't care anymore whether you live or die, and if this has gone on for at least two weeks with no relief, it's time to consider whether you've fallen into major depression. Check Appendix F for a complete list of signs and symptoms of major depression.

If you are suffering from major depression, you need spiritual, medical, and counseling help. Let's look at each.

- **Spiritual help.** You need the support of your pastor and Christian friends who love you and care about you. Isolation is the depressed person's worst enemy. A depressed person just wants to be alone and can run the danger of becoming isolated from the world. Spiritually, we are much more vulnerable to attack from the kingdom of darkness when we are alone. We need love. We need care. We need people. Even if you have trouble being with people, make sure you have people who are interceding for you daily. Don't shut out those who can help you.

- **Medical help.** When your body has been in a depressed state for at least two weeks, it is virtually impossible for your body biochemically and neurologically to get back on track on its own. Your doctor will prescribe antidepressant medication. Here are some things you need to know about antidepressant medication:

It is not addictive.

It will not give you a high.

If you are not actually depressed, it will have no effect on you.

If you are biochemically depressed, you will start to feel better.

The medicine has to build up in your body, and you may not see improvement for a few weeks.

If you are suicidal, tell your doctor because there are specific antidepressants to avoid if this is the case.

Just as you built up the medication in your body slowly, you need to wind down from it slowly. Never go off an antidepressant "cold turkey" because your body will have a negative reaction.

Some antidepressants have sexual side effects; orgasm becomes nearly impossible to achieve. If you don't want your sex life hampered, tell your doctor so he can avoid prescribing you those antidepressants.

Not all antidepressants help every depressed person. Your doctor may have to try you on a few before finding one that works well for you personally. Don't give up if the first one isn't helping—go back to your doctor.

- **Counseling help.** People fall into depression usually because life has overwhelmed them. Medication alone won't cure depression. You must get at the root cause of what triggered the depression. Find a professional Christian counselor to help you on your journey to emotional well-being. Check Appendix D for information on finding a counselor.

Generalized Anxiety Disorder

According to the National Institute of Mental Health, about four million adult Americans suffer from Generalized Anxiety Disorder (GAD) in a given year. Chances are, most of those people have children, and many have toddlers. Generalized Anxiety Disorder often accompanies depression. When you start getting relief from depression, underlying anxiety can surface.

If you are suffering from GAD, you have had excessive anxiety and worry for no apparent reason, for at least six months. Your ongoing exaggerated tension interferes with your daily functioning. You are easily fatigued, tremble, have headaches, are restless and irritable, have sleeping problems, feel shaky, have an exaggerated startle response, or have ongoing nausea or diarrhea.

For detailed information on the symptoms of Generalized Anxiety Disorder, refer to Appendix F.

If you are suffering from Generalized Anxiety Disorder, as with depression, get help:

> **Word from the Wise**
>
> "Share each other's troubles and problems, and in this way obey the law of Christ." (Galatians 6:2)
>
> The Apostle Paul tells us that it is the law of Christ that we share our troubles and problems with each other. Don't hesitate to share yours.

- **Spiritual help.** Meet with your pastor for spiritual encouragement and prayer. Ask your Christian family members and friends to pray daily for you. Don't avoid church or fellowship.

- **Medical help.** Talk with your doctor about your symptoms. She can help you with some medications to take the edge off your anxiety.

- **Counseling help.** As with depression, consult a Christian counselor to get to the bottom of your anxiety. Anxiety is not a biochemical problem like depression, but, like depression, it's one way the body reacts to stress and unresolved issues in life. Talk with someone who can help you sort out the things that are troubling you.

Issues from Your Family of Origin

While marriage has probably already elicited unresolved issues with your family of origin, parenting may bring up more issues.

Not a Problem for All

Many people raised in abusive families are able to completely turn it around with their own children. They just pour out love on their kids and are never at risk of treating their children the way they were treated.

Toddler Tales

> My friend's dad grew up with parents who showered him and his brothers with love. I was shocked to learn that both of his parents had been victims of physical abuse as children. They both swore one thing to themselves: "I will never treat my children the way I was treated!" And they didn't.

Knowledge Is Enough for Some

If the parenting you received was less than admirable, you may find that you are not only short on ideas of how to parent your children in a healthy way (one of the reasons you're reading this book), but that you are treating your children the way you were treated even though you don't like it.

Educating yourself with resources like this book gives you more parenting tools than your parents had. You will find more resources on parenting in Appendix E. Sometimes just learning new things and putting them into practice is enough for parents to start parenting well.

Knowledge Not Enough for Others

Sometimes it's not enough just to learn healthy and loving ways to parent. You may still find yourself reacting to your kids in ways you regret. For some, knowledge is not enough.

If you find yourself being just like your abusive mom or dad, it's time to get professional Christian counseling and to take immediate steps to ensure your children's safety. Refer to Chapter 22 for options.

> **Dr. Mom Speaks**
>
> Stopping abusive behaviors to your children requires you to confront and release the pain from the memories of what your parent did to you, replace the abusive behaviors with healthy behaviors, and resist the devil's temptation for you to repeat the abusive behavior.

Issues from Your Victimization

Besides family dysfunction impinging on your parenting, past victimizations can affect your parenting practices, decisions, and reactions to your children. Parents who were sexually or physically abused may find that these experiences are interfering with their responses to their own children. You may start having flashbacks of your own trauma.

Post-Traumatic Stress Disorder and Acute Anxiety Disorder

If you have had a severe or terrifying physical, sexual, or emotional event and were unable to deal with the trauma when it occurred, you may suffer from post-traumatic stress disorder.

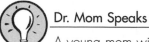

Dr. Mom Speaks

A young mom with two or three little kids at home who is not able to feed her children, do their laundry, or clean their house needs help. Your children still have needs. If you can't meet their needs, find someone else who can, and get help for yourself.

Word from the Wise

"Why am I so discouraged? Why so sad? I will put my hope in God! I will praise him again—my Savior and my God!" (Psalms 42:5, 6)

If you start feeling like David did, start both praising God and seeking help from others.

The disorder can be triggered by life changes, like having your children and parenting your children.

If you start having flashbacks or nightmares about the trauma or start feeling severe emotional, mental, or physical distress when you are exposed to things that remind you of the trauma, it's time to seek professional psychotherapy.

In terms of parenting …

- Nightmares can cause you loss of sleep, which means less patience with your toddler.

- Flashbacks can cause you a temporary inability to deal with your children, which means less patience for your toddler.

- Intense emotional or mental distress can leave you feeling numb or detached, which means an inability to be sensitive to the needs or requests of your children.

- Feelings of jitteriness or a heightened startle response mean you may over-react to your children and leave them feeling confused or scared.

- Overwhelming feelings of panic or fear can leave you holed up in your house with your tots instead of getting out to the playground or getting your grocery shopping done. Your kids still need to play and eat.

Effects of Mental Health on Parenting

Depression affects your ability to parent your children. Babies, toddlers, and preschoolers are at great risk of experiencing the negative consequences of your poor mental health because they depend on you to meet their needs.

Toddlers are a handful. You need to keep track of them every moment of the day. You need your energy, you need patience, you need lots of love, and you need good parenting skills. When parents lack in any of these, they can be …

- Short-tempered.
- Mean-spirited.
- Impatient.
- Intolerant.

They can err in ...

- Punishing their child.
- Shaming their child.
- Denying their child affection.
- Refusing to play with their child.
- Refusing to speak to their child.
- Not disciplining their child.
- Not guiding their child.
- Not feeding their child.
- Not creating routines for bedtime and potty time.

Toddler Tales

Reflecting on her preschool years, one teen said, "My mom should never have had kids. She never wanted to take care of us. She didn't even feed us! She was always impatient and seemed to resent us all the time. She made me feed my brother when I was five and he was three. She made me change his diapers and everything. She should never have had kids!" Take the proper steps now, and your teen will have fond memories instead.

When you are not doing well mentally, you have your own needs. It's hard to give to someone else, even your toddler, when you don't have anything to give.

It's okay for you to take the time you need to heal yourself. The quicker you get healthy again, the faster your children will start enjoying your company again.

It's better to take time away from parenting to look after yourself in the short run; it will pay dividends for you and your toddler in the long run.

Safety and Sanity Tips

If your condition is chronic or serious, sometimes the best thing you can do for your child is to entrust him or her to others for a time.

The Good News!

All of the mental conditions mentioned here have been found to respond success-fully to a combined intervention of psychotherapy and medications. As psychother-apy progresses, the need for medications decreases, and eventually you won't need either.

Spiritual Defense

Depression, anxiety, anger, and a whole host of other symptoms can be exacerbated by the evil one. We need to be on the alert. We only want to deal with our root prob-lems, not a demonically orchestrated exacerbation of our symptoms. When your symptoms rear their ugly head, issue these commands:

- "In the name of the Lord Jesus Christ, and with his power and authority, I hereby command all demons that have rights and grounds to me to be com-pletely bound and separated from all of your functions right now!"
- "In the name of the Lord Jesus Christ, I rebuke every demonic spirit attacking me right now, and I command you to go and stand before the Lord Jesus Christ for him to deal with you personally—go now!"

Say these in a spoken voice, not loud, but out loud. Don't freak out your kids or others; say them when alone, or go to the bathroom and whisper them under your breath.

If they help reduce the severity of your symptoms, you should consult with a Christian who knows something about spiritual warfare. (Go to www.power2serve.com for further information and online counseling.)

All Things Work Together

As Romans 8:28 says, "And we know that God causes everything to work together for the good of those who love God and are called according to his purpose for them."

No matter what has happened to you or what is happening to you, good can come from it. The Lord will help you work your situation to the benefit of yourself, your marriage, and your children. Continue in your pursuit of him, no matter how you feel, and use the resources that he's made available to you: your pastor, Christian friends, your doctor, and a Christian counselor.

The Hemorrhaging Woman

The Lord Jesus himself shows us the way to emotional healing. The Lord's desire for all of us is to be "whole" and healed people. Remember the hemorrhaging woman. The woman who had been bleeding for 12 years needed two things:

1. Physical/medical healing
2. Mental/emotional healing

The woman was physically healed when she first touched the edge of Jesus' garment (Luke 8:42–28, Mark 5:24–34). The power of God flowed to her, and her bleeding stopped. But that was not enough!

Jesus called her back. When she came back, trembling and falling down at his feet, she declared in the presence of all the people the "whole truth" of why she had come and how she had been healed. As an untouchable woman, she had endured a lot of emotional pain over those 12 years, and she needed to declare all of her pain before others and before Jesus Christ. After she did this, Jesus told her that her faith had made her "well." The best translation of that Greek word is "whole."

For the woman to be whole, she needed a medical healing and she needed an emotional healing. Only with both interventions was she then a "whole" person.

Seek Jesus. He will lead you, guide you, and be with you as you walk through the healing that you need.

Remember Romans 8:35: Nothing can ever separate you from the love of Christ!

Consent for Medical Care

Authorization of Consent for Medical Care for My Infant Children

I/We, _____ (name of parents),

of _____ (street address),

_____, (name of city/town) _____ (province/state), _____ (ZIP/postal code), am/are the custodial parent(s) having full legal custody of my/our children named here,

_____ (name of child), a minor child, born on _____ (date of birth)

_____ (name of child), a minor child, born on _____ (date of birth)

_____ (name of child), a minor child, born on _____ (date of birth)

_____ (name of child), a minor child, born on _____ (date of birth),

authorize _____, an adult in whose care the minor child has been entrusted (name of parent of babysitter if babysitter is a minor), and who resides at _____ , to perform any acts which may be necessary or proper to provide for the health care of the minor child, including, but not limited to, the power (i) to provide for such health care at any hospital or other institution, or the employing of any physician, dentist, nurse, or other person whose services may be needed for such health care; and (ii) to consent to and authorize any health care, including administration of anesthesia, x-ray examination, performance of operations, and other procedures by physicians, dentists, and other medical personnel except the withholding or withdrawal of life-sustaining procedures.

Parent/Guardian Consent and Agreement for Emergencies

As parent/guardian, I consent to have my child receive first aid by facility staff and, if necessary, be transported to receive emergency care. I will be responsible for all charges not covered by insurance. I give consent for the emergency contact person listed above to act on my behalf until I am available. I agree to review and update this information whenever a change occurs and at least every six months.

This consent shall be effective during the following "Initialed Dates":

1. _____ (Date), _____ (Initials)

2. _____ (Date), _____ (Initials)

3. _____ (Date), _____ (Initials)

4. _____ (Date), _____ (Initials)

5. _____ (Date), _____ (Initials)

6. _____ (Date), _____ (Initials)

By signing here, I indicate that I have the understanding and capacity to communicate health-care decisions and that I am fully informed as to the contents of this document and understand the full import of this grant of powers to the agent named herein.

Signed,

_____   _____

_____   _____

Signatures of Parent(s)   Date

Appendix
B

Information to Leave with Your Babysitter

Parents' Names, Address, and Phone Numbers

Mother's name: _____

Father's name: _____

Home address: _____

City: _____

State: _____

ZIP: _____

Directions to our house: _____

Nearest cross streets: _____

Our home phone: _____

Mother's work phone: _____

Cell phone: _____

Pager: _____

Father's work phone: _____

Cell phone: _____

Pager: _____

Children's Pertinent Information

1. Child's name: _____

   Date of birth: _____

   Known allergies: _____

   Medications: _____

   Medical conditions: _____

   Food not allowed: _____

2. Child's Name: _____

   Date of birth: _____

   Known allergies: _____

   Medications: _____

   Medical conditions: _____

   Food not allowed: _____

3. Child's name: _____

   Date of birth: _____

   Known allergies: _____

   Medications: _____

   Medical conditions: _____

   Food not allowed: _____

4. Child's name: _____

   Date of birth: _____

   Known allergies: _____

   Medications: _____

   Medical conditions: _____

   Food not allowed: _____

Medical Insurance/Medical Provider Information

Family doctor's name and phone: _____

Pediatrician's name and phone: _____

Dentist's name and phone: _____

Medical insurance provider: _____

Insured's employer: _____

ID number: _____

Group number: _____

Hospital to go to in case of emergency: _____

Address: _____

Directions: _____

Emergency room phone number: _____

Neighbor Contact

Name: _____

Address: _____

Phone number: _____

Cell phone: _____

Emergency Services Numbers

Emergency services: 911

Police department: _____

Fire department: _____

Gas company: _____

Electric company: _____

Poison control: _____

Where We'll Be

Name of place: _____

Address: _____

City, state: _____

Telephone: _____

FAX: _____

Text message on cell phone by e-mail: _____

We plan to return: _____

Where Things Are

First-aid supplies are kept: _____

Fire extinguisher is kept: _____

Ipecac syrup is kept: _____

Contact us if: _____

Appendix C

Guidelines for Hiring a Babysitter

Referrals

Check with neighbors, friends, day-care staff, other mothers who take their kids to day care, your pastor, and other moms and dads at church—ask for a few referrals.

Call the people you have been referred to, but make your own assessment of them.

Applications

Create your own application form and ask potential sitters to fill it out. This is an employee-employer relationship. You are hiring someone for wages. Ask for three references.

Checking References

You need to ask the references what they know of the babysitter's actual experience with children the ages of your children:

How long have you known the babysitter?

Under what circumstances?

What are the babysitter's strengths?

What are her weaknesses?

Have you seen her play with children? Read to children?

Have you ever seen her discipline children?

Do you know of any parents who have discontinued her services?

Classes and Courses

What does your potential babysitter know about first aid?

What does she know about children the ages of your children?

Has she taken any leadership training courses?

Has she taken a babysitter's course?

Interviews

Never hire a sitter over the phone. Invite her for an interview, perhaps more than one.

The Dry Run

Have your babysitting candidate come and spend a few hours with your kids while you do some work in another room. See how the kids react to her. See what she does to engage the kids and show interest in them. Does she appear to like your children? Does she seem to be "acting" nice and "acting" patient, or is it genuine?

Discipline and House Rules

Appraise your sitter of how your family handles disciplinary issues, and instruct her in what she should do if your children act up while you're out.

Make sure she is aware of your "house rules." Kids love to tell their babysitters they can do things they actually aren't allowed to do.

House Walk Through

Walk her through your house and point out any known trouble spots that she should be aware of. Make sure your sitter knows all the doors and windows that should be locked when you are out.

Finding a Counselor

Marriage and Family Therapists

A lot of people might print in their telephone ad, in their brochures, or on their business cards that they do family counseling/therapy. Some states and provinces have licensing for family therapists, and some don't. The licensing authority may or may not require them to specifically have a degree in family therapy. You can find out in many ways if a therapist is well trained specifically in family therapy.

The American Association of Marriage and Family Therapy (www.aamft.org) has a listing on its website of all of the clinical members of AAMFT. All of these people have advanced training in working with couples and families.

Besides clinical members of AAMFT, there are associate and affiliate members. These people aren't allowed to be listed on the AAMFT website. This doesn't mean they aren't well trained, only that they may not have finished their supervision hours since they finished their training. If you have the name of a therapist, call the state or provincial arm of the AAMFT (for example, the Indiana Association of Marriage and Family Therapy, the Alberta Association of Marriage and Family Therapy, and so on) and ask if the person you know of is an associate or affiliate member. Of course, you could just ask the therapist personally.

The AAMFT accredits Master's degrees and Doctoral degrees that meet their training standards. Make some calls and try to find out who in your area has taken their training at an AAMFT–accredited school. You can ask the therapist directly about this. Because of the licensing in different jurisdictions, the AAMFT graduate might be licensed as a psychologist or mental health counselor, which would give you no indication of the AAMFT training. These are the questions you need to ask.

Many psychologists and counselors have not taken a single class in their training on family counseling. And one class of this subject is nothing like taking a full training program for two or three years in this specialized area! You can ask the therapist specifically if he or she has had classes in family systems and child development.

After you know of the person's training, you can ask how long that person has been working in this profession. It's perfectly okay for you to know the level of experience a person has before you agree to pay to see him or her. Feel free to ask as many questions as you need.

Of course, word of mouth is highly important in finding a therapist. Try to find someone who will make a recommendation for you based on personal knowledge of the therapist and his or her effectiveness.

Try to make sure that you see a licensed mental health professional when possible, but do ask the questions. Many licensed people became licensed because of "grandfathering." This means that they were doing counseling work (not necessarily with adequate training) long before the jurisdiction brought in licensing. They were all given an opportunity to license without taking a licensing exam, many of them without ever having their work supervised. This is scary for the consumer because you may ask how long a person has been licensed or in the profession, and that person may have been around for a long time—but his or her training has been inadequate. If such a person has a good reputation for successfully treating people, go and see him or her. Otherwise, feel free to ask about the courses, classes, workshops, and training seminars taken related to the area of expertise you need.

Appendix
E

Resources for Parents

Books on Parenting from Christian Publishers

Barnhill, Julie Ann. *She's Gonna Blow!: Real Help for Moms Dealing with Anger.* Eugene: Harvest House Publishers, 2001.

Chapman, Gary D. and Ross Campbell. *The Five Love Languages of Children.* Chicago: Northfield Publishing, 1997.

Dobson, James C. *The New Dare to Discipline.* Carol Stream: Tyndale House, 1996.

Leman, Kevin. *Bring Up Kids Without Tearing Them Down: How to Raise Confident, Successful Children.* Nashville: Thomas Nelson, 2001.

Sears, Martha and William Sears, M.D. *The Complete Book of Christian Parenting & Child Care: A Medical & Moral Guide to Raising Happy, Healthy Children.* Nashville: Broadman & Holman Publishers, 1997.

Books on Parenting from Other Publishers

Faber, Adele and Elaine Mazlish. *How to Talk So Kids Will Listen, And Listen So Kids Will Talk.* New York: Avon Books, 1999.

Frankel, Alona. *Once Upon a Potty.* New York: HarperCollins, 1999.

Gomi, Taro. *Everyone Poops*. La Jolla: Kane/Miller, 1993.

Keirsey, David and Marilyn Bates. *Please Understand Me*. Del Mar, California: Prometheus Nemesis Book Company, 1984.

Maccoby, Eleanor. *Social Development: Psychological Growth of the Parent-Child Relationship*. New York: International Thomson Publishing, 1980.

Murkoff, Heidi and Laura Rader. *What to Expect When You Use the Potty*. New York: HarperCollins, 2000.

Neville, Helen and Diane Clark Johnson. *Temperament Tools*. Seattle: Parenting Press, Inc., 1998.

Internet Resources

Medical Information

WebMD (www.webmd.com)

Excellent medical information on every topic, including sexuality issues. Many other web-based health sites use WebMD articles and information.

Suite 101 (www.suite101.com)

Many articles and links pertaining to a large range of topics, including physical and mental health.

Parenting Websites

All of these sites are rich resources for parents:

Christianity Today (www.christianitytoday.com/parenting)

Christian Mommies (www.christian-mommies.com)

Parenting (www.parenting.com)

Mommy Guide (www.mommyguide.com)

Kid Source (www.kidsource.com)

American Baby (www.americanbaby.com)

Parenthood (www.parenthoodweb.com)

Dad and Me (www.dadandme.com)

PageWise (www.essortment.com)

Top Baby Pages (www.topbabypages.com)

At Top Baby Pages, you can do a customized babysitter checklist online and then print it for the sitter.

Safety Sites

U.S. Consumer Product Safety Commission (www.cpsc.gov)

Click on 4kids and check out the warnings on children's products and clothing, and get safety tips.

Safety Alerts (www.safetyalerts.com)

Check for product recalls.

American Association of Poison Control (www.aapcc.org)

You can enter your ZIP code and find out the number of the Poison Control Center nearest your home. Or, call 1-800-222-1222.

Blankees Poisonous House Plants (www.blankees.com/house/plants/poisonous.htm)

U.S. Army Center for Health Promotion and Preventive Medicine (chppm-www.apgea.army.mil/ento/PLANT.HTM)

Mental Health Sites

American Psychological Association (www.apa.org/psychnet)

Information for the general public on getting help.

American Association of Marriage and Family Therapy (www.aamft.org)

Links to find a local therapist.

American Association of Christian Counselors (www.aacc.net)

Christian Association for Psychological Studies (www.caps.net)

Christian Counselor locator.

Church Angel (www.churchangel.com)

Find a Christian therapist.

Christian Counselors Directory (www.christiantherapist.com)

Psychotherapy Finances Therapist Directory (psyfin.com/directory)

Postpartum Support International (www.postpartum.net)

Information and support for women suffering postpartum disorders.

Appendix F

A Brief Glossary

altruism   Helping, rescuing, sharing, comforting, and defending others without expectation of reciprocity. Selfless concern for the welfare of others.

autonomy   The ability to act independently.

behavioral reinforcement   Training a behavior into someone through systematically reinforcing each movement that approximates the desired behavior.

bonding   The heartfelt attachment between two people in a nurturing relationship.

boundaries   Limits to acceptable behavior.

brain power   The ability of the brain to learn new things.

conceptual thinking   Thoughts about ideas or concepts. Thinking of things that are not tangible, that you cannot touch—for example, "above," "below," "around," "under."

concrete thinking   Thinking about things that exist in reality that you can see and touch.

conduct disorders   Stealing, running away, fire-setting, destroying property, fighting, lying, and behaving cruelly to animals or people.

depression   A neurophysiological condition that, if severe enough, impairs everyday function and requires medication for recovery.

developmental delay   When a child's physical development lags behind the norm for his age.

discipline   Training implemented to produce specific behavior or to develop one's moral or mental maturity. Training to produce self-control.

emotional intelligence   The ability to monitor and react appropriately to one's own emotions and the emotions of others.

emotional language   Words and phrases that describe the internal reactions to external events or internal thoughts.

emotions   God-given physiological internal reactions, positive and negative, to occurring events.

entity   Something that has existence and being.

external control   When people other than the self control one's thoughts and behaviors.

extrovert   A person who gains energy from external sources and stimuli.

family therapist   A mental health professional with specific training in family systems, the marital dyad, and child development.

feelers   People who make decisions based on what they feel.

flashbacks   Previous memories that come unexpectedly into the mind.

generalized anxiety disorder   A mental condition in which the person is nearly paralyzed with constant worry and anxiety.

genitalia   Sexual organs.

"good enough" parents   Parents who provide a balance between nurture and comfort of their infant, yet who allow enough frustration that the child strives to learn.

good-touch/bad-touch   A school program teaching children what touches to their body are good and what touches to their body are bad, along with instructions on what to do if they receive a bad touch.

industrious years   The years when children are between the ages of 6 and 12.

inner healing   The healing of the emotions caused by past abuses or emotional pain through inviting Jesus Christ and the Holy Spirit into the memory and seeking their comfort, healing power, and restoration of the soul.

initiative   The ability to begin or follow through with an activity or objective.

insecure   Lacking self-confidence and stability. Feeling unsafe.

internal control   When one's thoughts and behaviors are controlled by the self.

internal dialogue   Conversing with oneself through thought.

introvert   A person who is energized by his or her own internal dialogue and solitude.

intuitive   Knowing or sensing without having to use rational thought.

judging   The lifestyle orientation based on decision making.

learning disability   The inability to learn at the same pace or in the same way as most others of the same age.

locus of control   How a person makes a decision based on either an internal locus of control (that person's own thought processes, values, and ideas) or an external locus of control (someone else's thought processes, values, and ideas).

morality   Defined standards that determine right and wrong behavior or thinking.

overstimulated   When a person's ability to cope collapses due to an excess amount of stimulation in the environment.

parent co-op   A group of parents who work together to share child care.

pedophile   An adult who is sexually attracted to children.

perceiving   The lifestyle orientation based on gathering information.

phonological knowledge   Knowing how speech sounds go together to form language.

presexualized   When a child is exposed to adult sexual information or experiences.

regression   Return to a previous level of development.

role-play   Pretending to be other people in mind, thought, and action.

secure attachment   When an infant is emotionally bonded to his or her care-giver and feels that the world is safe.

self-esteem   How good one feels about oneself.

sense of self   Comprehension that a person is a unique entity, separate from others.

sensing   A person who gathers information by making physical contact with the environment.

separation anxiety   The fear experienced when an infant or toddler is separated from his or her primary care-giver.

sex offender   An adult who violates another person through sexual activity.

sexual abstinence   The decision to not engage in sexual intercourse outside of marriage.

sexual abuse   Nonconsensual sexual contact by another person. Children are too immature and legally unable to give informed consent to the sexual advances of older (or bigger) children or adults.

sexually desensitized   When overexposure to things of a sexual nature causes one to lose conscience about what is right or wrong about various sexual acts or practices.

socialization   The process of learning how to become well-functioning human beings with sensitivity for others and the world we live in.

speech pathologist   A trained professional who helps children with speech defects.

temperament   A person's manner of thinking, behaving, and reacting.

thinker   A person who makes decisions based on thoughts.

traumatized   Subjected to psychological, physical, or sexual trauma.

trust   Firm reliance on another person or God.

verbal interaction   A conversation or dialogue between two people.

Appendix
G

Prayers for Dealing with Spiritual Concerns

Anointing a Room or House with Oil

If your toddler is having nighttime spiritual disturbances or you want to walk them through inner healing, you can anoint their room or your house with oil for spiritual protection.

With any type of oil, make a long stroke on the top and sides of the doors and windows of the room or house you want to anoint while praying over each stroke: "I pray for the protection of the blood of Jesus over this door/window." You can do this from inside your house. Anointing a room or house is a one-time event.

Daily Prayers for Spiritual Protection for Your Home

If your family is under demonic attack, pray daily prayers of spiritual protection over yourselves and your property, home, and children. Your home life with your son or daughter should become more peaceful and your child should become better behaved.

Pray quietly:

Father God Almighty, I ask that you put a hedge of protection angels around our home right now and that you would send warrior angels to stand guard at any holes that may be in the hedge. I ask Father that you would envelop our home with a wall of fire so that the light of the Lord Jesus Christ would shine brightly. Father, please send your angels to remove all spirits in our home that are not of you and cover all of the protection around our home with the blood of the Lord Jesus Christ.

Spiritual Disconnection from Victimization

The following prayer instruction is provided as a sample prayer. I suggest both Mom and Dad say the prayers and command aloud together. The speaking of this command and this prayer should be done in private or with your pastor. Your child does not need to be present or involved. In fact, your child should not be present as it may be confusing or frightening to them.

Command:

In the name of the Lord Jesus Christ and with his power and authority, we, (parents' names), take authority over all the kingdom of darkness on our (son or daughter) (name of child)'s behalf, and we renounce and command to be made broken all rights and grounds that any and all demons have gained to (him or her) through (identify event), and we command them all to be made broken right now!

Then pray:

Father God, we ask that you would pour out the blood of the Lord Jesus Christ to cover that access-way that the kingdom of darkness gained to our (son or daughter) right now and seal it up completely, and make it impenetrable to all evil forces. We ask this in Jesus Christ's holy name. Amen.

This command and prayer should be said for each and every incident that may have caused traumatization.

Sometimes we don't know, and will never know, if a particular trauma or event has opened our child to the kingdom of darkness. If there is a possibility, issue the command.

Prayers for Inner Healing

I recommend you do these prayers at your home, where your toddler is comfortable. These prayers presuppose that you have already anointed your home with oil and that you have prayed the prayers of daily protection over your property.

Speak out loud:

In the name of the Lord Jesus Christ, I command all demonic spirits that have rights and grounds to me (my wife and my daughter) to be completely bound and separated from all of your functions in me right now.

Each person involved should say "I agree" out loud after this. Revise according to who is there with your toddler.

Pray:

> Father God, Lord Jesus, Holy Spirit, please come now and be with us. Please let us sense your presence now.

Pray:

> Lord Jesus, bring your healing touch and your presence to us, lead us and guide us as we pray for (name of child) for healing and restoration.

Tell your tot that the Lord Jesus is with you in the room. Ask your child to please tell Mommy and Daddy and Jesus how they have been hurt by the event(s) in question and encourage them to feel free to cry and be sad about it.

Wait patiently for your child's response.

Gently encourage them to share what's on their heart because it will make them feel better. You can ask some open-ended questions such as these:

- What happened to make you feel so bad?
- Who is it that made you feel so bad?
- If your heart could talk to Mommy and Daddy, what would your heart say?
- If your eyes could tell us what they saw when you were hurt, what would they say?

If they do not want to speak about it at this time, leave it alone. They will talk when they are ready. If your son or daughter hasn't been able to talk about their hurt, stop here. If your child has talked and cried and let out some emotional pain, continue with the following prayers.

Pray:

> Lord Jesus, please come to (name of child) and gently remove the fiery darts of the enemy that came to (name of child) through (name the actions/event).

Wait a few moments peacefully together, then ask:

> Lord Jesus, please come and heal the emotional wounds that (name of child) has sustained.

Wait a few moments peacefully together, then ask:

> Holy Spirit, please come and fill up all (name of child's) wounds that have released their pain. Fill them up with the Holy Spirit.

Wait a few moments peacefully together, then ask:

> Lord Jesus, please come and seal up these wounds with a covering of your precious blood so that they are completely impenetrable to the kingdom of darkness.

Pray:

> Father God, I ask for all the blessings of heaven to come to (name of child) right now. Lord Jesus, I ask that you would be with (name of child) every day and continue to help (her or him) heal from the things that have happened. Amen.

Diagnostic Spiritual Assessment

If some sort of demonic force is causing your little one's disturbance, it is easy to determine. It takes little more than a few prayers and commands to make the assessment. Try this spiritual thermometer to take the spiritual temperature of your little one.

When your child gets into the mind-set or state that you are concerned about, in another room, out of earshot of your child, say the following command (it can be whispered):

> In the power and authority and the name of the Lord Jesus Christ, I command all demons that have rights and grounds to my (son or daughter), (say their name), to be bound and separated from all of your functions in (him or her) right now!

Then go back to the room and see what state your toddler is in. If your child's disposition has changed, issue the command a number of times in different circumstances and see if it is effective each time. If it is, there is a demonic problem.

Please, never issue these sorts of commands in the presence of your little one. Children can too easily believe that their parents think they are evil. If it's a demon, it's a demon—it's not your toddler! If this spiritual thermometer indicates that there is a demon, the situation can be dealt with fairly easily.

Because your little one is still a minor, you have the spiritual authority to protect him or her and to walk through deliverance on your child's behalf (if need be). Please note that minor children can always be represented by their parents for deliverance and never need to be in attendance for ministry to be effective.

Please go to www.power2serve.com for detailed instructions on how to walk through deliverance on behalf of your children and say special prayers for the adopted child. Or write to Power2Serve Resources, P.O. Box 932, Lumsden, Saskatchewan, S0G 3C0 Canada, for more information or go to www.power2serve. net, info@power2serve.net.

Index

U–V

W–X–Y–Z